GOLDEN BOY

the life and times
of Lew Hoad,
a tennis legend

Larry Hodgson
and Dudley Jones

First Published 2001
by DSM
The Studio
Denton
Peterborough
Cambs PE7 3SD

British Library Cataloguing in Publication Data
A catalogue record of this book is available form the British Library

ISBN 0 9536516 4 9

Copyright © 2001 Larry Hodgson and Dudley Jones

The rights of Larry Hodgson and Dudley Jones to be identified as the authors of this work have been asserted in accordance with the Copyright, Designs and Patents Act 1988.

Produced by
DSM
The Studio
Denton
Peterborough
Cambs PE7 3SD

Printed in Finland by WS Bookwell

In memory of Lew Hoad

For Matthew and Cristina Hodgson who are part of this story, and Lisa and Matthew Jones for all their help and encouragement.

Acknowledgements

The authors would like to thank: Joe Stahl for his generous assistance and encouragement; Gordon Forbes; Steve Flink; Pancho Segura; BBC Wimbledon for a video of the '57 final; Manolo Santana; Paloma Garcia-Verdugo Rodrigues; Ashley Compton-Dando; Peter Sampras; Neale Fraser; Ashley Cooper; Rex Hartwig; Ted Schroeder; Salvador Gallardo Gómez; Joseph Barnatt; Peter Risdon; Stephen Bourne; Jack Kramer; Frank Sedgman; Brian Evans and Paul Luper (for technical assistance); and our publisher, Paul Holness, for his faith in this project and his invaluable support. We would also like to thank Jenny Hoad for access after Lew Hoad's death to papers, cuttings and photographs.

Picture Credits

Preface

I have played tennis and keenly followed the game for over forty years. For me, as for so many others of my generation, Lew Hoad was a childhood idol. Though I only saw him play on a few occasions, I can still vividly recall the astonishing power of his serve and volley game, and his electrifying ground strokes. In 1988, I paid my first visit to the Campo de Tenis, the tennis club he established in southern Spain, and was struck by the beauty of the setting and the friendly, relaxed atmosphere. I made another three visits to the Campo in the '90s but Lew was only there on one occasion, and there was little opportunity to talk to him.

When I heard of his death, I wondered if anything had been written about him since *My Game*, his autobiography, published in 1957. I knew that *My Game*, which I can still recall reading as a teenager, only covered his career as an amateur player. Subsequent enquiries revealed nothing had been written about his later life. I toyed with the idea of writing a biography of Lew, but then the day job intervened, and the idea was shelved. Two years later, I was listening to a Wimbledon commentary on the car radio. Sampras was playing and Christine Jaynes turned to Frew MacMillan and said: 'Tell me, Frew, isn't Pete Sampras the most complete player you've ever seen?' Frew paused, then replied, 'Well, he's certainly up there with the greats, but no, I'd have to say the most complete player I've ever seen was Lew Hoad.' Thanks Frew – you rekindled my interest in this project.

It was some time before I became aware that Larry Hodgson, a close friend of the Hoad family for many years, was also researching a book on Lew. Eventually we met, decided to pool our resources, and this was the beginning of a fruitful collaboration which we hope does justice to the memory of a great Champion.

Dudley Jones

Foreword by Peter Sampras

Wimbledon Champion 1993-1995, 1997-2000

There are certain players you remember for more than their tennis victories. Lew Hoad conducted himself as a champion, both on and off the court, He was someone I looked up to and admired. I heard about Lew's death shortly after my 1994 victory over Goran Ivanisevic, my second successive win, same as Lew. Although flushed with victory, I became very sad. I thought the game of tennis had lost a true gentleman.

Pete Sampras

Contents

Chapter 1

A great Champion is born - A great Champion dies

It was exactly 4.05pm on the Centre Court clock. The reigning champion had been on court for nearly two hours in a temperature of 116 degrees, serving aces at more than 125 miles an hour, and coping with the lightning-quick deliveries of the man hoping to seize his crown. He'd withstood that barrage and was only two points away from victory. Once again, his opponent made a desperate charge to the net. Leaning back, his weight perfectly balanced, the champion hit swiftly under the ball, the follow-through sweeping high over his shoulder. For the third time that set, a perfect lob sailed over the head of the six feet-four giant the other side of the net, and plopped on the baseline. Match point: he stood poised on the brink of his second consecutive Wimbledon Championship title. When a dejected, heart-broken Goran Ivanisevic played only a token shot on his next return, the match was his. A broad smile lit up his face, he tossed his racquet into the crowd, a treasured memento for some lucky fan, swiftly followed by a sweat-soaked shirt.

Never the most demonstrative of players, Peter Sampras was justifiably elated. He'd captured the Wimbledon singles title for a second time and consolidated his position as the world's number one player. The score was 7-6, 7-6, 6-0, the first time anyone had won a fifth set to love in the men's final at Wimbledon since Fred Perry in 1936.

A thousand miles away, Lew Hoad lay on his couch in his little whitewashed cottage on the Costa del Sol, and grinned. He knew a great Champion when he saw one, and now Sampras had won twice in a row, just as Lew had all those years ago. Strewth, he thought, Sampras even played like him. That pleased him. As the pictures from England flickered in the corner of the room, Lew felt his strength ebbing away. His wife, becoming alarmed by his worsening condition, frantically summoned his doctor, and Hoad was rushed to hospital in Malaga. At ten minutes past seven on 3rd July 1994, Lewis Alan Hoad died.

Back in England, Sampras's elation evaporated when the news of Lew's death was conveyed to him. He idolised the 'old Aussies' and tried to play like them, and uphold their standards of integrity and sportsmanship. Now the man many regarded as possibly the greatest, certainly the most flamboyant and outrageously gifted player of them all, was gone. Sampras's pride was tempered by grief as he made his way to the Champions' Dinner that night, rejoicing over his second Wimbledon title yet mourning the loss of a man who'd endeared himself to crowds all over the world. The casual approach of this blond, green-eyed Australian might have occasionally frustrated coaches and friends, but anyone fortunate enough to have witnessed that combination of awesome power and dazzling shot-making of Hoad in his prime, could only mourn the passing of a great player and a fine sportsman.

Chapter 2

Promising beginnings and early retirement

Almost half a century earlier, Australia emerged from the Second World War having lost its innocence. During the war 120,000 servicemen and women had given their lives for the British Empire. Appalling losses for a small population, which despite its size had never wavered when the call came from Mother England. In the previous four years, thousands of soldiers and civilians had fallen into the hands of the Japanese - 15,000 in Singapore alone. An attack on Darwin by Japanese bomber aircraft had resulted in heavy casualties, Japanese submarines had surfaced in Sydney harbour, and the whole of Australia nervously awaited a full-scale invasion. Many children were evacuated from the coast and cities to relatives in rural areas.

But when the invasion finally came it was very different from what people had expected. One morning, grey warships with huge white letters and numbers painted on their hulls, crowded the harbours and ports. Unfamiliar aircraft criss-crossed the skies. Thousands of troops, speaking in strange accents and dressed, not in Australian dark green, but sand-coloured uniforms, stormed ashore and set up camps along the coastline and further inland.

The Americans had landed. A new friendship was forged. Though there were problems, misunderstandings, and occasionally mistrust, it was a friendship that looked set to last. Australians and Americans, both blunt-speaking, straightforward, ex-colonial nations, 'liked and admired each other'.

Generous aid poured into Australia from America. By the end of the war some sixty per cent of Australian imports, previously supplied by Britain, came from the United States. American influence over the Australian economy increased whilst that of the war-weary British inevitably dwindled. Australia looked to America as a role model, and America viewed Australia as a staunch ally and co-helper in the defence of the Pacific. And something that linked both nations was their passionate enthusiasm for sport. Americans, however, didn't play cricket, and so some other game had to be found to pit these two new friends in friendly (and, sometimes, far from friendly) rivalry. In Australia, because many men had still not returned from the war, coaches and organisers for team games were hard to come by, and Australians increasingly turned to a sport that required little space and organisation, that men and women could play together, and that appealed to all ages. Discarding its 'sissy' image, tennis became *the* game to play.

Whilst there had long been a tradition of keen competition between America and Australia in the Davis Cup, the sport – as in Britain – tended to be the preserve of a small, wealthy elite. After the war, however, it quickly cast off that exclusive image in Australia and became a game played by the masses. In America the same process took place, albeit at a slightly slower pace. In Britain, on the other hand, the 'old school tie and varsity' tradition that Fred Perry railed against in the 1930s, continued to pervade the ruling bodies of tennis (as, arguably, it still does today). This partly explains Britain's relative failure to produce top-flight players: the sport has never been democratised in quite the same way as in these other countries.

The ease with which any Australian kid, regardless of social background, could pick up a racquet and find a court to play on, suited a shy, quiet little boy with white hair and green eyes, just fine. Lewis Alan Hoad's family had recently moved into 43 Wigram Road, a small terraced house in the working-class suburb of Glebe, Sydney. Lew's father, Alan Hoad, a fourth generation Australian, was the son of a chemist from the New South Wales country town of Quirindi. He'd come to Sydney from the bush at the age of six and developed into a fine all-round sportsman at school, winning medals in swimming and diving competitions, playing football in the first team, and becoming a first-grade ice hockey player. Lew's father also used to love going up into the mountains and skiing with his cousin, Bill Day, an Olympic skier. One sport he'd never played, though, was tennis and he always told Lew he was the world's worst tennis player.

In his autobiography, *My Game*, Lew recounts the tough time his father experienced during the Depression when he was out of work for two years. Like many before him, Alan Hoad was drawn by the dream of 'striking it rich', so he set off prospecting for gold just outside the New South Wales country town of Goulborn. Unfortunately his dream of untold riches was never realised, and it became a family joke that in three months gold-digging, he found only eighteen shillings worth of gold. Then he got a job as an electrician, and one day at a Masonic Lodge Christmas tea met an attractive young woman who worked on the hosiery counter of a big Sydney department store. Her name was Ailsa Lyle Burbury, though she was always known as 'Bonnie', and seven years later, in 1934, the couple were married. In late November of that year, Lew was born. There were two more sons, Graham (nick-named 'Kelly' after the Australian bushwhacker) born in 1936, and Larry in 1938.

In those carefree days before the fears of a Japanese invasion curtailed social activities, the Hoads were keen swimmers and every Sunday the family would go to Wiley's swimming baths at Coogee for a day in the sun. They became as brown as berries and were rarely out of the water, unless it was to eat. The outdoor life and constant exercise made them fit, strong, and healthy. A family friend, Dr Emery Barcs, later described them as looking like 'the nearest thing to a group picture of a happy family. Alan, the father, fair, handsome, athletic, barely thirty; Bonnie, the mother, with the figure of a beach-wear model and the face of a Hollywood starlet; three little boys, fair urchins, who swallowed sandwiches almost bigger than themselves, and who could scarcely walk, but swam like fishes.' In many ways they were the archetypal 'Aussie' family: blond, tanned, good-looking, fit – and mad about sport.

When they weren't spending time at Wiley's Baths, the three brothers would often play in the busy street outside their house, and Bonnie became increasingly worried by the thought of her boys dodging cars and heavy lorries. Then she had an idea. The courts of Hereford Tennis Club in Glebe lay just behind the Hoads' house, and from an early age Lew would sit at his window seat at the back, gazing in fascination at the people on court. Bonnie realised she had found the perfect way of keeping her eldest son away from traffic.

Lew was given an old discarded racquet, which he christened the 'onion bag', and for the next seven years a racquet was rarely out of his hand. Everywhere he went, even around the house, he'd be swinging the 'onion bag', practising his strokes. Often, he'd rise at five o'clock in the morning and pound a ball against a garage door in a lane beside the tennis courts. This garage door, he always said, was 'his first opponent'. Half way across the world, a little American girl, Maureen Connolly, also destined to become a great Wimbledon champion, was honing her strokes against *her* garage door. At other times Lew would hit against a wall, unaware that only nine miles away in the Sydney suburb of Huntsville, a boy who'd turn out to be one of his greatest rivals – Ken Rosewall – was also practising against a wall.

In those early days money was tight: Lew would play barefoot to avoid wear-and-tear on his one pair of sandshoes. When eventually the 'onion bag' began to disintegrate, there was a lot of scrimping and saving in the Hoad household before enough housekeeping money could be spared for a new racquet. To provide Lew with something other than a garage door to play against, Bonnie took up the game but soon realised she was no match for her son. Later on, however, she was to win the ladies singles at her local club.

The player who most influenced young Lew's game was Joe Harris whom he used to watch for hours on end from the grandstand seat at the back of his house. Joe's fluent strokes were reminiscent of Jack Crawford's, a famous Australian tennis player of the time, and he was recognised as the best player for miles around.

It wasn't long before Lew's tennis skills started to attract attention, but many observers commented on how small he was for his age. In his early teens, he was undeniably short – there's a photograph of him around this period where he's cradling a tennis racquet that appears almost as big as him. It's difficult to reconcile the diminutive figure in the photo with the powerful build of the Wimbledon Champion of 1956 and 1957. When a newsreel firm suddenly appeared one day to take shots of this talented youngster so freakishly small and young, they asked Harris to hit with him.

In his autobiography, Lew recounts how Harris – whose job as a tram guard often meant he wasn't working during the day – generously devoted much of his free time to help develop Lew's game. But he also goes on to claim that his style was entirely natural, something that nobody, in fact, has ever seriously disputed.

One day Lew returned home and proudly announced, 'Mum and Dad, quick. Come and look, I can serve hard!' His parents were persuaded to go to the courts to watch him, and there he demonstrated the service action that remained fundamentally the same throughout his playing career. With virtually the same action, he was able to hit a flat, 'American kick', or swinging serve – and the serve was invariably preceded with a little foreplay of 'kissing' the strings of the racquet face with a ball before the service toss. His serve was beautiful to watch – and fearsome to face. Like most of his game, it wasn't coached, it just came naturally. Referring to his tennis achievements in later life, he said: 'It's not the system, it's not in the coaching, it's not in anything except you. You must want to do it – and practice, practice.'

It is interesting to speculate whether Hoad, with his innate talents, would have developed such a distinctively fluent, powerful game had he been nurtured in the tennis climate of the 1980s or 1990s. Nowadays, promising youngsters are sent to tennis academies or centres of tennis excellence and they come under the watchful eye of a battery of coaches. Occasionally some trace of an individual style survives, but usually their game is moulded according to the prevailing fashion, or current coaching orthodoxies.

Lew was right-handed, and because he had had no formal coaching, never learned to turn his left shoulder towards the net when hitting a forehand, or his right shoulder when preparing for the backhand. He would face the court square on, with the same open stance for forehand and backhand, and use his forearm to hit the ball in front of his body – like a table tennis player.

Although he went on to develop an elegant, more orthodox style when he became a successful tournament player, he would still sometimes revert to that table tennis technique – with a short backswing and a wristy hitting through the ball – to confound his opponent. Such a technique required a very strong forearm and like Rod Laver, Hoad's right forearm was much thicker and more muscular than his left (with Laver it was the other way round because he was left-handed).

Playing this way there was little room for error; you smacked the ball as hard as you could, whether you had the slight build of an undersized boy or, later, as in Hoad's case, the burly physique of a lumberjack. When he reached the top ranks of tennis, this uncompromising style brought gasps from the spectators if his shots went in, and frustration for Lew if he missed the target.

By the time he was eleven he was beginning to do well in his local district competitions; he was dedicated to sport and had no interest in 'girls, marbles or stamps, just winning tennis matches'. The rapid improvement in his game soon outweighed the difficulties posed by his lack of height.

When Alex McPherson, a lively Scot who was President of the Tennis Association covering Lew's district, came to take a serious look at the youngster, he commented: 'I saw a tiny, wee laddie, thin as a stick, with a racquet that came up to his armpit. He looked like someone who was too erratic to become a good player.' Asked by Lew's father what should be done, he replied, 'Take the boy home and feed him on porridge.'

Around this time Lew played in a tournament where his first round opponent was two years older than him and, at five feet nine inches, a foot and a half taller, but Lew still triumphed. A newspaper report of the match said his forehand and backhand sometimes lacked consistency but were hit with confidence, and that his knowledge of the game and tactics were superior to a lot of older boys. However, he was still only four feet four inches, and felt that this was a definite handicap. His father helped him with a strenuous exercise regime to build strength and hopefully add inches to his height. He joined the Glebe Police Boys' Club and every day went there to work-out with weights, and train for a variety of sports. Gymnastics, where he represented the Club team; boxing – he became State champion and eagerly followed the sport throughout his life; table tennis, where again he was to become State champion; cricket; swimming; and wrestling.

The body responded and, at the age of twelve, he won all the tennis events open to him in the Balmain district. The word went out, here was a tennis prodigy. What Lew and the other people in his area didn't know was that in another part of Sydney a boy of the same age was also being acclaimed as a future champion. His name was Ken Rosewall.

The Sydney tennis fraternity decided that perhaps these two boys should meet. At this time, the Americans had come to Australia and had just thrashed the Aussies, 5-0, in the first post-war challenge of the Davis Cup. They decided to stay in Australia for a while to help cement the new friendship, and foster the sporting rivalry between the two countries by playing some exhibition matches. So the two boys dominating junior tennis in Sydney were called upon to play a curtain-raiser to entertain the crowd (and perhaps give the Americans a taste of what might lie in the future) prior to an exhibition match between the two national teams.

Excitement mounted in the Hoad household, and for days before the match Bonnie fed her son on raw carrots to improve his eyesight! Every care had to be taken about her son's appearance. 'She always sent me to the court immaculately dressed,' recalled Lew, 'shorts neatly pressed, and she must have spent hours at the washtub on my things. She even ironed my shoelaces. We were all very excited at Wigram Road about the match.'

When he got to the ground, Lew's eyes met those of a boy even shorter than himself with a thin, serious-looking face, and a mass of black hair. Then they both looked up at the sea of faces around them. It must have been an intimidating sight. There were thousands of people in the stands; many, of course, were there for the exhibition matches by Davis Cup players, but a fair proportion of the audience – doting families and supporters, and rival tennis groups from different parts of Sydney – had come to cheer on Hoad or Rosewall.

When play started, Lew hit the ball as hard as he could, and it soon became clear that the 'little blond kid' had the heavier weight of shot. Unfortunately, Rosewall's racquet, seemingly too big and heavy for him to control, was always in the right place to steer Hoad's cannonballs back to the sidelines, or deep to the baseline. It was an entertaining set but Rosewall won it, 6-0. When the umpire asked the crowd if they wanted another set, they clamoured for more. The second set followed a similar pattern to the first. Although most of the games went to deuce, Rosewall again won 6-0.

Lew's family was more disappointed by this defeat than he was. He wasn't upset, just frustrated because he couldn't work out where he'd gone wrong. Then he watched a singles between the two great Americans, Jack Kramer and Ted Schroeder, who had been the architects of their country's Davis Cup victory. It dawned upon him that incredible power could be harnessed to precise control: 'They hit the ball as hard as they could – the way I really knew I wanted to hit it. But my eyes couldn't believe it – they had control over the ball. I just couldn't believe it.'

After the match, Lew found himself sitting next to Schroeder at tea in the clubhouse. The American told him not to be disheartened. 'I'll have my money on you next time you play that dark-haired kid,' said Schroeder. 'I lost just as badly as you when I started. Who's coaching you, Lew?' Lew looked at his father who he knew couldn't afford money for a coach. 'Nobody,' answered his father in tones full of regret. 'That's a damn shame,' replied Schroeder.

Had Ted Schroeder placed that bet on Lew beating Ken Rosewall next time they met, he'd have lost his money. One must assume Schroeder – a man with a reputation for tactical know-how on the tennis court, canny business investments, and shrewd calculation in a poker school – would have made it a small bet. In fact, not only did Lew lose his next match to Ken 6-0, 6-0, he lost the next four to him by the same humiliating score, including three different age-group finals in one afternoon in front of a nearly full house at the famous White City ground.

Years later, Kramer recalled watching the Australian youngsters: 'Ted and I were to play an exhibition and these two little kids, two 12-year-olds, were the prelim. We were amazed at the way they could play. Their games were already formed: Lew the attacker, Kenny peerless at the baseline. It was wonderful stuff.'

Then, suddenly, at the ripe old age of twelve, Lew retired from the game. He said it was because he couldn't find boys of a reasonable standard to play with him. His mother thought hearing others describe tennis as a 'sissy's game' probably discouraged him. Given the macho culture of Australian sport, there was probably some truth in this explanation though it's unlikely to have been the only reason for his premature retirement. Whilst he maintained the decision had nothing to do with the defeats by Rosewall, it's difficult to believe he wasn't a little disheartened by a succession of 6-0, 6-0 scorelines.

For the next eighteen months he concentrated on other sports and interests – especially pigeon racing, which he became very fond of. Given the solitary nature of the sport and its lack of physical activity, it's hard to think of anything further removed from tennis or, indeed, another of his passions, boxing. There were, of course, other sports that would strengthen his body: he played Rugby League for the Police Boys' Club and his school; he also became a good track athlete, winning championship medals for the 100 and 200 yards sprint events, the long jump, and throwing the cricket ball.

The greatest joy for the family, however, was when he was awarded a trophy and travelling bag as the 'Best and Fairest Sportsman' at the Glebe Police Boys' Club. His mother always said, 'I was proud the day Lew won the Wimbledon Tennis Championships, real proud. But not as proud as I was the night they gave him that travelling bag. Dad and I, and the two youngest boys, went along to the Police Boys' Club to see him get his prizes and things. Then out of the blue they gave him a trophy and that travelling bag for being the fairest boy in the Club. The prizes he won that night didn't give him a swelled head. They didn't change him then, and they haven't changed him since. But it was my proudest moment of all – and I cried.'

His father had always instilled in his sons the sportsmanship ethic: you didn't brag about your triumphs and you accepted your defeats with a good grace. Alan agreed with Kipling's tests of manhood, especially the injunction that when you met Triumph and Disaster you 'should treat those two imposters just the same'. Often, over an ice-cold beer, Lew would sweep a huge hand through his mass of blond hair, grin and tell friends that the lectures he got from his father about 'swollen heads' probably made him more diffident than he should have been.

After about a year in 'retirement', Lew started meeting boys who played tennis locally and competed in tournaments. They would talk about their matches and it wasn't long before they re-awakened his appetite for the game. Sometimes he'd stop and linger outside the Hereford Club courts behind Wigram Road, drawn by the pick-pock sound of ball against racquet strings and court surface. There might be a game going on between a couple of good players, and he'd experience that familiar longing to pick up a racquet.

Those crushing defeats by Rosewall still burned deep in his memory and he wanted revenge. Also, he couldn't erase from his memory that match played by Kramer and Schroeder. If only his desire to hit the ball ever harder could be harnessed to the kind of control they possessed. He'd enjoyed competing at athletics, rugby and cricket, gaining many medals and trophies in these sports, but nothing quite matched that rush of adrenalin you got from hitting a perfect ground stroke, a crunching volley or a service ace.

Tennis has been described as 'three dimensional chess'; in Lew's case, it was more a cross between a Beethoven symphony (powerful, majestic, and rhythmical) and ballet (graceful and fluid). Of course, there are powerful players with muscular build and weight of shot who could never be described as graceful and stylish – Thomas Muster and Jim Courier come to mind. They are heavyweight sluggers. Lew was more like Mohammed Ali. He may have had a heavyweight boxer's physique, but he 'danced like a butterfly and stung like a bee'.

Bonnie, conscious that Lew had never really lost that passionate desire to play tennis, persuaded him during his 'retirement' to regularly accompany her to the White City to watch the big names of tennis in action. One day the people in the stands noticed this blond-haired former prodigy mimicking every shot the stars played as he sat or stood in the stadium. They became so engrossed by his eager excitement that soon all eyes were on him, not the players on court.

It wasn't long before, once again, a racquet was constantly in his hand as he roamed around the house. His father nurtured this interest by starting a book of tennis cuttings that Lew pored over at night. Finally the lure of tennis proved too strong, and he took up the game again.

Soon, Bonnie had to practically drag him from the courts. In the first year of his comeback, Lew won six district titles. To try to ensure he didn't again retire prematurely, the now devoted Alec McPherson asked Adrian Quist, former Australian Davis Cup star and director of the Australian Dunlop Sports Company, to give Lew a job. In those days the Australian system was to select young sports stars as soon as they could leave school, and place them with sports goods firms. This not only kept them off the streets, it gave them pocket money, and plenty of practice time. Lew, who disliked everything about school except the sports periods, left as soon as he legally could and became an odd-job boy, and eventually a racquet stringer. He strung racquets till his arms hurt. But his hands became hard and tough and he earned two pounds eight shillings a week.

It is worth noting that the Americans had an entirely different system of grooming their youngsters for sporting stardom – although it too produced superb sportsmen and women. The American idea was (and still is) to encourage their promising juniors to progress through High School, Junior College, College and thence to University so that they acquired not only the aggressive competitive skills necessary to prepare them for top class tennis but also a sound education. That is why many American tennis players have become wealthy agents, promoters, lawyers and businessmen after their playing career has ended. Certainly, Lew could never claim to be a businessman, and never wanted to be one.

* * *

By the time he leaves school, Lew is physically transformed. The daily exercises with his father and brothers, the competitions to see who could do the most push-ups, sit-ups and pull-ups ('He's done thirty – now you do forty'), the workouts at the Police Boys' Club with weights and punch bags, and the strenuous sessions in the swimming pool, had finally paid off.

Having retired as the 'Mighty Atom', he returns to tennis tall, broad-shouldered, fit and tough. He looks like a young lumberjack or truck-driver and, as someone who loved boxing, he did occasionally wonder whether he should have pursued that interest professionally. Had he done so, he could never have got away with being as lazy in the ring as he often was on the tennis court. Those lapses in tennis concentration (occasions when his mind would go 'walk-about') that were to dog Lew throughout his tennis career and frequently cause frustration to family, friends and advisors, would have been disastrous in the boxing ring. But with his carefree philosophy on the tennis court, he remained unfazed and always shrugged off unexpected defeats by lesser opponents.

Typical of this lack of concentration was the time shortly after his return to tennis when Lew became so interested in some pigeons he saw circling the court that he completely 'switched off' from the match. On another occasion, having been driven ten miles to compete in a final, he was left to walk home by his father because his play had been so lackadaisical. National selectors called in to watch Lew said he was potentially 'first class' but also 'erratic'. One suggested he would never beat Rosewall – from whom, indeed, at that stage, he'd never won a game. Rosewall described how when they became doubles partners, Lew would sometimes become so interested in a match on an adjoining court that they'd quickly lose a number of games before he started to focus once more on the game in hand.

The turning point came in the State Junior Championships. The third round of the singles once again saw Hoad (who was unseeded) and Rosewall pitted against each other. Lying in bed the night before, Lew contemplated the match with mounting excitement. He should have felt nervous, apprehensive – after all, he had never beaten Rosewall, had been thrashed on almost every occasion, even though the score didn't always reflect the respective abilities of the two boys. However, now he felt an increasing confidence in the power of his strokes, and more importantly his ability to control them.

The next day he had his first taste of a match where everything seemed to come together. His first serve shot through, surprising Rosewall with its speed. When that failed, he had his kicking, swerving second serve to fall back on, a serve that reared up, making it difficult for opponents to steer back low returns to the feet. The ground shots began to consistently arrow down the lines or cross-court, and the volleys were punched away imperiously. When everything clicked like this it was all so easy, the ball zinging off the strings, body and racquet moving in perfect harmony. Rosewall tramped dejectedly off the court, beaten 6-3, 6-2. On the Saturday, his fifteenth birthday, cheered on by his family and Balmain Club members, Lew defeated John Blacklock in straight sets to give him his first important championship title.

As a result of this win, Lew was invited to play some exhibition matches to provide practice against top-class players, and on one of these occasions met a man who was to become a life-long friend, an exile from Czechoslovakia, and a future Wimbledon Champion – the great Jaroslav Drobny. In a letter to the authors, Drobny described his first meeting with Lew in 1949, and pays tribute to the man he loved and respected:

I was asked by some Australian officials if I would hit a few balls with a promising junior and give them my impressions, which were: this lad could be a world beater. Here was this strong boy with blond hair and a big grin and an arm I could see was made of steel. He said 'Hi, Mr Drobny' and shook my hand. I couldn't hold anything with that hand for several hours and counted myself lucky that I was a left-handed player. Since then I always tried to avoid his friendly steel handshake. You could tell right away that here was a future tennis champion which, of course, he became in a very short time, winning everything in the tennis world.

For me, Lew was the most talented player I have ever seen and also the most attractive player to watch or play against. He had the most beautiful style, hitting the ball very hard and with ease from any position. And he was a great sportsman. I never saw him protest at anything. Lew was admired by the public all over the world for his dynamic play. And he was loved by all in tennis, opponents included, for his easy way and friendship. You know Lew and I became very good friends over the next forty-five years. I was very, very fond of him and will miss him very much – and his steel handshake.

Another European entered the scene, Mike Szabados, the Hungarian world table tennis champion who had come to live in Sydney. He repeatedly tried to get Lew to give up tennis and concentrate on table tennis because he was convinced that he could become world champion. Lew resisted these overtures, however, and his decision was swiftly vindicated by a series of tournament victories, which showed his increasing consistency and maturity and earned him a place in the New South Wales team – the youngest player ever chosen to represent his state. In these heady days, Lew even took a set off the American Dick Savitt, who was to win the Wimbledon singles title only a few weeks later.

Then the New South Wales tennis authorities made a surprising selection that established one of the all-time great doubles partnerships. They asked Lew and Ken Rosewall to team up together as a trial combination. No two players could be more different in style or temperament. One built like a young bull, blond hair bobbing, free and easy, hitting the ball as hard as he could, and all the while grinning cheerfully. The other with slicked-back black hair, small and thin, cautious, canny, apparently lacking emotion, steering balls over the net with chess-like precision, and with a serve that seemed no harder than a schoolgirl's.

Were the selectors crazy? They were like chalk and cheese. This partnership would never work in a million years. Everything about them was just so different. Why, they didn't even talk to each other. Nevertheless, as Lew later commented: 'From the first game we played together we blended as a team. It was just something natural – or unnatural! Our styles were so different that on a doubles court they locked into each other like a jigsaw.' Separated by only three weeks at birth, but a million miles apart in everything else, the 'tennis twins' who were to rock the tennis world were born.

Whilst travelling with the New South Wales team, a meeting took place that would have profoundly important implications for the development of both their careers. They were introduced to Harry Hopman who was to guide them as captain, guardian, guide, and stern taskmaster, on and off court, throughout the rest of their amateur careers. Hopman exercised what many regarded as an excessively authoritarian control over Australian Davis Cup teams. Members of these teams would be fined for a variety of offences: being out late, swearing, speaking out-of-turn or answering back, being disrespectful, appearing on or off the court in scruffy rather than smart clothing – and even for using the wrong cutlery at dinner. Lew said, perhaps jokingly, that Hopman pocketed the money from these fines for himself.

* * *

Lew is now sixteen, he's five feet nine inches tall and weighs twelve stone. His power-hitting is the talk of the town. In one match he hits sixteen clean aces and ten other serves which just couldn't be returned. But his first mentor and boss at Dunlop, Adrian Quist, had a problem: though Lew always walked on court in the peak of physical condition, he sometimes forgot, as we have seen, to bring his concentration with him. At various times over his playing career he would lose to people he ought to have beaten because of a loss of concentration, or a laid-back attitude towards the game – or both.

The New South Wales team went on to the Australian Junior Championships and Lew reached the final. This was when he first experienced a drink problem. He became involved in a milk-shake drinking contest! Five boys put two shillings in a pool for the winner to take, and paid for their own drinks. They proceeded to drink five pints each, by which time the shop had run out of milk.

The next day Lew was to play the final against Ham Richardson, a promising 17-year-old American with some fine wins to his name. It's a hundred degrees in the shade at noon and soon Lew begins to feel sick. The stands start to shimmer and heave – and so does he. At set all, an interval is called and Lew, hand clasped to mouth, weak from the heat and the diet of milk-shakes, approaches Quist and says, 'I'm sorry, Adrian, I feel terrible, I think I'd better quit.' An angry Quist shoved him under a cold shower, and while Lew waited to throw up and give up, Quist gave him a blistering lecture about his stupidity, and his frequently casual attitude towards tennis. How could he do this before his most important final? Quist was practically tearing his hair out. Lew's stomach turned to knots of pain, the milk-shakes came back into his throat. He returned to court and won the final set 6-1. Such tragicomic situations were to continue throughout his life.

Further trouble loomed. He was about to become embroiled in a controversy that could have threatened his future career. In 1952 it was announced that the teenage 'tennis twins' would be included in the Australian national team, captained by Mr Hopman, that was to tour the world that year and play at Wimbledon. Lew 'couldn't believe it' (his favourite expression for all things good or bad). He and 'Muscles' – the affectionate nickname given to Rosewall because of his apparent lack of them – were going to play for their country against the world's proudest and toughest tennis nations. Lew was visibly moved by the news.

Then, out of the blue, the storm broke. With only a month before the team was due to leave Australia, he developed flu, but typically felt he couldn't let his doubles partner down by defaulting. Walking on court, he could barely see or breathe. He carried a handkerchief into which he constantly spluttered, and another to wipe his streaming eyes. To make matters worse, at the end of one rally something flew into his eye. He put up his hand to try to clear the eye and a ball-boy, thinking this was a signal that Lew was ready to serve, tossed him a ball. It was almost on him before he realised it and he 'instinctively flicked at it with his toe. Perfect contact was made and the ball sailed way into the crowd.' Feeling so groggy for the rest of the match, Lew remembered little further, and completely forgot about the incident with the ball.

It was decided he should have a holiday with his family before the team left. On the way back he had to change trains and listening to the radio in a station buffet was amazed to hear he'd been reported for misconduct over the kicked-ball incident. He was accused by Lawn Tennis officials of not caring, not trying to win and, incredibly, of 'disgraceful court demeanour'. Western Australia administrators, it was said, could not believe a first class player capable of such an exhibition. For once in his young life, Lew was worried.

Looking back at the incident now it is difficult to understand what all the fuss was about. From the nature of the official allegations, one presumes Hoad wasn't castigated for kicking the ball into the crowd. This was not, after all, like the hapless Tim Henman, who lashed out in frustration at a ball with his racquet at Wimbledon a few years ago and inadvertently hurt a ball-girl who was struck by the ball. In Hoad's case, neither spectators nor officials were in any danger. It seems kicking the ball must have been interpreted as a gesture of submission, but this was to ignore both Lew's character and his physical condition.

Nevertheless, the furore grew with Hopman, Quist, and the New South Wales Tennis Association defending Lew, and other factions within the tennis establishment demanding his withdrawal from the overseas team on the grounds that he was clearly not fit to represent Australia. One typical comment was: 'We cannot have players like that at Wimbledon. Such conduct would discredit Australia's name throughout the world.'

Lew began to sense his dream of playing on the lush green lawns of Wimbledon vanishing fast. The controversy rumbled on for days with officials, fans, and newspapers, taking sides, making demands, offering suggestions. The phlegmatic Hoad household was plunged into gloom, especially Alan who had always placed such importance on sportsmanship, loyalty and patriotism – though he knew his son was innocent and being unfairly maligned. Lew was hauled to Melbourne, to the headquarters of tennis. He was shown into a room full of grim-faced men who made little comment other than demand he apologise. He was happy to oblige, and simply replied, 'I apologise.' After a long silence, the Chairman rose, and said: 'Good luck on your first overseas tour – and be a credit to Australia.' And that was the end of the affair.

To restore his name, and make amends, Lew fought hard in the National Hard Court Championships that immediately followed. He never grinned or smiled because he was trying so hard to keep his wayward concentration under control. He beat Rosewall in the final in five sets – his first national title. Combining with Rosewall, the 'twins' as they were known (because they were born within eighteen days of each other) easily won the doubles and the newspapers proclaimed the dawning of a new era for Australian tennis.

The next few days were hectic. Passports and papers, kit and clothes were handed out. Working-class Lew Hoad was given a special financial grant by Dunlop. Even food parcels were prepared in case the starving English (rationing was still in force in Britain) were unable to feed the visitors properly. The 'twins' went to the gymnasium where Hopman's top coach looked them over and prepared a training regime.

Lew didn't need any more bodywork, he needed stamina and additional speed to accompany the power. He was given a programme of sprinting, running and road work every day. Rosewall, on the other hand, would clearly benefit from body-building. He'd have to use weights, bars, lifts, pushes and pulls. There were hard men out there waiting for this young pair. They had to be ready.

Departure day came, and in Hoad's words, 'I went up the aeroplane steps with the team, turned and waved to my family. I grinned a big grin of reassurance. But my mother began to cry and Dad just looked. I vowed I would do everything to do well, to be a credit to my family and my country. I was proud to be playing for Australia. It's a feeling which never left me when I was playing for my country and whatever disappointments I caused when I was playing as me, Lewis Alan, I always gave all I had when I was playing for Australia.'

Years later, John Newcombe, Wimbledon champion and World No 1 would say: 'Lew was as Australian as meat-pie, Swan (heady Aussie lager) and Holden (the home-produced Australian people's car).'

Chapter 3

Hopman, a French love affair and heroic exploits at Wimbledon

First stop was England for training under the strict discipline of Hopman, whose record as the most successful Davis Cup captain of all time will be covered later in this book. Lew remembered Hopman as a 'tough ole' b. But he was also a father-figure to us – and had to be with two raw kids on his hands, away from home for the first time.'

Hopman got a bad press for the way he supposedly treated both the boys and more experienced players in his charge. Since being appointed as the Australian Davis Cup captain in 1949, his methods and his handling of players had attracted both hostility and support, but it is worth noting that his most vocal supporters were often the very players he was supposed to be victimising.

Like Neale Fraser, Wimbledon Singles Champion in 1960 and Doubles title-holder in 1959 and '61, who waited patiently in the wings as understudy and reserve. He regarded Hopman as a father-figure and credits him with instilling the right values and manners in his young charges. Then there was Fred Stolle, French and US Champion and three times Wimbledon finalist, who was told he wasn't good enough to represent his country (but later would prove his captain wrong). He described Hopman as a 'bastard,' adding 'but I came to respect him so much that when I wanted to send my son Sandon to a tennis camp I sent him straight to Hop's.' [1]

Newspapers, however, called him 'a fanatic' and 'sadist', and accused him of 'acting as if he was on a Holy Crusade'. One even described life in the Australian team as 'like being on a chain gang'. Reporters following the team around wrote that Hoad was 'forced' to do hours of non-stop road work until he was drenched in sweat. The truth is, Lew always sweated, and invariably had to have his shirt peeled off after a long match. Later, some commentators blamed the back injury that cut short his career on Hopman's insistence that exhausting weight-training regimes in the gym be maintained despite the fact that Hoad's upper body strength was clear for all to see.

There was one other thing reporters noticed about Lew's relationship with Hopman. His mentor would only have to glance at him or say a word, and he would jump to it. But Lew respected older men and always wanted to do the right thing – it was the way he'd been taught by his parents.

It's easy also to exaggerate the oppressive nature of the captain's stewardship. For example, the players regarded Hopman's much publicised system of fines for their 'indiscretions' as no more than an amusing idiosyncrasy which raised team morale. Using the wrong knife or fork at dinner would lead to a small deduction from the official twenty-five shillings a day 'incidental expenses' – expenses often referred to, derisively, as 'haircut money'. Swearing, appearing at dinner without a tie, or misbehaviour in a match, would cost the offender between six pence and twenty-five shillings.

In retrospect, such restrictions might sound either absurd or tyrannical but they probably helped players become familiar with the niceties of etiquette when attending social functions, and they possibly contributed to the reputation acquired by Australian tennis teams as exemplary sporting ambassadors for their country. And the players themselves took it in good part, laughing rather than complaining about the fines. Certainly, Lew's abiding memory of that long overseas tour was that it had been 'great fun', whilst the improvement in his play and tactics on tour appeared to vindicate Hopman's approach. Perhaps Bonnie and Alan were the most grateful beneficiaries of the captain's fatherly influence over his young charges because he regularly enquired how long it had been since Lew had written to his family, and encouraged him to write immediately if a letter was overdue.

The team flew from London to Paris, and the French Championships. Immediately, Lew was captivated by the French: by their charm, cuisine, their clothes and sense of style. He loved Paris and its atmosphere, and this was the beginning of a love affair that lasted for the rest of his life. These feelings were reciprocated: the French took to their heart this good-looking, blond Australian whose flamboyant, spectacular tennis seemed to epitomise Gallic flair. Although few players with a powerful serve and volley (strengths nullified by the slow, dusty, red clay courts at Stade Roland Garros) relished the gruelling matches and the demands on stamina and patience that lay in wait for them at this tournament, the French Championships became one of Lew's favourites.

Later he was to comment: 'Every year I say I'll never play Paris again. I'm a short rally player. Your arm can nearly fall off in Paris. The balls are heavy, they water the courts, and you're always playing some guy nobody's ever heard of – who keeps you out there for four and a half hours. But in the evenings. Wow! ... Paris is a *great* tournament!' Significantly, the only title to elude the most accomplished power player of recent years, Pete Sampras, is the French.

It was to be four years before Lew won his French title and on this, his first trip, he lost in the second round. Probably his most vivid memory of the visit was Hopman taking the team to a saucy nightclub in the Place Pigalle where Lew, who never quite lost his shyness with women, blushed at the sight of the scantily clad mademoiselles. Though he grew up in a Sydney suburb, Lew was, in many respects, always a 'good ole' country boy' who worshipped his mother and respected his father. Indeed, in his autobiography, he records his pleasure at buying a charming bonnet for his mother in a Parisian shop – and then worrying about whether she would like it. As far as tennis was concerned, he enjoyed his first European tour and though suffering defeat at the hands of the talented South African, Eric Sturgess, in the singles in Paris, there were some encouraging results in the doubles with Rosewall.

To England then for the Queen's Club tournament – the traditional warm-up for Wimbledon. Rosewall and Hoad had good wins in the singles against Eric Sturgess and the American, Ham Richardson, respectively. Lew enjoyed playing on the fast, manicured lawns of Queen's Club which were the perfect preparation for Wimbledon, and he was pleased that Frank Sedgman, the top Australian player and hot favourite for the Wimbledon title that year, won at Queen's.

Next stop, Wimbledon.

It's difficult for any player - let alone a shy, unassuming 17-year-old Australian - not to feel intimidated as he enters the gates on Church Road, Wimbledon, walks up past the Players' Gallery, and pauses to gaze at the names of the past title-holders on the Roll of Honour Board. It's partly the sheer weight of tradition, one's awareness of the rituals that have to be observed, such as the bows to the Royal Box on entering and leaving the Centre Court. Partly the awe-inspiring sight of those lush, green, grass courts, the paths between them thronged by excited crowds all competing to catch a glimpse of their favourite players. At Wimbledon there are fans dressed in sweaters and jeans who have queued all night, backpackers from destinations as far apart as America, Australia and the Far East, mingling with tennis devotees from the world of show business like Peter Ustinov, Charlton Heston, and Cliff (now Sir Cliff) Richard.

Lew was overwhelmed. 'Bloody hell, I'd never seen anything like it in the world,' he told friends. For the first time in his life he felt nervous. It was not just the intimidating atmosphere of Wimbledon that bothered him, it was his first round singles opponent, the Italian, Guiseppe (known as 'Beppi') Merlo. He was recognised as a maestro with the racquet, a tennis magician who could bewitch, torment, and confuse his victims, luring them to destruction. Especially on the slow, clay courts of the Italian Championships in Rome, playing Beppi was like being a fly gradually enmeshed in the web of a spider. Even on a fast grass court –

not his favoured surface – he represented a formidable challenge, a man always tough to beat.

Lew's description paints a vivid picture of Merlo: 'He is a little man with tiny, dancing feet, who takes no backswing, plays with a loosely strung racquet like my old Onion Bag, and uses two-handed shots.' True to form, Beppi chipped and sliced the ball throughout the match, blocking everything back, taking the pace off the ball, and waiting for Lew's errors. Hoad's nervousness caused him to make several, and it took him five sets and two-and-a-half hours before he finally overcame the Italian.

Three rounds later he ran into the man who, having hit with him in Australia, predicted a great future for Lew – Jaraslav Drobny. It was the young Australian's first match on the Centre Court, but it was familiar territory to his opponent who had previously reached four semi-finals at Wimbledon and was second favourite to win the title. Lew didn't play badly; he aced his opponent fourteen or fifteen times but Drobny was able to call upon his vast experience, and proved too cunning for Hoad, winning in four sets. Lew wasn't bothered because he had learned something: he realised he loved that fast surface. And the *Daily Express*, referring to the impressive performance by 'Lew Hoad, a blond Viking with a Melbourne surf bather tan and complexion,' went on to quote Drobny's generous tribute to his opponent: 'My luck was in today. I don't want to play this boy in two or three years time.'

The next day, the Saturday of the first week, Hoad and Rosewall, the 'twins', walked onto the Centre Court for their toughest challenge as a doubles pair. There, waiting to gobble them up, was the glowering, crew cut American, Gardner Mulloy, and his countryman and reigning Wimbledon Champion, Dick Savitt. The young Australians had been disappointed when they looked at the draw to see that in the second round of the doubles they were matched against the No 2 seeds. However, Hopman told them that though everyone expected the Americans to win, he thought they had a fighting chance of beating them.

It was a boiling hot day. In the packed stands the temperature registered over ninety degrees, and it's always hotter on the court. Back in Wigram Road his father and mother lay in bed with the lights out, listening to a short wave broadcast of the match. Before the knock-up, Savitt flashed a smile at the young Australians but Mulloy, well versed in the art of 'psyching' his opponents, just stared down at them, lashing his racquet from side to side like a tiger's tail. Lew vaguely remembered reading something at school about Christians being thrown to the lions in Roman amphitheatres. He felt jittery and glanced at Ken who was tight-lipped, pale and apprehensive.

'Are you ready, gentlemen? Play.'

The Australians got off to a shaky start and nerves were clearly inhibiting their play. But it soon dawned on them that they were faster round the court than the veterans the other side of the net. Mulloy at thirty-eight was four years older than the combined ages of the boys. Then Lew and Ken broke Savitt's serve in the 'vital seventh' game, surprising the Americans with some dazzling returns. The next game, Hoad's service, and he hits two aces. They had won the first set. The crowd – hardly able to believe their eyes – were growing more and more excited. They had been cheering at every change of ends, and the applause was often so prolonged that the players had to wait before the match could be resumed. Rumours of a possible upset began to fly around Wimbledon.

Mulloy and Savitt conferred and decided to try and hit their way out of trouble. The Australian boys ran and chased down everything, sometimes clashing racquets and bumping into each other in their desperate attempts to retrieve the ball. In the eleventh game Mulloy lost his serve, only for Hoad to follow suit. At 6-6 the youngsters raised their game another gear and played some dream shots. Making light of Savitt's booming serves, they punched stinging returns to the American's toes. One shot in particular brought the crowd to their feet, and if ever a shot won a set it was here: a cannonball serve of Savitt's looked unreturnable – surely Hoad couldn't get a racquet on it? But incredibly he hit a screamer down the line, past the flailing racquet of Mulloy at the net. Rosewall then served some rare aces in his service game to win the set, 8-6, and give the youngsters a two sets to love lead.

Mulloy looked as if he could murder them; Savitt shook his head in disbelief. The crowd went wild. But the Americans were not second seeds for nothing, and they showed steely determination and brilliant team-work to claw their way back into contention, winning the next two sets for the loss of only four games and levelling the match. Vivian Jenkins in the *News of the World* commented how, with everything resting on the final set, 'one could feel the electric atmosphere which comes to Wimbledon at its greatest moments.'

Years later, after a number of beers with friends had loosened his tongue, Lew re-lived the experience: the tension you could almost cut with a knife; a fever-pitch excitement with the cheering, clapping crowd almost out of control; the sudden silences like a curtain falling. In that fifth set, one of the most dramatic climaxes to a match ever seen at Wimbledon, there were breathtaking winners, thunderous aces, and incredible passes and gets. The four players, said Lew, were often so close to each other at the net that, 'You could smell each other, almost hear our hearts straining and pounding.'

Games went with service until at 4-5, Rosewall prepared to serve. Though Gardner Mulloy and Lew had both somehow survived three game points against them on their serves, there was always the fear that Ken with his weaker serve might be the first to crack. The fear seemed well-founded; match point for the Americans at

30-40. Somehow it was saved, as Mulloy netted. In the eleventh game the 'twins' sensed their moment of destiny had arrived.

Recalling the match, and that game in particular, Lew smiled wistfully, and said: 'I loved it. I loved every shot I was playing. And in that game, Kenny hit the two greatest backhands I have seen in tennis. The first sent Mulloy to the floor as he tried to cover it. Then – in the next point, Dick lobbed Kenny and practically hand in hand we dashed back. Kenny slid to a stop, almost colliding with the netting at the back of the court, turned and hit an unforgettable backhand drive which flew like an arrow between Gardner and Dick as they raced to the net. They were astonished – and so was I. Kenny just looked up, like he was expecting rain or something. He often did that.'

With spectators on the Centre Court and crowds packed together on the concourse outside now almost hysterical, Lew prepared to serve for the match. A hush descended. 15-0, 30-0, 40-0. Three match points and nothing was going to stop Lew finishing with a love game. 'Game, set and match to Hoad and Rosewall,' shouted the umpire trying to rise above the deafening noise of the crowd, '6-4, 8-6, 1-6, 3-6, 7-5.'

Lew, again: 'Kenny threw the jockey cap he was wearing into the air and I was grinning at him like a bloody idiot. The entire Centre Court stood and cheered for minutes. Gar and Dick came slowly to the net. Dick had a big grin on his swarthy face but Gar looked surly. Four hands shook. Then they put their arms around us. It was the greatest match Kenny and I had ever played and we'll always remember it. Some officials said it was one of Wimbledon's greatest games.'

At the post-match news conference, Gar was still looking surly, but when asked what he thought about the 'twins' he laughed and said, 'Great, that's what. Those kids are great.' Consolation for Mulloy came five years later when he became the oldest player ever to win a Wimbledon doubles title. Thousands of miles away in Wigram Road, Glebe, Australia, they heard the news on the radio. Lew's father cried.

The next day the boys awoke to discover they were headline news on the sports pages of newspapers all over the world. In England, *The Times* declared that never before had two of the world's best players been defeated by 17-year-olds. With the headline: 'Two Aussie Lads Shock US Stars,' *The People* called the result 'a sensation' and the *Sunday Graphic* described the match as a 'Teenage Turn-up. Frenzied spectators see Australian boys scarcely out of school blast second seeded pair.' The *News of the World* referred to, 'sweltering spectators nearly melting away with excitement'.

The youngsters were fêted wherever they went. Immediately after the match they were changing in their dressing room when Mr Clement Attlee, former Prime Minister and Leader of the Labour Opposition in the House of Commons, came rushing in and said to Harry Hopman, 'Where are those two boys of yours? I'd like to congratulate them on such a great win.' Hoad tried to dissuade the politician, saying he was still under the shower and dripping wet. 'Nonsense, my boy,' retorted Attlee. Barging into the shower room, he grabbed Lew's hand, told him what a tremendous win he and Rosewall had pulled off, and left, a slightly bedraggled figure with damp trousers.

Fan mail for the 'twins' poured into their hotel and in the second week of Wimbledon they were introduced to well-known people like Field-Marshall Lord Montgomery, and invited into the Royal Box to meet the Duchess of Kent. Overnight they had achieved the celebrity status of pop stars today. Looking back at this reception almost half a century later, it might seem amazing that such a fuss should have been made of Hoad and Rosewall's victory. Today, a similar Wimbledon upset might warrant little more than a by-line in a tennis report. Doubles matches now occupy such a lowly position in the tennis firmament. They usually get squeezed out of the television schedules at Wimbledon – partly, it's true, because of always being scheduled so late in the day. And yet tennis aficionados, and most keen club players, will tell you that there are few singles matches that compare with the entertainment, visual spectacle of rat-a-tat-tat rallies, and the variety of good doubles play.

Unfortunately, the top men players now tend to shun the men's, and especially the mixed, doubles, preferring to concentrate all their energies on the more prestigious, and far more lucrative, singles title. Ultimately it comes down to money and the tennis game, the *singles* game, represents, par excellence, the dominance of market forces and the triumph of bourgeois individualism. The public can be whipped up to a frenzy of partisan support for their favourite, and matches are played out in a gladiatorial atmosphere where the quality of play is less important than the result. Wimbledon now resounds to hysterical cries of 'Come on Tim' – or 'André' – or 'Pete'.

In Hoad's day, the players often entered all three events. The singles title was the most important title, but they enjoyed playing doubles events, and doubles titles still carried considerable prestige. And though Hoad might have had his ardent young female fans who, just like fans today, were obsessed with seeing their idol win, the manner of that winning was still regarded as important.

Equally important to British crowds at Wimbledon then was the adherence to traditional values of sportsmanship and fairness, and this applied especially to the way in which they supported British players competing against foreign opponents. The '50s are, however, a world away – a world that has disappeared, and will never return. Its passing was sharply registered in the crowd's response to the women's final of 1977, Jubilee year. Admittedly British fans had been brought up on failure, had become inured to English players losing gallantly, so the vociferous support of Virginia Wade was understandable. Even so, would a Wimbledon crowd in 1952 have cheered double faults by Betty Stove, Wade's opponent in the final – as crowds did in 1977?

The last great singles player to compete in the doubles events was John McEnroe. He clearly loved playing doubles, and never regarded competing in this event as a handicap in winning the men's singles. Interestingly, when he teamed up with Steffi Graff for the mixed doubles in the Wimbledon Championships in 1999, Graff disappointed the crowd (and, possibly, the Tournament Committee who saw this pairing as a dream ticket) when she pulled out of their semi-final doubles match because of her singles final the next day.

Hoad and Rosewall's fine run in the doubles continued through the next two rounds. In the semi-final, however, they lost in four sets to Eric Sturgess and the American with film-star looks, Vic Seixas. This match was marred by disputes between Seixas and the umpire. In fairness to Seixas, it should be pointed out that it wasn't just the crowd's noisy cheering of the Australian youngsters that caused him to become nettled. Following a bad call that deprived Hoad and Rosewall of a winner, he felt aggrieved when his deliberate mistake on the next point was not reciprocated with a similar gesture from the Australian pair when a similar incident occurred a few games later.

Hoad clearly had some sympathy for Seixas, and the description of this incident in his autobiography leaves it unclear whether the Australians' refusal to concede the later disputed point was because they didn't feel the linesman had made an obvious mistake. Of course, it's typical of Hoad, with his belief in sportsmanship, that he should gloss over this and present his opponent's argument with the referee in the best possible light.

In defeat, the 'twins' had certainly not disgraced themselves. The *Sunday Graphic* commented:

> *The narrow margin by which Sturgess and Seixas won was an eloquent tribute to the skill and courage of their young opponents; but what it does not show, is that the Australians on two occasions had a point for the fourth set and if Hoad had not smashed out of court on the first, they must have won it.*

The report continued:

> *As before, their volleying was brilliant, Hoad's in particular being at times almost miraculous, and their tenacity was such that Seixas and Sturgess had to make a titanic effort to shake them off.*

Wimbledon finished on a high note for the Australian team that year because Frank Sedgman won the singles title at his fifth attempt, beating Drobny fairly comfortably in four sets. Then Hopman and his team flew to the United States for the American season, played in some of the wealthiest country clubs in the world. It was an eye-opening experience for Lew who couldn't believe the opulent lifestyle of the Americans, especially when competing in the Pacific South West Tournament which was close to the glamorous world of Hollywood. Harry Hopman's wife, Nell, who was travelling with the team, recalled how many film stars who were ardent tennis fans would not only flock to see them play but also arrange lavish parties for them.

When Ken Rosewall beat Seixas to take the singles title, Stewart Granger and Jean Simmons had been the first to rush over and congratulate him. Other regular fans from the movie colony included Humphrey Bogart and Lauren Bacall, Audrey Hepburn, Ginger Rogers, Debbie Reynolds and Marlene Dietrich. In an interview for an Australian newspaper, Lew described Jean Simmons as, 'the best looking girl,' he'd ever seen and 'just as good off-screen as she is on it.' However, in the same interview, he also said 'he didn't care for American girls because they talked too much,' and 'Australian girls dressed better.' Nevertheless, Lew and Ken were great admirers of Debbie Reynolds who gave the latter an autographed photo as a keepsake after his singles win.

A newspaper photograph from this visit shows Hoad and Rosewall (plus Stewart Granger) bare-chested surrounded by a bevy of Hollywood beauties. What particularly impressed Hoad was that the Australian team were offered The Stone House, built by actor Lewis Stone, to live in. Lewis Stone was his mother's favourite actor, and she'd christened her son after him.

Both Rosewall and Hoad reached the quarter-finals of the singles of the US Open where Mulloy had his revenge over Rosewall, and Lew was beaten by Sedgman who went on to take the title without dropping a set throughout the tournament. Hopman said he was pleased with the boys: they had done pretty well on the tour. He himself had come in for a good deal of criticism about the way he handled them but he felt vindicated by their successes. Now it was time to go home. When they landed at Sydney airport there were families, friends, fans, officials, and a scrum of reporters and photographers awaiting them.

When the team was interviewed, they all said they were tired and wanted a holiday, which provoked a fresh storm of criticism of Hopman's training regime. Lew felt this was unfair. Hopman had done wonders for his game on the tour. 'Hard work was essential for someone with my lazy mind.'

Hopman was asked what the 'twins' had done when they weren't training or playing. He replied: 'They read comics mostly. The only difference is I think Rosewall understood them.' Fortunately Lew, like most Australians, had a good sense of humour.

Chapter 4

Davis Cup preparations

When the 1952-1953 Australian tennis season started, Lew was still not eighteen. He had acquired an international reputation and his electrifying shots, good looks, natural charm and self-effacing modesty, had made him into the golden boy of Australian tennis. Unfortunately he got off to a miserable start with a string of inexplicable losses to lesser men. Once again the papers rounded on Hopman, saying the tour players had been over-worked, 'over-tennised' and, at the age of eighteen, the tour youngsters were now over the hill! When Hoad and Rosewall had a bad loss, one newspaper carried the headline: 'From whizz kids to was kids'. Hoad was accused of not enjoying his tennis; you no longer see him grinning or laughing on court, people said. But Dunlop boss, Adrian Quist, rose to his defence. He pleaded for understanding: 'Hoad's innate shyness is almost an embarrassment to him. At times crowds have mistaken this for superciliousness. What he needs is to be given confidence in himself.'

Lew described his own attitude at the time in terms of his concern to get his game right. He knew a lot was expected of him, and also of Rosewall, especially after their dramatic debut at Wimbledon. But it was harder for him than it was for Kenny who had no problem with either his concentration or controlling his emotions on court. 'It's difficult to grin,' confided Lew to friends, 'when you're getting your head together.' Also, he was working on his ground shots, trying to increase his control and consistency. At the same time his service action required some fine tuning: his action had barely changed at all since he started playing tennis, but he wanted to eliminate the double faults that sometimes crept into his game. He worked on the stretch and leap in his overhead, which, in time, became so powerful that it once took a huge divot out of the Wimbledon Centre Court grass – much to the concern of the ground staff. Essentially, Hoad was trying to come to terms with the responsibilities that advisors and senior administrators in the game sought to impose on him.

After a dismal start to the season, it came as something of a shock when he heard that he'd been selected for the 1952 Davis Cup team. It was only the second time an 18-year-old had ever been selected for an Australian Davis Cup team. Clearly it was his doubles performances rather than his singles play that had earned him a place. When Rosewall phoned to congratulate him, they bemoaned the fact that they were to be split-up as a doubles partnership for Australia.

In fact, Rosewall had only been selected for the training squad, not to play in the rubbers. Ken McGregor and Frank Sedgman, the two leading stars at the time, were the backbone of the team, with Mervyn Rose as first reserve. So if someone was injured, Hoad would get a game in the doubles. What was important was that he was involved in all the Davis Cup activity: training, team-talks, and hitting balls every day for two weeks with other members of the team to ensure they would all be in tip-top shape for the matches against Vic Seixas and Tony Trabert. It was invaluable experience.

As the Davis Cup matches grew nearer, Lew noticed that Sedgman and McGregor became rather secretive. Maybe what he hadn't noticed was that Jack Kramer, the American professional tennis promoter, was also in town at that time. The Australians won the Cup 4-1 and after the final rubber, Sedgman and McGregor announced that they had signed with Kramer and were to turn professional.

The Australian public and the tennis authorities were shocked. There was uproar – facing an uncertain future, all the country had to rely upon now to mount a challenge in the Davis Cup were the 'twins'. When the supremo of Australian tennis, Sir Norman Brookes, asked Hopman: 'What will we do now?' he simply replied, 'Give me the boys for twelve months and everything will be all right.' Preparations had to begin very soon because it would not be long before the national team left Australia for another gruelling overseas tour – with the added incentive of Davis Cup places to come for Lew and Ken, plus their reunion as a doubles pair.

Both the European and American legs of the tour were less than remarkable as far as Lew's singles play was concerned. Feeling the intensity of expectations aroused by the previous year's tour, he won only two singles tournaments. However, the Hoad and Rosewall doubles partnership flourished. They won four national doubles titles: Australian, Italian, French and Wimbledon, and were just pipped in the US Doubles - a great disappointment for the 'twins' as the Grand Slam of five titles had never been achieved before.

At this time, the major figures on the tennis scene were the two Americans, Trabert and Seixas. Tony Trabert, crew cut, six feet tall, honing his big game to perfection after two years in the US Navy. And Vic Seixas, dark, good-looking, someone who could be a difficult customer on court to officials, fans and opponents, but charming and witty off it. Trabert had beaten Seixas in the finals of the US Singles, and two of the world's greatest players were about to try and snatch back the Davis Cup from two teenagers for whom this would be their first Davis Cup outing.

Australian hopes were raised, however, by a transformation in Lew's singles record once he was back on his own shores. As the 1953 Davis Cup Challenge Round approached he notched up a string of victories, including one over Rosewall that set the pattern for his future dominance over his long-time rival.

Then the Americans arrived and, full of confidence, declared: 'We've come to take the Cup home.'

* * *

How did the Davis Cup, this competition that generates such passions and such fervent nationalistic feelings, come into being? It's generally agreed that the idea of a cup competition between tennis teams from different nations was the brainchild of a wealthy young American tennis player, Dwight Filley Davis. The adjective 'wealthy' is really superfluous since tennis at the turn of the century was almost exclusively the preserve of an affluent elite; it was a relatively new game and one only affordable by people from a wealthy, upper-class background.

Inheriting the family merchandising business, Dwight's father, John Davis, had expanded it by opening new offices in America, France, England, and Germany. By 1882 his properties in St Louis alone were worth over a million dollars, and he had become a director of several banks as well as founding one of his own. But when John Davis – reputedly the richest man in Missouri – died in 1894, he bequeathed his son more than just a very considerable fortune; Dwight also inherited his father's patrician code of honour and belief in public service. As E. Digby Baltzell points out, in later life, Dwight Davis:

> served on the boards of almost every cultural institution of importance in St Louis [his home town] and on many at national level; he went with the Missouri National Guard to France in the First World War, winning the Distinguished Service Cross for 'extraordinary heroism in action.' Calvin Coolidge appointed him Secretary of War and Herbert Hoover made him Governor-General of the Philippines.[1]

Dwight Davis first tried playing tennis at the age of fourteen, just a few months after his father's death. His mother had taken him for a holiday to the fashionable Oceanside Hotel near Magnolia in Massachusetts, and he played on the clay courts of the Essex County Club. It wasn't long before young Dwight was hooked on the game. Returning with fellow team members from a Californian tournament in the fall of 1899, he conceived the idea of a trophy to stimulate international competition:

> Just as the team reluctantly started eastwards, the International Cup races for the America's Cup were being sailed; the newspapers were full of the

preliminary tryouts and then of the races themselves. Putting two and two together... this thought occurred to me: 'If team matches between different parts of the same country arouse such great interest and promote such good feeling, would not similar international contests have even wider and far-reaching consequences?' [2]

However, Dwight Davis's claim to have first thought of an international competition was later disputed by an Englishman, Charles A. Voigt. In an article for *Lawn Tennis and Badminton* in July 1912, Voigt described meeting Davis some years before the initiation of the Davis Cup at a tournament at Niagara-on-the-Lake. Apparently there was a daily paper called *The Lark* which was devoted to the tournament and engaged in gossip and social chitchat about the players. According to Voigt, *The Lark* contained frequent references to Dwight F. Davis's 'strolls in the shrubberies' with 'the belle of the place'. Having named some of this young lady's other admirers, Voigt insists that none was really able to compete with Davis:

> *I remember there was great rivalry over her favours, but neither Whitman's blonde curls, nor Wrenn's fascination, nor young Beal Wright's spotless high collar, (he, too, was in the running), nor Scott Griffin's diamonds (to 'cut diamonds' was a larkish expression for cocktails and other liquid refreshments) nor the bookays of honey-suckle which a foreign count laid at her feet, could cope successfully with Dwight Davis. He cut out all others easily and won a love set. 'Who on earth is this young sport?' I remember enquiring one evening as the couple passed out of the ballroom onto the balcony and from thence wandered off into the moonlit gardens. 'Why that's our young multi-millionaire, Dwight Davis, of St Louis,' was the reply. So rarely had I had the good fortune of meeting a millionaire... and such a young one into the bargain that my first observation was: 'A millionaire, is he? If so, why don't you people get him to do something for the game? Put up some big prize, or a cup?' I verily believe that passing remark laid the foundation of the Davis Cup! We had just been discussing the possibilities of international visits and matches, and I had ventured to observe that, if properly put before the Associations of the two countries, the affair would no doubt soon become a fait accompli. Next morning 'The Lark' recorded scraps of the conversation. Davis read and heard about it, and so did all the others, and when the matter was seriously brought up a few years later, Dwight Davis came forward and offered to present a trophy for international competition. And this is the true story of how the Davis Cup originated.* [3]

The light-hearted tone and the Gatsbyesque expressions with which Voigt laces his narrative do not mean one should dismiss his claim out-of-hand. A chance remark from the Englishman could have lodged itself in the back of Dwight Davis's mind, and he may even have forgotten where it came from. What cannot be disputed is that it was Davis who possessed the energy, the will, and the financial resources to convert this idea into a reality.

The Davis Cup began, auspiciously, in the first year of the twentieth century. The formula arrived at for the schedule of matches has remained the same ever since. Played over three days, the contest involved five matches - four singles and a doubles. Two singles were played on the opening day, a doubles match on the second, and the reverse singles on the final day. A team consisted of four players: the singles had to be played by the two players nominated, but there could be an entirely new combination for the doubles – or the doubles pairing could draw upon one or both of the players selected for the singles.

In that first year of the Cup, the British Isles, who were the only challengers, sent a team of three players to the States: A.W. Gore, the 32-year-old Wimbledon Singles Champion of the previous year; E.D. Black, a tall Scot in his late twenties; and H. Roper Barrett, a 26-year-old London solicitor, generally acknowledged to be a shrewd tactician. They were pitted against a much younger US side. Malcolm Whitman, at 23, was the oldest member of the team and he would play No 1 singles. Dwight Davis was No 2, and was 21, the same age as his doubles partner, Holcombe Ward.

When the British team docked in New York they were slightly dismayed to find that there seemed to be no-one to greet them. Having no practice facilities available, they decided to visit Niagara Falls on the Canadian border, a spectacle which, according to Roper Barrett, 'beggared description'. However, when the 'Dauntless Three', as the British team were dubbed, finally arrived at Boston, 48 hours late, there were no complaints about the hospitality of their American hosts. Instead, complaints were reserved for the conditions of the courts on which they were to play, conditions which exacerbated the problems the British team had in handling the twist serve of their opponents. Fortunately, Roper Barrett's recollections of this contest survive; whilst he's scathing about the courts and the balls used, his lively account includes an aside which indicates that – like so many talented players who came after him – he had an eye for the pretty girls:

Now, as to the conditions of play at Longwood, the venue of the international matches. The grounds were abominable. The grass was long. Picture to yourself a court in England where the grass has been the longest you ever encountered; double the length of that grass and you have the courts at Longwood at that time. The net was a disgrace to civilised lawn tennis, held up by guy ropes that were continually sagging... As for the balls... They were awful – soft and motherly – and when served with the American twist came at you like an animated egg-plum... We had never experienced this service before and it quite nonplussed us. The spectators were most impartial and the female portion thereof not at all unpleasant to gaze upon… The umpires, who sat perched on tables, and the linesmen discharged their duties most satisfactorily. Indeed, we had nothing to complain about in regard to American sportsmanship and hospitality…[4]

Given their problems both in adjusting to the court conditions and coping with the Americans' twist serves, it's not altogether surprising that the British Isles' team were beaten 3-0 (at this stage, with the remaining rubbers of only academic interest and players pressing commitments elsewhere, the match was abandoned). Perhaps the British team was a little complacent and underestimated their opponents.

Certainly this was not the best team that might have been fielded. Overshadowing the contest for Britain was the continuing Boer War. Although neither of their two best players, the brothers Reginald and Laurie Doherty, were in the army, they still found pressing reasons for absenting themselves from the tie. If the Boer War provided the British LTA with a readymade excuse for any shortcomings in the team's performance, the Americans had an even more legitimate excuse. Two of their most experienced players, William Larned and Robert Prenn, were recuperating from injuries sustained while in action with Teddy Roosevelt's Rough Riders in Cuba, and were therefore unavailable. Thus the young and untested American team could feel immense pride in their achievement; they had demonstrated admirable fighting qualities and ensured that in the inaugural year of the competition, the handsome cup donated by Dwight Davis would remain in the USA.

A photograph of the winning team shows Dwight Davis standing, hand on hip, behind a table, upon which rests the Davis Cup – his 'Little Pot' as it was affectionately known. Seated on either side of him are his two team-mates. There's a casual elegance about Davis's pose, and an air of self-belief that privilege, breeding and ability invariably promote. Amanda Hooton, in an article on the Davis Cup for the *Sydney Morning Herald* Magazine (11th September 1999) describes how the sterling silver cup, commissioned by Davis from one of the most exclusive silversmiths in Boston, gradually increased in size with the passage of time:

At 33 centimetres high, it seemed more than adequate to the task of recording the victors and the vanquished each year. But Davis had reckoned without the passage of years. Today the cup stands on a tray, which stands on a base, which stands on another base, with a third base waiting in the wings. It looks like a cake a stripper leaps out of.

Back in the beginning, however, it was simply a Georgian-style bowl, decorated with primroses.

There was no challenge in the following year and in 1902 a strong British team was narrowly defeated, 3-2, by the Americans. However, in 1903 the Doherty brothers, Britain's two-man team, succeeded in bringing the Cup back to Britain where it remained for the next four years.

By 1905 the competition had widened to include not just America and the British Isles but also France, Belgium, Austria and – significantly – Australasia (Australia and New Zealand). Two of the three-man Australasian team were to become famous figures in the world of tennis: Norman Brookes and the New Zealander, Anthony Wilding. Although the team eventually lost to the Americans, 5-0, the match was much closer than the score suggests, and Brookes and Wilding, in particular, served notice that they would be a force to be reckoned with in the future. Sure enough, they returned to England only two years later to secure victories at Wimbledon – first in the All England Championship and then in the Davis Cup Challenge round. Brookes won the singles title and the doubles title with Wilding at Wimbledon, and the pair went on to defeat the British team, 3-2, and take the Davis Cup back to Australia where it remained for the next five years.

Australasia had won the Davis Cup for the first time but the result was not the easy victory some had anticipated. In fact, the contest is remembered more for the heroic resistance of the British team, represented by veterans Arthur Gore and Roper Barrett, aged 39 and 33 respectively. On the first day Brookes and Wilding won their singles matches against Gore and Barrett and, on the second, Australasia led by two sets to love in the doubles and had reached 5-3 and match point in the third. Somehow or other the British pair staved off defeat, saving the match point and going on to win the match, 13-11, in the fifth set.

Gore then defeated the inexperienced Wilding in the reverse singles to leave the contest poised tantalisingly at two rubbers each. Brookes, however, never faltered in the final match against Barrett, crushing him in straight sets.

Tony Wilding was an imposing figure: tall, good-looking, and incredibly fit. He set female hearts aflutter and when British Prime Minister Asquith rose to announce that 'Captain Anthony Wilding had died in the trenches of Flanders', the loss was felt keenly not only by the entire tennis world but by many who had no particular interest in tennis. Norman Brookes, however, is the figure more relevant to our narrative since almost half a century later – as president of the Lawn Tennis Association of Australia – he was to play a part in the Lew Hoad story.

Brookes, often known as 'The Wizard' by his contemporaries, was a slight, pale figure of average height. Though lacking the robust good health of his partner, Anthony Wilding, he was a natural sportsman who seemed to excel at all games. In his memoirs, Wilding paid tribute to his friend's sporting abilities:

> *A more versatile games man I have seldom met. He can make his hundred break at billiards fairly regularly. He is on or near the plus mark at golf. He was one of the finest left-hand schoolboy bowlers in Australia, and if he had stuck to cricket his appearance in test matches must only have been a question of time. I remember staying with Brookes at his home in Melbourne when the croquet championship of Australia happened to be taking place. Brookes invited the winner to play him a match on Sunday, and a dreadful act of sacrilege was committed – the tennis court was marked out for croquet. The champion came, saw, and was badly defeated.[5]*

Like Dwight Davis, Norman Brookes came from a wealthy background, and he inherited his father's sense of fair play and sportsmanship, qualities that were to characterise later generations of Australian tennis players. Baltzell provides a fascinating account of Brookes and his background:

> *The Brookes [Norman and his wife, Mabel] eventually became one of the first families of Melbourne, in the state of Victoria, where the first lawn tennis championship tournament in Australia was held in 1880. Norman Brookes was knighted in 1939 and his wife was made a DBE (Dame of the British Empire) in 1953…*
>
> *Norman's father, William Brookes, arrived in Melbourne from Northamptonshire in 1852, an orphan of 18 with nine pounds in his pocket. In the best traditions of the success sagas of our own [America's] Horatio Alger and England's Samuel Smiles, he soon made a place for himself in the sun, methodically building up a fortune in railways, bridge building, shipping, paper milling, and sheep ranching. A religious man of simple faith, plain tastes, and absolute integrity, he insisted that Norman earn his own living and treat tennis and his other games as secondary pastimes. Just as Norman was about to enter Melbourne University, for example, his father put him to work in one of his paper mills, where he began as a clerk licking stamps and ended up as chairman. At the same time he became one of Victoria's business, civic, and sporting leaders. Already in his thirties, Brookes was attracted by a young lady of 17 who was a member of one of Melbourne's distinguished families of far older wealth than his own…*
>
> *Throughout their married life, both Sir Norman and Dame Mabel dedicated themselves to the best interests of lawn tennis. In 1926 Brookes was made president of the Lawn Tennis Association of Australia, a post he held for 29*

years before retirement in 1955. Brookes came back to Europe in 1914, winning at Wimbledon in June and taking the Davis Cup back to Australia in August. After the war, he devoted his time to business and tennis administration. But he was still playing first-class tennis in his forties: in 1919 he won the US Doubles Championship (at the age of 42) with his pupil, Gerald Patterson; and in 1924 (at 47) he won the Australian Doubles Championship with John Anderson, who also won the singles that year.[6]

Amanda Hooton is obviously right in maintaining that most Australians have never heard of Brookes, their first national sporting hero. He is, she writes, Australia's original quiet achiever. When Brookes won Wimbledon in 1907, 'Everyone was stunned: no foreigner, let alone an Australian had ever beaten the Brits there before.' Perhaps she's also right to claim that Brookes, being laconic, self-deprecating and naturally gifted, exhibited traits that Australians like to imagine are inherent not only in their athletes, but also in their national identity.

In addition, she says, 'he refused to give in, which according to the English ethic of tennis, seemed slightly unsporting. Australians loved it. It was thanks to Brookes that guts got suddenly glamorous. His victories showed how we liked to win: coming from behind, sweating blood. We didn't mind if our players were carried unconscious from the field – as Brookes very nearly was – so long as they won before keeling over.'

Various things, argues Hooton, could be read into that Australian Davis Cup victory of 1907. That it helped, for instance, to forge a national sporting psyche, and establish that iron-jawed tradition of Australian tennis players; it could also explain New Zealanders' resentment of the way their contribution tends to be ignored. After all, it was New Zealand's cup too – not till 1923 did the two nations enter the competition separately.

What was incontestable was that it initiated a pattern of success that lasted a long time. 'Brookes continued to win,' says Hooton, 'and Davis's 'old tin pot' remained in Brookes' Melbourne home (with a two year hiatus) for nearly a decade and a half.' In fact, in the first century of the Davis Cup's history, America and Australia have emerged as the most successful nations. Apart from the dominance of France (with the magnificent 'Four Musketeers': Borotra, Brugnon, Cochet, and Lacoste) who won the Cup six years running between 1927 and 1932, Australia's record of twenty-six wins is second only to America's thirty-one.

Chapter 5

A Davis Cup Captain for all seasons – Harry Hopman

In achieving Davis Cup success, the role of the captain has been seen as pre-eminent. Upon the captain rests the responsibility of preparing the squad, selecting the team, and – the only time this is permitted in tennis – dispensing tactical advice, encouragement, and generally attending to the player's needs during each change of ends. It's widely acknowledged that the captain's seat at the side of the court is one of the 'hottest' in any sport. In soccer, for example, the team manager only has the fifteen-minute break between halves to advise and support his players. The Davis Cup captain lives every moment of the match alongside his players. He has to be a shrewd psychologist for no two players have the same make-up, react in the same way to intense pressure. He has to gauge when to comment, and when to stay silent; has to be able to read the game and the opponent; and needs to be aware of that occupational hazard for coaches: trying to dispense too much advice on tactics, shot selection etc. The last thing a captain wants to do is confuse the player with a plethora of instructions at changeover of ends.

Judged by any criteria, Harry Hopman emerges as the greatest captain in Davis Cup history. He had had a fine record as a doubles player and represented Australia in the Davis Cup in 1928, 1930 and 1932. This coincided with the period of French dominance, however, and his team returned to Australia empty handed.

Hopman was first appointed Davis Cup captain in 1938-39, but when World War Two ended he decided to concentrate on his job as a sportswriter. In the following years, Australia lost to the Americans in the Challenge Round four years running (1946-49). What should not be overlooked in recording these defeats, however, is that the commendable Australian preference for allowing the code of sportsmanship to overrule official regulations may have affected the outcome of the match in 1947.

Apparently, in the second rubber, a masseur had been summoned to treat Ted Schroeder who was suffering from cramp in his right arm. Fred Perry in the radio commentary box realised that this violated the rules and immediately informed

Alrick Man, the American captain. An embarrassed Man consulted with the match referee and rushed over to offer Roy Cowling, the Australian captain, the match by default. Schroeder had by this time beaten John Bromwich in four sets but Cowling refused to accept the offer stating that as far as the Australians were concerned, Schroeder had fairly won. This incident epitomised the tradition of good sportsmanship long associated with the Davis Cup, demonstrating that it was possible for the intense rivalry between these two nations to be maintained without losing sight of the Corinthian ideals that inspired the competition.

When Harry Hopman was once more appointed Davis Cup captain in 1950, Australia hoped that he might be the man to stem the tide. And how he repaid their belief in him! In the next eighteen years, Australia won the Davis Cup fifteen times. Not only that, but players who were members of the Davis Cup squad coached and captained by Hopman, won thirteen singles titles at Wimbledon, and these same players were losing finalists on twelve occasions – including eight where they were defeated by their own countrymen. It's a record for a Davis Cup captain that will probably never be surpassed.

Having said that, it might have been a different story if the top American players, Bobby Riggs, Ted Schroeder, and especially Jack Kramer and Pancho Gonzales, had not abandoned the amateur game and joined the ranks of the professionals. Many commentators would pick Kramer and Gonzales for their shortlist of all-time top tennis players. As Alan Trengove points out in *The Story of the Davis Cup*, it's doubtful whether Frank Sedgman and the talented crop of young Australians that succeeded him, players like Lew Hoad, Ken Rosewall, Ashley Cooper and Neale Fraser, 'would have blossomed so quickly if they had been obliged to make their way, from the start, against those who had turned pro.'

But while nobody could really dispute Hopman's claim to be the most successful Davis Cup captain the world has ever known, questions remain about his captainship and his coaching ability. Some would contend that he was simply the fortunate beneficiary of an Australian tennis system that produced a constant stream of gifted players like Hoad, Rosewall, Cooper, Fraser and, later, Fred Stolle, Mal Anderson, Roy Emerson, John Newcombe and Tony Roche. It's unlikely he would ever have been able to stamp his firm authority on his young protégés had there not been this production line of great players to replace those who turned pro or bucked against his stern rule. As for his coaching ability, Roy Emerson, whose record of the most wins in major tournaments has only recently been broken by Pete Sampras, said that he didn't teach them that much because most of the players had their own coaches anyway. However, he added, 'Once you were on the Davis Cup squad, he taught you everything tactically and demanded peak physical condition.'

On the other hand, Ashley Cooper, the 1958 Wimbledon Singles Champion, recently told the authors of this book (admittedly forty odd years after being a member of Hopman's squad) that he received no great tactical insights or revelations about opponents from Hopman. Rex Hartwig, Hoad's doubles partner in many Davis Cup matches, was another who was sceptical about Hopman's coaching ability. 'If Hop was such a good coach,' he commented, 'how come he never did anything to improve Rosewall's serve?'

Again, Hopman's team selection was an aspect of his stewardship that was occasionally called into question, though more often than not hindsight proved him right and his detractors wrong. As we shall see, the decision to substitute Hartwig for Rosewall as Hoad's doubles partner in the 1953 Davis Cup, a decision for which he was heavily criticised when the pairing failed miserably, was one imposed on him by the Australian selectors.

What really distinguished the Australian captain was his shrewd understanding of his players, a psychological acuity about the best way to motivate them or prepare them for the big match. Thus on one occasion he made sure that Mal Anderson won at poker the night before a vital challenge match because that would raise his spirits and boost his morale. He knew also how to spot a promising youngster, to recognise world class potential in a player others might have been tempted to dismiss. As Hooton says, 'He could pick a future champion at a thousand paces. He watched Rod Laver as a 'scrawny little kid in a bush hat with bandy legs,' and told Roy Emerson: 'This kid will win Wimbledon one day.' Laver won it four times.'

Finally, he was a strict disciplinarian who regarded physical fitness - being in peak physical condition - as a prerequisite of a successful Davis Cup squad. Undoubtedly the incredible fitness levels and stamina of Australian Davis Cup players, whether they were playing for their country or themselves, was one of the most important factors in their amazing record of victories. Come the fifth set in a closely fought contest and the fitter player will be a fraction of a second faster to the ball that makes all the difference between winning and losing.

Hopman regularly put his squads through punishing training routines involving road runs, drills on court with two against one, and weight training in the gym – till they were on the point of collapse. Though the results appeared to justify this spartan regime, some have questioned the extreme pressures placed upon players. Ken Rosewall, for example, has suggested that Hoad's later problems with a back injury may well have been exacerbated by Hopman's insistence that he spend time in the gym lifting weights that were too heavy and placed an excessive strain on the kidney muscles and back.

What helped the Aussies to survive and prosper under this exhausting schedule, argues Arthur Ashe, the 1975 Wimbledon Singles Champion, were two factors:

> *First of all, and simply, the Australians are good athletes; they are athletes who happen to be tennis players. They didn't learn in country clubs. Secondly, though probably more important, it is part of their culture to endure. By their own definition, they are a nation of 'mutton-punchers' and 'sod-busters' and so it was relatively easy for them to accept the Marquis de Sade exercises that, in the main, Harry Hopman devised.*

Ashe goes on to provide a perceptive appraisal of the Australian captain:

> *Hop is the father figure of Australian tennis – or the godfather figure. He was captain for most of thirty years, beginning in 1938, and while he had been a world-class player himself, he made his mark as a team leader. He wasn't just a captain, he was everything: coach, administrator, trainer, warden, chaperone. He even wrote his own newspaper scoops. He is the one constant in the Aussie story, and while many of the guys who played for him still hate his bloody guts, they all give him credit.*

> *Of all Hopman's training devices, the most maniacal is the two-on-one drill: just two guys on one side of the net hitting to the target player on the other. It's as simple as it sounds and it's a universal procedure now, but it's absolutely the most gruelling exercise.[1]*

But important though these training methods were, says Ashe, what was even more crucial was the team camaraderie and the sense of continuity Hopman created. The younger Aussies who haven't developed under Hopman's watchful eye, he argues, don't possess the same spirit and outlook. This is partly attributable to the influence of money, and partly to a change in culture:

> *Hopman probably couldn't run things his way any more. He treated newcomers to the squad with contempt. Here was some hotshot kid, junior champion, the comer, and Hopman made him into an errand boy, an orange squeezer. The reserves on the team didn't hit a ball unless Hopman deigned to let them. On the other hand, if he thought one of his stars needed work, he'd bring out a reserve and use him as a ball machine for as long as it suited his purposes.[2]*

Induction into the Davis Cup squad clearly involved the negotiation of difficult *rites de passage* and the picture that emerges is reminiscent of those military academy films, in which a young rookie soldier is licked into shape by the sergeant/commanding officer, who is a martinet, but a fair one. The officer – Hopman – eventually instils in his young recruits the kind of training and camaraderie that enables them to overcome all odds. The rookie is transformed into an 'officer and a gentleman'.

When considering the disciplinary code – against which Hoad occasionally rebelled by staying out late and having a few too many beers – one should always bear in mind that Hopman's squad generally regarded his rules with an amused tolerance. The fines, for example, for swearing or ungentlemanly behaviour, were too trivial even in those days to make much impact on a player's pocket. Yet some critics saw them as evidence that Hopman's authoritarian control of his squad was like Captain Queeg's over his crew in *The Caine Mutiny*. Given that Alan Hoad had always been quick to nip any unsporting behaviour in the bud, Lew tended to look upon Hopman not as a tyrannical bully but as a father-figure – as he so often did with older men whom he respected. Hoad, Neale Fraser and Roy Emerson have all emphasised that with so many youngsters regularly in the squad, Harry was, essentially, *in loco parentis*, and that one of his great achievements was to turn his charges into fine ambassadors for their country. Ashley Cooper says he set an example by not drinking or swearing, and that he joined in with the training routines. Also, the responsibility of speaking at dinners was rotated so that each player acquired some experience of this daunting task because Hopman knew this was a role they would often be called upon to fulfil on foreign tours.

But not all players responded to his strict, dictatorial regime. Mervyn Rose, one of Hopman's Davis Cup team, a man with a mercurial temperament, dry wit, and a non-conformist attitude, had a dog he christened 'Hop'. 'Why'd you call that mongrel 'Hop', Rosie?' enquired one of his friends. 'Well,' replied Rose, 'it's so whenever it's passing I can have the satisfaction of giving it a good kick.'

And not all players were prepared to put up with Hopman; some even abandoned Australian tennis forever and went elsewhere to win their spurs. Ken Fletcher, an accomplished player seeded No 3 at Wimbledon one year, left for England; Bob Hewitt, never one to obediently knuckle under to authority, emigrated to South Africa who he represented very successfully in Davis Cup matches; and Martin Mulligan went to live in Rome and played for Italy.

Confident that the conveyor belt of Australian tennis would produce comparable or even better replacements, Harry could afford to ignore such defections. On some occasions, however, his method of asserting his control over a player could amount, at best, to insensitivity and, at worst, to bullying and psychological intimidation. Hopman provides a good example of this in his own book, *Aces and Places*. He explains that Ken Rosewall is left-handed in many ways, and then goes on to recount a time in 1952 when the team, wanting a break from tennis, headed for a beach just outside New York City:

At the last moment one suggested taking a tennis ball to throw about in the water, and on the beach, so I warned against too much strong throwing because of the US championships coming up the next day.

'You're not talking to me, Hop, are you?' queried 'Muscles' (as he was known to the team in that first overseas tour).

'And why not you, Mr Rosewall?' I asked.

'Only because I'm a left-handed thrower, Hop,' said 'Muscles', delighted to have caught me out.

Rosewall was really a baby in the team that year, so I asked Ken McGregor, sitting beside him in the car to punish him. 'Big Mac' put a headlock on him, chiefly I think to hear the little fellow's cry of 'Help me, Lew.' [3]

Note the curious and ambiguous phrasing of 'really a baby in the team that year', particularly in the context of Hopman asking McGregor to 'punish him'. And again the reader is left uncertain about the tone of voice in which such comments were made, or how to interpret Rosewall's cry of 'Help me, Lew.' Without hearing Rosewall or seeing the expression on his face, it's impossible to know whether it was a serious plea for help. If Rosewall said it in a falsetto voice, then he was clearly joining in with the fun. As it is, the reader might well conclude that Rosewall was a 'wimp'. The whole account, which leaves a slightly sour taste in the mouth, is quoted in Peter Rowley's book about Rosewall's life in tennis, *Twenty Years at the Top* (written with Rosewall).

Rowley – one presumes with the player's approval – made no bones about Ken's antipathy towards Hopman, which he claimed could be traced back to this 'amazing' incident. 'The suppressed violence,' he says, 'of the tennis world comes out in the crude camaraderie and rough jokes among the stars' manifested here. Ignoring the ambiguity of the 'baby' reference (Hopman might argue that he simply meant Rosewall was one of the youngest members of the team), Rowley continues: 'If Rosewall was indeed a 'baby', punishing him was hardly the way to mature him. As Rosewall was possibly the most talented junior player in the world... he deserved respect.'

Another dominant figure in the world of tennis critical of Hopman was Jack Kramer. In his biography, *The Game* (a fascinating account of both his career and major developments in tennis), he acknowledges the debt Australian tennis, and the Davis Cup squad in particular, owes Hopman, and he clearly respects his assessment of players and his tactical acumen. However, he also admits that the Australian captain has never been his 'favourite guy'. The reasons he cites for this are instructive, and some of his criticisms illustrate the diametrically opposed perspectives of the two men towards the game.

Hopman, says Kramer, has devoted his life to tennis; both his marriages were childless and his first wife was an accomplished player in her own right so that there were no distractions. For husband and wife tennis represented an all-consuming passion. But what really sticks in Jack's craw is that once one of his protégés left the amateur fold, 'Hopman would turn on him.' As soon as a player was out of Hopman's control – no matter how close to him he'd been, 'the guy was an outcast.'

'It was as if we'd never existed,' Rosewall said once. And yet if a pro tried to help Hopman and his old Australian team, Hopman would make use of him.

Kramer cites an occasion when Frank Sedgman, by then a pro, offered to help train the Australian team. Hopman accepted his offer, but asked him confidentially if he'd go easy playing Hoad and Rosewall because what they both needed was their confidence boosted. Sedgman gladly agreed, only to find that Hopman in his newspaper column had boasted, 'how his kids could whip Sedgman and this proved once again that amateurs were better than pros'.

Such a devious ploy was bound to anger Kramer, a proud man whose belief in the superiority of the pros to the top amateurs was not only well-justified, but crucial in maintaining public interest in the professional game, and thus the financial viability of pro tours. If you look at the incident from Hopman's point of view, however, and ignore the ethical dubiety of the Australian captain's behaviour, it might be regarded as a legitimate method of boosting the morale of his players for the Davis Cup challenge they were facing. Of course, he might also have been bitter about the way Kramer had 'poached' former Australian Davis Cup stars, and wanted to discredit pro tennis. As Kramer points out, 'He battled open tennis to the bitter end.'

Chapter 6

Shootout at Kooyong

In 1953, the Australian tennis authorities fixed on Kooyong in Melbourne for the Davis Cup venue and spent just over £800,000 to make it the 'Wimbledon of Australia'. The old stand, built in 1946 for the last Challenge round held there, was demolished and work on constructing a new stand began. Towering seventy feet high, this stand would increase the capacity from 10,000 to 17,500 – which was to be a world record for a tennis crowd.

Hundreds of staff and builders worked round the clock for four months to get things ready. Workers slept in the grounds; thirty-four ball-boys and a similar number of umpires were selected from hundreds of applicants. Out of four hundred eager aspirants, one hundred and twenty-five young women were trained to marshal the expected record crowds in and out of the stadium and direct them to their seats. Careful plans were made for the checking of tickets – though these were sabotaged by wily Australians who, once through the turnstiles, put their tickets in the lunch boxes and bags they had brought with them and dropped them from the stadium to friends waiting below.

Excitement was at fever pitch. As Richard Evans points out in *The Davis Cup*, 'Beating England at cricket had always been the Australians favourite pastime. Now beating the Americans at tennis was becoming a passion of equal proportions.' Thousands of fans even turned up for the draw to decide the order of play. Lew drew Seixas for the first match on court at 1.15pm on Monday, 28th December.

The *Sydney Sun* was in confident mood: 'Lewis Hoad 'the strong man of Australia's team' is ready. His serve is now more powerful than any in the amateur game, his overhead is dynamite, and his drives, heavy with topspin, wait for the right shot to win. He is untroubled by reverses almost to the point of nonchalance. He has few mannerisms; although he'll throw his racket when a hard-played stroke goes wrong. When you watch him you are probably seeing a world-champion in the making.' Lew also believed he'd improved his ground strokes to a point where they now matched the rest of his game.

When Hoad and Seixas walked on court in their national blazers, 17,000 people – the biggest crowd ever – rose to applaud them. Thirty-one flags representing the countries that had entered the Cup that year fluttered all around the ground and the two national anthems were played. It was a daunting moment for the teenager. But he was perfectly relaxed and hit the ball with such beauty, power and precision that Seixas was quickly tumbled out in three sets.

The Australian victory celebrations were short-lived. If the tension of the moment hadn't got to Lew, it certainly had Kenny. Nerves particularly affected his second serve which Tony Trabert eagerly latched on to as he cruised to a straight-sets win.

There followed a crisis meeting as the Australian selectors agonised over the doubles pairing for the following day. Arguments raged back and forth about the wisdom of selecting Rosewall; he'd been so nervous in his singles – would it undermine his confidence still further to pick him for the doubles? Hopman held out for Rosewall on three counts: one, he wasn't as nervous as he looked; two, to drop him obviously would damage his confidence; and three, why break up a tried and tested team that had won almost everything in sight, including the French title the previous year?

But Hopman was overruled and they pulled Rex Hartwig from the reserves to play with Lew. Unfortunately the new pairing – unfamiliar with each other's game and without match practice together – were only told of the decision a couple of hours before they were due to play.

It was clear from the start this experiment was not going to work, although later they were to prove a formidable combination, winning a string of doubles titles, including the Wimbledon doubles in 1955. At this stage, however, the problem was that basically they were both right court players. Also, as the match progressed, they became increasingly unsettled by the Americans' system of signalling during service games; this is where the player at the net signals behind his back to his serving partner to indicate whether he's going to cross and intercept the return of serve. Hoad and Hopman regarded this tactic – so much a feature of the modern game where all kinds of similar tactics are adopted to unsettle the receiver – as unsportsmanlike conduct. The Australians, out-of-sorts and unable to find any rhythm to their game, went down 6-2, 6-4, 6-4 to Trabert and Seixas.

Australia was shocked by the defeat, which was blamed on the selection of Rex Hartwig. The selectors were subjected to a torrent of abuse, with Hopman, in particular, singled out for criticism. This was hardly fair; he had opposed the dropping of Rosewall but had been overruled. However, he kept his silence and his dignity in the face of mounting complaints that the 'twins' had been put in an impossible position by the rank stupidity of old, out-of-touch selectors. Two teenagers had now been entrusted with the daunting task of turning this match around by winning both remaining rubbers against seasoned American opponents.

Switchboards were jammed as messages and calls flooded in offering support to Hoad and Rosewall. Time and again, well-wishers phoned to say that Australia looked to the youngsters in its time of need. This was a sentiment echoed by newspapers and radio stations, so that when Lew walked out on court with Trabert to try to bring the scores even, not just Melbourne, but the entire population of Australia was in a state of fever-pitch excitement.

As the game developed, the whole nation ground to a halt. Everywhere people crowded around radios: in parks, cafes, and in the streets where shops even put their radios on the pavement so more people could gather round and listen. Later it was reported that two seamen in Sydney harbour, caught listening instead of working, had been fired. Richard Evans provides another illustration of how powerfully the country's imagination was gripped by this enthralling clash:

> On Glenferrie Road, which passes the famous tennis club at Kooyong, a tram stopped one afternoon just after Christmas in 1953. Nothing extraordinary in that. They have been stopping there ever since. But never again has a driver climbed out of his cab and, putting himself in imminent danger of electrocution from the live pole, clambered onto the roof. From that vantage point he was able to relay to his passengers the precise score of the fourth rubber... between Lew Hoad and Tony Trabert.[1]

Amongst the crowd were Lew's mother and father; and sitting on the stairs, watching every shot intently, was a pretty teenager, Jenny Staley, who – along with other young girl players from Victoria – had been asked to act as an usherette. It was a dank, overcast day but nothing could dampen the expectations of Australian supporters.

As soon as the match began it was clear it was going to be a tight one. When they changed ends after Hoad's first service game, Trabert accused him of serving before he was ready. 'Forget it,' said Hopman, 'he's only trying to get you jumpy.' He was probably right but from that moment there was that slight element of 'needle' in the game.

Both players held serve until the twelfth game; then Lew had a marvellous opportunity to break his opponent's serve and seize the first set. Unfortunately – and uncharacteristically – he tried to play safe and the chance disappeared. Games continued to go with serve until, with Trabert serving at 11-12, Hoad's forcing returns earned him a set point. Trabert paused before serving, took a deep breath, and composed himself. His first serve was good and Trabert, a natural serve/volleyer, quickly followed it in to the net, but Hoad's chipped return forced him to volley up. Then, with the American anticipating a backhand pass down the line, Lew checked and hit a superb cross-court winner. With just over an hour gone, he was one set up.

By this time, though, it had begun to rain; just a fine drizzle but enough to make swift movement problematic. Trabert had already experienced difficulty in keeping his footing on the damp, greasy grass, but his request to Cliff Sproule, the referee, to change his tennis shoes for a pair with spikes had been refused. Lew was less troubled by the surface and anyway he disliked spikes, which he rarely wore because they didn't allow him to slide into his shots. Many players would find it hard to believe that in those days wearing spikes when grass courts were damp was quite a common practice. Of course, there are now very few grass tournaments left, and certainly the Wimbledon committee would be appalled at the prospect of having their hallowed lawns churned up by spikes.

In the second set Trabert, following his captain's instructions, began to charge the net at every opportunity but Lew, remaining cool and focused, directed a stream of passing shots from the back of the court. At 4-1 down Trabert again requested permission to wear spikes but when this was granted, still found himself unable to prevent Hoad closing out the second set, 6-3. The Australian crowd was jubilant: young Hoad was playing 'out of his skin', his game so finely honed that it was virtually free of errors.

However, with the court getting wetter by the minute, even he began to experience difficulty in moving and turning swiftly, and one particular rally ended in a heavy fall as he went for a wide shot. The balls also were becoming very heavy which increased the strain on these two powerful servers; in addition, balls are always inclined to stay lower and shoot through more on grass, and the drizzle simply accentuated this tendency.

When he went 4-1 down in the third set, Lew bowed to the inevitable and changed to spikes. Having never practised in them before it's hardly surprising that his balance was affected, and his movement around the court lost its usual fluency. Trabert took the set, 6-2, and the players repaired to the dressing room for the regulation break after the third set.

Lew changed his sodden clothes and talked tactics with Hopman. Both men realised that the tide had turned in the match. Lew said he was uneasy about the spikes which he felt interfered too much with his movement, but his captain was adamant. 'Persevere,' he said, 'you'll get used to them.' Though Lew was less sure, he reflected that Hopman's judgement had never let him down in the past. In the fourth set Trabert raised his game to new heights, varying the pace of his strokes, chipping and slicing returns as he advanced to the net so that the 'soft' returns died at Lew's feet, making it almost impossible to dig them out. The tall, crew cut American secured the fourth set with relative ease, 6-3, to square the match.

With poor light adding to the players' problems, the referee inspected the court. It was becoming badly cut up but with both players reluctant to stop at this stage of the match, play was allowed to continue. In the second game of the final set an incident occurred that initially had the crowd holding their breath. Forgetting for a moment that he was wearing spikes, Lew tried to slide into a shot. The spikes gripped; he fell headlong and lay face down on the grass.

At this moment Harry Hopman revealed what a shrewd psychologist he was. He leapt from his chair, and having checked that his man was not really injured, picked up a towel and threw it over Lew's head. 'Come on, Musclebound,' he yelled at the prostrate figure. 'You can't lie there forever.'

It was an extraordinary thing to do – if Australia lost this match, they lost the Davis Cup; to abuse his own player with the match so finely poised seemed a fatal misjudgement, and yet it worked. Hoad looked round amazed, then burst out laughing – only to be joined by the whole stadium, Americans included. The incredible tension that had built-up was relieved; Lew relaxed and he always maintained that when he was relaxed he played his finest tennis. It might have been instinctive response from the captain or it might have been entirely calculated. Given Hopman's record, the latter seems more likely.

There was no falling off in the quality of Trabert's game, however; he was winning his serve more comfortably than Lew, and Hopman tried every trick he knew to keep up Hoad's spirits. When a broken string forced him to change his favourite racquet for a new one, his captain turned a potential misfortune to advantage by telling him that the increased tautness of dry strings would aid his shots on a wet court. And so it proved: as Lew says in his autobiography, 'Immediately I felt how much more zing I got on the ball – it sped away.' On another occasion he advised his young protégé to 'chip the ball wide and make Trabert lunge – stretching and bending low will take a lot out of him.' This also was sound advice: stamina and fitness is an important factor in the final set of most five-set matches.

Gradually the match moved to a climax with the tennis on both sides of the net reaching new heights. Later Hopman declared that when Lew mastered the spikes 'the already superlative tennis became the best of their respective careers. The rallies were awesome.'

At 5-6, Trabert, who had previously been within two points of victory, prepared to serve. He will always remember that last game: 'My first service was perfect, hard and deep to Hoad's backhand but he passed me down the line by an inch. The next point I volleyed his return but he stepped back and simply blasted the ball at me and I hit it out. Just by an inch.' At 0-30 down, Trabert took a deep breath before his next serve. There then occurred an unfortunate incident that left him bitterly reflecting on the poor sportsmanship of the crowd. Steve Flink provides a graphic account of what happened in his book, *The Greatest Tennis Matches of the Twentieth Century:*

> *Trabert hit a hard first serve, which missed its mark. He then went for the wide second serve in the deuce court, attempting to avoid the Australian's lethal backhand wing. The serve was out.*

> *The double fault put Trabert at 0-40, but neither he nor Hoad heard the call. They played the point out with Hoad finally hitting an apparent winner. Trengrove [a distinguished tennis journalist and writer of a book on the history of the Davis Cup] reported that few in the crowd had heard the linesman cry 'fault', and they thought Hoad had won the point with a placement. Trabert realising he had double-faulted and was now triple match point down, believed the crowd had cheered his double fault in a breach of traditional tennis civility.*

> *As Trabert said forty-six years later, the incident still lived in his memory, 'I thought it was unfair for them to clap my double fault. They say in retrospect that Lew hit a forehand down the line that would have been a winner and that is why they were clapping. That is all history and hindsight.'* [2]

> *Either way, Trabert was understandably distressed at the time, placing his hands on his hips for a long moment, looking up disapprovingly at the crowd. At triple match point, his percentage first serve was directed deep to Hoad's backhand.*

Now Lew takes up the story. 'His serve was good and instead of blasting it as Tony seemed to expect, I came in, took it early and chipped across his body, skipping like a schoolgirl as I didn't think it would clear the net and the jump was a mental effort to help it over. Tony sprawled in an effort to get it but when the ball squelched into the wet grass I knew he wouldn't make it.' After three hours the match was over; each man had won exactly thirty-one games.

Spikes, a joke, and dry strings made the difference.

Lew looked over to Trabert and, to his amazement, saw that this mighty champion, this tough, American, was in tears. To come back and square the match after being two sets down had taken immense resilience and determination, and he was emotionally and physically drained. Lew later acknowledged that without the American's tremendous fight back, this contest would never have entered the annals of Davis Cup history. And then the American captain, Bill Talbert, came over, shook Lew by the hand, and said, 'Great match, Lew. Congratulations.' It was a fitting testament to the sportsmanlike traditions of Davis Cup rivalry.

In the stadium, the tension had become so unbearable that Alan Hoad missed the end of the match. Bonnie cried for joy, while an exultant Jenny Staley was jumping up and down with excitement.

The first of many tributes that poured in from all over the world, came from an onlooker. As Hoad was leaving the court, a spectator shouted to the Australian Prime Minister, Robert Menzies, who was sitting in the stand, 'Give him a knighthood, Bob!' Lew's compatriot, Jack Crawford, former Australian and Wimbledon champion, referred to Lew's 'sensational Davis Cup debut'. He thought it was not only the 'best Davis Cup tennis he'd ever seen, but that this clash of giants proved that Hoad was the best player in the world'.

Up to then Lew Hoad had been good. Now he was great. But when the euphoria subsided, everybody realised the responsibility of securing a famous victory and retaining the Davis Cup still rested heavily on the slight frame of Ken Rosewall. Hoad had created the opportunity for Australia to turn the match around; now the nation had to rely on 'Muscles', his 'twin', to complete the job by defeating Seixas the next day. Would the task be beyond Rosewall, given his nervy performance in his opening match? Any fears expressed were misplaced; inspired by Hoad's example, he dispatched Seixas with clinical precision in four sets, 6-2, 2-6, 6-3, 6-4. When Rosewall's winning shot clinched the tie, the crowd went mad and threw their cushions in the air. At the courtside, standing calmly by his chair, a phlegmatic Harry Hopman looked on, a self-satisfied grin on his face.

Trabert gave what many felt was the best summing-up on the match: 'I've been playing tennis since I was six,' he said. 'But this is the first time I've been beaten by two babies and an old fox.'

Lew received more than a thousand letters of congratulation. He replied to them all personally in a hand that was just like his play: strong, well-formed, and graceful. The letter Lew treasured most was from a nurse who said that one of her patients, a paralysed little girl, was left alone to listen to the radio broadcast of the match. Towards the end there was interference and the volume faded. The little girl was so excited that she forced herself out of bed to adjust the knobs. It was the first time she had moved in years.

Lew, short as a boy, can barely reach over the net

Lew, in his prime, reaches for glory

Before the crucial '52 Davis Cup Doubles: from left to right, Harry Hopman (Capt.),
Rex Hartwigt, Lew Hoad, Vic Seixas, Tony Trabert, Billy Talbert (Capt.)

A great interception at the net by Lew in the '53 doubles

A dramatic shot - framed against a sea of faces, Hoad makes a backhand smash in the epic singles duel with Trabert in the '53 Davis Cup

A victory salute after Hoad's defeat of Trabert in the '53 Davis Cup

A backhand volley at full stretch

The "Terrible Twins" - Ken Rosewall and Lew Hoad

Lew sets hearts aflutter at New York airport, 1954

Movie-star, Victor McLaglen, gets to grips with the "twins" in Hollywood

The girl who made Hoad "broody" and "moody".
Young Jenny Staley at the White City club in Sydney

Lew and Jenny after their "secret" wedding

The newly-weds at Wimbledon

Harry Hopman's Davis Cup squad in Hollywood:
Back Row (left to right): Rex Hartwig; Dorothy Malone; Lew Hoad; Gig Young
Neale Fraser; Ken Rosewall. Front row (left to right): Roy Emerson; Ashley Cooper

Hoad being congratulated by his "twin" after the 1956 Wimbledon final

Davis Cup ties are never easy - especially against Italy

Lew struts his stuff on the Centre Court at Wimbledon

1956 - Hoad in pursuit of the Grand Slam. He's captured the Australian, French, and Wimbledon titles and now he's after the American at Forest Hills. Here he's taking a sneaky look to see how his eventual opponent, Ken Rosewall, is doing on the practice court

The Duke of Edinburgh presenting Hoad with his 1957 trophy after he's demolished
Ashley Cooper in less than an hour

Lew and Jenny with baby Jane

Chapter 7

Serving his country, a brush with death – and on tour again

The day he beat Trabert, Lew had two visitors. The first was Bob Menzies, the Prime Minister (later Sir Robert and Warden of the Cinq Ports in England) who was beaming and chuckling. He pumped Lew's hand (always a risky operation!) and congratulated him on having done a 'national service' for all his countrymen.

The second visitor was a smartly dressed young Army officer, not much older than Lew. He seemed completely in awe of the Australian idol standing before him. Managing to stammer a few words of congratulation, he received a warm smile and then felt an iron paw crush his hand. After he'd recovered from Lew's legendary vice-like handshake, he informed him he was now obliged to do another kind of national service for his country. Like all boys of his age, a three-month stint of national training in the Army awaited him. Amazingly, Rosewall was exempted when it was discovered he suffered from flat feet!

So on 13th January 1954, Lewis Alan Hoad, tennis hero of 43 Wigram Road, Sydney, became 2/730536 Hoad L.A., Private, A Company, Australian infantry. He joined in a blaze of publicity which he hated because of his inherent shyness and his sincere belief that he was 'just another ordinary bloke'. But he loved the Army, meeting boys from all over the country and all walks of life; he loved the companionship and the mates he made; he loved the hard, simple, outdoor life. He even contemplated joining full-time and combining an Army career with tennis. He knew once tennis was over he could never settle to an office job – and with his limited education, this was possibly the most he could expect. And he knew that, with his temperament, he would never make a businessman: he was too open and honest, too trusting and generous. He'd give anything he had to anyone who asked – all admirable traits that would cost him dear in later life.

During his amateur days as a tennis player, he sometimes received requests to go to Hollywood and be groomed to become a movie star. With a physique like a lumberjack, astonishing good looks (not unlike Robert Mitchum's), blond hair and green eyes, some felt he would be a 'natural', especially in Westerns. Lew laughed. Nothing would persuade him to endure the Hollywood lifestyle, the phoneyness and the backbiting. Later, a friend was heard to remark that if a dime was thrown into heavy traffic, a certain well-known player would dive into the road to retrieve it. If, on the other hand, you offered Lew a million bucks to cross an empty street, and he didn't feel like it, he wouldn't do it. Materialism and greed formed no part of his nature. He was content with the comradeship of close mates, sharing stories over a few, or maybe several more, beers. And, of course, expressing himself on a tennis court.

It was in the Army that Lew had his first brush with death. Whilst out on manoeuvres with his training platoon, he suddenly felt a sharp bite on his arm. The approved treatment was applied: earth wetted with spittle plus an aspirin; then wait five minutes to see if it works. Five minutes later he went white, his knees buckled, and his heart began to race. He was rushed to hospital where doctors drained a pint of poison from his arm. The bite he'd received was from the deadly Funnel Web spider. He was in a coma now and doctors were fighting for his life though they felt it was a hopeless task. When he awoke three days later, he'd lost a stone in weight; looking in the mirror, the haggard face with sunken eyes and deathly yellow skin that greeted him was hardly recognisable. It took another two weeks to get him on his feet and doctors said it was only his supreme physical fitness that pulled him through.

On another occasion during his National Service, he was pleased to be selected to line the route when the Queen and the Duke of Edinburgh toured Sydney. But after a day standing in one spot in the blazing sun in his thick uniform, Lew collapsed. Later in the Queen's tour, he had recovered sufficiently to play an exhibition match at Kooyong in front of the Royal visitors and then be introduced to them. Newsreel footage and photographs of the time show a patently apprehensive Hoad, standing rather stiffly to receive a silver tray as a memento from the Queen. The Duke, always more at home chatting to athletes than official dignitaries, asked him how he found the Army life. 'It's fine,' replied a nervous Hoad. And when the Duke also enquired whether he'd been among the soldiers lining the Sydney streets recently, he confirmed he was.

An Australian newspaper reporter described the scene. 'Lew, who has faced many an Australian crowd with natural, carefree confidence became suddenly nervous when it was his turn to meet the Queen. Carefully he approached the Royal couple to receive his trophy, but he was laughing again when the Duke spoke to him.'

After three months of basic training, marches, drills, and a battle with a spider, Lew had completed his Army service and said goodbye to his mates. He'd enjoyed their company because they were young Australians from all walks of life – a refreshing change from the restricted tennis circle he'd always mixed with.

There was a hectic scramble as he prepared to join the Australians on another gruelling overseas tour to Europe, America, and back to Australia to defend the Davis Cup. Hopman believed that no title was beyond the team he had assembled in 1954: Hoad, Rosewall, Hartwig and Rose would sweep all before them. And youngsters Neale Fraser, Roy 'Emmo' Emerson, and Ashley Cooper would go along for the experience, waiting in the wings for the moment when their time would come to perform on a Davis Cup stage.

For Lew, however, the worst year in his tennis life so far was about to begin. He'd not played competitive tennis for three months, had not had time to practise, was not match fit, and once his mind began to wander and he got off to one of his notoriously lackadaisical starts, that was it. And his mind, as we shall see, certainly wasn't on the game – or the tour.

The team flew to Paris for the French Championships where they learned that Hoad had been seeded number one. Lew groaned. It was an impossible expectation for someone who hadn't played much and had been seriously ill. He got to the last sixteen only to be beaten by the veteran, Gardner Mulloy.

Mulloy also delivered another blow. Hoad and Rosewall were playing a doubles match against Mulloy and Budge Patty. Ken put up what may, in these circumstances, accurately be described as a 'hospital' lob. Normally this would be the cue for Lew and partner to scurry backwards. But Lew stood his ground defiantly at the net, and Mulloy smacked him straight in the face with a mighty smash that fractured his nose. With blood streaming from his nose, Lew was almost lifted off the ground by the force of the impact, and he crashed backwards.

The court was engulfed by Frenchmen. Mulloy feared that Lew would ingest blood and drown in it – if he wasn't suffocated in the throng first. He cried out for people to stand back and get assistance, swishing his racquet at them furiously when they ignored him. Patty, who spoke fluent French, ordered a ball-boy to fetch water and when the startled boy appeared to hesitate, an irate Patty lashed out at him with his towel. There was pandemonium. Eventually Lew was carried away, but it was his two opponents he had to thank for stemming the flow of blood.

Twenty minutes later, he returned to the court – with nose swollen and black eyes already beginning to appear. He could hardly see and had a pounding headache. If he and Rosewall were shaken, their opponents seemed even more distracted and, amazingly, lost the match in four sets.

At Wimbledon a few weeks later, Lew remained glum, surly, and out of sorts. He knew he'd not had enough competitive tennis to sharpen his game. In the quarter-finals of the singles he met Drobny again, and once more the wily veteran gave him a tennis lesson, winning 6-4, 6-3, 6-3. When the match finished, Drobny told reporters, 'I have never felt so good. The only thing I am sorry about is that it was Hoad I beat again because I like him more than any other player.'

Drobny had adopted England as his home, and he became a firm Wimbledon favourite. Twice he'd been runner-up and advancing years made it unlikely he could still gain the much-coveted Wimbledon crown. Standing between him and the title in 1954 was Ken Rosewall. The crowd saw Ken as a spring chicken whose turn would come in the years ahead. They weren't to know that just over two years later he'd join Jack Kramer's professional tennis troupe, and his chance of a Wimbledon singles title would be lost forever. He had defeated Trabert in five sets in the semi-finals and his tennis was so outstanding in the last two sets, he was an odds-on favourite to beat Drobny in the final.

Odds-on favourite with pundits and bookies maybe, but not with the crowd. Their sympathy was entirely with the older man. And the crowd's tidal wave of emotional support for Drobny seemed to affect the outcome of the match for Rosewall clearly found it disconcerting and played well below his best form to lose in four sets. A protest about the partisan nature of the crowd's response was sent by the Australian tennis authorities, and brought an apology from officials of the All England Club to Hopman.

Unfortunately, when the scenario was reversed seventeen years later, the crowd did not get the result they all wanted. Then, the 39-year-old Rosewall, by common consent one of the finest players never to have won Wimbledon, met a brash young American, Jimmy Connors, in the final and suffered a crushing defeat.

Lew's miserable year dragged on in America where he did little to make new friends. There was something obviously wrong. And the wrong (if that's the right description for it) can be summed up in three words – Jennifer Jane Staley. For Lew had not only been bitten by a deadly spider, he'd been bitten by the far more deadly love bug.

Chapter 8

Love is in the air... and it brings problems!

So far we have kept Jenny Staley in the wings, but she'd begun to play an increasingly important role in Lew's life. He first met her when she and other outstanding players from her area, Melbourne, were sent down to Sydney to play in the New South Wales Championships. When they were introduced he was thirteen, and she, being eight months older, felt entitled to say things to him like, 'Stop parting your hair in the middle, and part it on the side.' Lew, who was awkward in the presence of girls and tended to shy away from them, didn't know how to respond. Clearly at this stage they made little impression on each other; Lew continued to part his hair in the middle. Truth to tell, he was somewhat in awe of her. Unlike him, she didn't appear to dislike school.

Jenny's first date was with Ken Rosewall, and it wasn't long before she and Lew were going out on double dates, or with groups of friends. They also met at tournaments and he began to feel increasingly relaxed in her company. He found he could talk to her – yes, actually talk to a girl. On sunny days they would often watch each other practise or play, and on rainy days they would go to the movies.

Although her development as a player wasn't as spectacular as Hoad's, she made swift progress through the junior ranks. She won a string of state titles, and after reaching the final of the Australian Championships, became the country's No 2 woman player. She'd grown from a skinny, leggy young teenager into the best-looking girl on the Australian circuit, with dark hair, big brown eyes, a lissom figure and shapely legs. Her photo frequently adorned the front covers of newspapers and magazines. Writing in *Australian Tennis* in 1954, Thelma Long, the Australian No 1, paid tribute to her impressive debut in senior tennis:

> *Jennifer lost to me in all three principal championships and reached the finals of the Victorian and Australian singles in doing so. [She also won] the South Australian Singles championship. All these performances and subsequent high ranking are a just reward for Jennifer who has worked at her tennis with considerable effort and purpose. There are still some weaknesses to be eradicated from her play, but we all hope Jennifer will continue to make*

further outstanding improvement. The remarkable success achieved in her first year of senior tennis should give her the necessary encouragement to strive for even greater honours.

Jenny was unusual in that she played tennis with her left hand but did everything else right-handed. She had been educated at Melbourne Grammar School and left school with her Leaving Certificate, a higher qualification than Lew had obtained. Originally intending to become an artist, she attended art school - until tennis took over. However, she retained her artistic flair and temperament, and the whitewashed, converted dove-cote surrounded by trees, flowers and bushes which she and Lew shared in the grounds of the Campo de Tenis in southern Spain, is a miniature museum of artefacts, screens, paintings and furniture collected from around the world. And the paintings by Jenny that used to hang on the walls of the restaurant and lounge at the Campo revealed a talented amateur artist. She was the only girl Lew was ever interested in. It was a love that burned as brightly forty years on as it had all those years earlier when a glittering tennis career lay before them both.

Coming from a middle-class background – her father was an accountant – Jenny was used to a more sophisticated lifestyle than Lew, and she soon began to exercise an influence over him. That he had inherited his parents' conservative views comes out strongly in an interview he gave for a Sydney newspaper when he was nineteen. He had been asked for a 'Man's Angle on Women' and his responses are revealing.

To begin with he was critical of the shorts most girls wore on the tennis court. 'They wear them too short,' he complained. 'Some girls can wear shorts, but others can't wear them at all. Myself, I prefer girls in skirts.' It was clearly important for a girl to be unaffected: 'I think the main thing about a girl is to be herself. Most of the girls you meet at cocktail parties try to push themselves to attract attention and talk for the sake of saying something. They should act naturally and talk as they do normally – that's much the better way.'

Warming to his theme, he observed that American girls had a tendency 'to talk too much.' Not surprisingly, on to the topic of sport, his views became more progressive. 'I think girls should play quite a bit of sport… and it's a good idea for them to get out of the home and learn as much as they can from the outside world.' Perhaps feeling this was all going too far, he paused, then added: 'They can learn to cook after they get married.'

When it came to dress, appearance and new social trends, however, Lew reverted to a typical working-class Puritanism. He didn't like stockings on young girls – 'they don't look too good.' And he didn't like high heels, preferring girls in flat shoes. He didn't approve of girls smoking either, believing that 'they should only drink in moderation, and not beer. A Martini may be alright.' Another dislike was make-up: 'Give me a natural complexion any time.' He liked girls in sports clothes best and preferred skirts and blouses to evening frocks. Concluding the interview diplomatically (but, one senses, honestly) Lew declared that, in his opinion, Australian girls dressed better than their American counterparts and 'must be the best-dressed in the world – AND the best looking.'

Sometimes, though, old-fashioned attitudes could appeal to a modern young woman. Jenny was impressed by Lew's insistence upon carrying her tennis bag for her. One of the men on the circuit had told the girls if they were strong enough to play tennis, they were strong enough to carry their own bags. She was surprised when Lew, ever the gentleman, disagreed. Under Jenny's guidance, however, he became more relaxed in his views. He hated to see her smoking but when she persuaded him to try a cigarette, he discovered he quite liked it. It was at her home that Lew had his first beer, and he liked that too!

Inspired possibly by evangelical zeal, he went on to introduce fellow team-mates to a beer culture. Neale Fraser remembers Lew persuading him to try a 'bevvy' or two on his first tour abroad. Most of the team turned out to be 'pretty fair drinkers' and some, like Lew himself, 'Emmo' (Roy Emerson), 'Newc' (John Newcombe) and Tony Roche broke world records. Amazingly, given his lean, wiry fame, the one with the most prodigious capacity was 'Emmo'. His team-mates all agreed that he had 'hollow legs' and could drink anyone under the table. Players from other countries, particularly the Americans – always their greatest rivals – would gawp as the Aussies quaffed their beers, then went on court, and demolished their opponents.

Respected commentators on the game of tennis have puzzled over the phenomenon of a country's top tennis players enjoying a reputation for unrivalled physical fitness combined with a Falstaffian relish for the 'amber nectar'. Jack Kramer acknowledged that after the war, when the Aussies came to prominence, 'they did drink a lot of beer together,' adding caustically, 'everybody else started imitating them because they won, and it was easier to imitate their beer-drinking than their hard work.'

In his 1973-4 diary, Arthur Ashe noted, 'Hoad had the reputation as the most indomitable drinker,' but Newcombe and Roche were strong contenders. Ashe also pointed out that Aussies never ordered anything like a martini: 'Hell, they call you a 'lardy' (snob) if you ask for wine.' Furthermore, the beer culture had its conventions that had to be strictly adhered to:

> If you do join a group of them drinking beer, there is only one rule – the newcomer must be prepared to 'shout'. That means order your round. 'It's your shout mate. What's the matter – your arms too short or your pockets too

long?' Economic status has no bearing when it comes to shouting. The poorest man at the table is expected to match shouts with the richest.[1]

Of course, the convention of 'paying your way' or 'getting your round in' applies not only in Australia but also in Britain and America, and failure to observe this convention risks social exclusion. Amongst the Australian tennis players, though, it was also another illustration of that group solidarity that helped make them such formidable Davis Cup opponents. They were always a tightly cohesive team: they pulled for each other; helped each other; and, in a crisis, closed ranks against the enemy.

This group camaraderie was one of the things Lew missed most when he abandoned the amateur game and joined the pros. Admittedly it was a macho, 'blokeish' bond. Native Australian women, comments Ashe, know their place:

> *'Sheilas' they're called. 'Come on, you bloody Sheila,' Emmo will scream, pulling some other player's wife by the arm when inviting her to dance. Fred Stolle, he says, used to complain that American soldiers had been spoiling all the Sheilas by 'talking to them, listening to them, and spending money on them – making them think they were bloody queens.'* [2]

Ashe (half?) jokingly concludes that: 'The Australian idea of a great date is to take a Sheila to a pub, park her in a corner and then go over and drink all evening with the boys.'

The Aussies also enjoyed a reputation for being able to hold their liquor; when inebriated – or just tipsy – they rarely became objectionable or disorderly. Bud Collins, describing his life with the pros, singles out as the most jovial, 'Emmo and Fiery, Roy Emerson and Fred Stolle, who could turn any gathering up a few notches into high-proof, high jinks.' He recalls, in particular, the tours of America by 'Emmo and Fiery' in the summers of '65 and '66:

> *They were undeniable hits, unbeaten in doubles and dominant in singles. Attractive and gregarious, they played and laughed their way into the hearts of everybody watching. Emmo gleamed from head to teeth – patent leather hair and a Fort Knox line-up of gold fillings – a superb athlete covering court like a greyhound. Stolle, a big-serving cornstalk with maize locks, walked as though every step was the last. Together they were murder, hanging tough whether or not hung over.*[3]

The two of them developed a sort of split-shift program to get them through the American summer so that they either went to bed or stayed out all night. Their energy, says Collins admiringly, was prodigious. One morning, returning home from a party (at about 9.30am!) Emmo suddenly remembered they had a semi-final doubles match to finish. Their opponents were Jim Osborne and Jerry Cromwell, two lightening serving college kids from California, and the match was being played in an area known as the paddock because the grass courts were terrible, and returning serve was a nightmare for all concerned.

The college kids had won the first set, 24-22, but lost the next, 9-7. By this time it had become so dark, the match was suspended to the following morning at ten. Stolle recalls he and Emmo were 'a little fuzzy':

> *When we get to the club Cromwell and Osborne are out practicing. Bright-eyed and eager. They've got a big upset going, and they want to be right to start the last set.*
>
> *'You want to hit some, Emmo?' I ask him. 'God, no,' he wrinkles his face and blinks. 'Be right with you fellows,' I say to Cromwell and Osborne. Then Emmo and I run and jump into the club pool, hoping that'll clear our heads. We put on our tennis gear, walk to the court, and say, 'Let's go!'*
>
> *Cromwell says, 'You want to hit a few, don't you?' And Emmo says, 'Naw – couldn't stand it, mate. Let's just start and get it over with so we can go to bed.'*
>
> *'Well,' Stolle beams, 'that just bloody psyched those two right out, although it wasn't intended that way. Emmo and I couldn't stand to look at a bloody ball. We figured they'd go through us like salts, and we didn't care. But damned if they couldn't put a ball in court, and we won easy.'* [4]

According to Collins, they amended their approach for the National Doubles in Boston to a 'split formation: one-in-bed and one-in-the-beer'. 'If either of us decides to stay at the party, the other goes back to the hotel early and gets enough sleep for both of us.'

On another occasion, at a party that had gone on well into the night, there was a visit from the police. Stolle, standing guard over the beers in the kitchen fridge, commented to Joe Vay, a good player and local coach, that the police visit had been disappointingly low-key and relaxed. Vay, an engaging personality, had adopted the title of the Baron of Hungary, insisting he was such in exile. He proceeded to tease Stolle, saying it would have been amusing if the police had carted Fred off and he'd spent the day in jail instead of playing his semi-final doubles match:

> *'Ah, Baron,' Stolle replied, reaching for another Foster's, 'Emmo could win it without me. No fears. Who are we playing? Just bloody Reissen and Graebner in the semis, and probably Pasarell and Froehling in the final. No worries there that I can see.'* [both these pairs were generally regarded as formidable doubles teams!]

'Really?' said the Baron, sniffing at a cognac. The Baron and cognac were virtually inseparable. He also liked to make a bet, and, being Australian, so did Stolle. 'No problems, you say, Fred?'

'Absolutely none, Baron. I make Emmo and me two-to-one over anybody you can name.'

'What about later today? Marty Reissen and Clark Graebner. Not a bad team, Fred...'

'Two-to-one for twenty bucks, Baron?'

'Fred, you're on. You're a sportsman,' said the Baron, who spent the next few hours trying to be sporting himself, as a one-man bucket brigade keeping Stolle from burning up with thirst. 'Let's drink to your match,' the Baron kept saying, working hard to protect his wager. Stolle appeared to be working just as hard helping him.

As three o'clock in the morning approached, and they'd drunk the whole night through, Stolle murmured, 'Baron, I think I ought to ring up Emmo and tell him about the bet. I want him to know, so he realises how important his sleep is.'

'Capital idea, Fred,' the Baron whispered from the kitchen floor.

Fred dialled. After innumerable rings from the hotel switchboard, Emerson was on the line.

'Did I wake you, Emmo?' Fred inquired.

'Ah, no, had to be up to answer the phone. Lovely to hear your voice and know that you and the Foster's are well, you bloody idiot.' Stolle related the proposition with the Baron, offered Emmo half the action, and then hung up. 'No chance for you, Baron. Emmo's very clear-headed and determined,' he said, trying to help his adversary out the door.

Even muddle-headed, the Baron knew he had a sure thing. Never had he worked so strenuously to give himself an edge.

Stolle and Emerson together, however, were beyond the Baron's control. He sat in the stands groaning, perhaps more in recognition of his post-dawn squash than his losing bet.

'Baron,' Fred smiled as he collected his money, 'you should know that beer is like Popsicles to us Aussies. But the cognac doesn't seem to have agreed with you.' [5]

Love is in the air… and it brings problems!

When Lew came back from his 1953 tour, he started seeing Jenny regularly. Bonnie told the newspapers that he seemed for the first time to be 'interested in a lass – a nice little Australian tennis player.' But the interview this quote is taken from does not reveal the name of the 'lass'. She was, of course, Jenny Staley, the usherette who'd watched him beat Trabert in that epic Davis Cup match, and then been escorted by him to the Davis Cup Ball that very night. By the time he set out on the 1954 tour he was hopelessly in love. But on the eve of his departure he believed Jenny's affections had cooled. She was constantly on his mind and their separation became a major factor in his distracted performances on tour. He wrote to her frequently but was beset by nagging worries about her constancy. She saw several other men from time to time, and he fretted over the possibility that one of them would 'cut him out'.

His bad temper on court shocked his now legion of fans who remembered only the laughing, happy-go-lucky player of the previous year. So when Lew and the team returned to Australia, he walked into a hornet's nest of criticism. One former Australian Davis Cup player wrote, 'Is Hoad a hoax? He's certainly the year's biggest flop.'

Then the news of Lew and Jenny's romance got out and became headline news. Lew's bad play and bad ways were all attributed to her. One suggested that Lew had proposed and been turned down before he left, which was not true. Jenny, unused to the attentions of the press, was deeply upset. And Lew also was infuriated by this continual invasion of their privacy. In a match against Seixas, he became so bad-tempered he slammed a ball not just out of the court but out of the stadium. As the ball soared into the wild blue yonder, Jenny felt twenty thousand pairs of eyes turn to focus accusingly upon her. She felt bitterly ashamed, and refused to speak to Lew for some time.

Once again, he seriously contemplated quitting tennis. Fortunately for the tennis world, Hopman succeeded in dissuading him and gave both of them a long, fatherly talk. He said he knew exactly how they felt and advised them how to handle their tempestuous emotions as well as the press news hounds baying at their heels, thirsting for blood.

In another match shortly after this, the Queensland final against Rex Hartwig, Lew suddenly felt sick. The sun was blazing down and he could hardly see. He forgot the score, seemed unaware who was serving, and changed ends at the wrong time. The stands fell eerily silent and Hartwig, who had raced through six consecutive games and could see something was wrong, put a hand out to his pal. The umpire, Ron Leahy, enquired, 'Are you all right? You're just staring into space.' Later, Leahy told him: 'You continued to play, but all of the six thousand spectators could see you had little realisation of what was going on. I had to sit under a shade to carry on umpiring, but the heat still burned me up and left me in a pool of sweat.'

A ten-minute rest (subsequently extended to fifteen minutes) was called at the end of the third set. Ice cubes were applied to Lew's face, and an iced handkerchief tied around his neck. He knew that Jenny was watching in the stands. She would be going through agony. Summoning up all his strength in the final set, he made a superhuman effort to win and closed out the fifth set, 6-1.

It turned out that his sunstroke had been caused by the lingering effects of poison from the spider bite almost a year earlier. Throughout Australia doctors phoned, or wrote, to confirm that recovery from a Funnel Web's bite was a long process; hardly surprising in view of the fact that nobody else appears to have survived such a bite!

The Davis Cup tie was approaching, and Lew channelled all his energies into training. It was as if he was hewing wood, sweat streaming from every pore, teeth grimly clenched. Power and control, power and control – and concentrate, concentrate, concentrate. Watch those ground strokes, that's where the mistakes creep in. Slowly Lew felt his game returning to something like its old form. At the eve-of-Cup dinner, the Prime Minister, Bob Menzies, turned to Hoad during his speech and told him to forget his critics. And addressing both Hoad and Trabert, who were to play the opening match, he said, 'You are both great players. Without players like you, there wouldn't be any Davis Cup matches. Get stuck into it!'

The Sydney Stadium seating had been increased from 17,500 to nearly 23,000 and the biggest crowd in tennis history sat waiting. Thousands more had been turned away. Applause rang round the stadium as Hoad and Trabert walked on court.

Ultimately, the occasion proved too much for Hoad – and Rosewall. The pressures and expectations were just too great. Both played well below form (Ken was also in love!) and though they were trying as hard as they could, the Americans battled for every point as if their very lives depended on it. In the opening match, Lew, distracted by a strong gusty wind, lost to Trabert in a lengthy, four-set match. Then Seixas beat Ken, also in four sets. Worse was to follow. The next day Seixas and Trabert won the doubles to ensure the Cup's return to America.

There was one more sadness in that unfortunate year. Hopman decided to break up the 'twins' permanently. He calculated that if they were going to win the Cup back from Trabert and Seixas in 1955, he needed another strong server to partner Hoad. The problem was how to overcome Seixas' return in what usually proved to be the crucial doubles match. Powerful servers could get Seixas into trouble on his backhand side. But when faced with Rosewall's relatively weak serve, he could chip skimming backhands cross-court, and race in to dominate the net alongside Trabert.

From now on it would be Hoad and Hartwig – the failures of the previous year. Vindicating Hopman's judgement, they never lost another match the whole time they played together. Nevertheless, Australia sighed when it heard the news of the break-up of the Hoad-Rosewall partnership; despite their ups and downs, the country loved the 'twins' and had taken them to its heart. Lew was sorry too. Over the years they had grown apart in temperament, interests, friends, music, movies, everything. And, of course, they never remotely looked like 'twins'. But Kenny was Lew's mate and they never lost their mutual respect for each other's (very different) style of play.

As the year drew to a close, one night when Lew and Jenny were staying alone at a friend's house, he asked her to marry him and she said, 'Yes.' It was the only good thing to happen to him in 1954.

* * *

For Lew, 1955 dawned as a bright new, sunny prospect. He'd got his girl. And the prospect was made even brighter by the news that, for the first time since 1938, the Australians were going to send a women's team overseas that would include Jenny as the national No 2. They were both thrilled: this would mean they wouldn't have to spend months and months apart. However, because of their different schedules they would have to endure a period of separation. The women's team, managed by Adrian Quist, was travelling by sea, stopping off to play various tournaments, first in cities on the coast of Australia and then on the Continent, taking in the French Championships in Paris. The men's team missed the Continental tournaments and flew directly to London. Lew, waiting impatiently for Jenny to join him in London, found it difficult to concentrate on his preparations for the Queen's Club tournament and Wimbledon.

There was a joyful reunion on Jenny's arrival – and then Jenny told him to sit down because there was something serious she needed to talk to him about. She was pregnant; they would have to get married immediately. Lew was completely unprepared for this bombshell.

He was delighted by the news but he knew it would cause consternation amongst the bigwigs of Australian tennis. And the timing was unfortunate. It was just three weeks before Wimbledon, and apart from practice and playing at Queen's Club, Lew had to attend to all the arrangements. To begin with, there was no time to be lost in obtaining a special marriage licence from Caxton Hall. Then a wedding ring had to be purchased (an especially difficult task because in every jeweller's shop there seemed to be someone who'd recognise him); and permission from his family was required since, in those days, at the tender age of twenty, he needed parental consent.

He cabled his parents in Australia: 'Want to marry Jenny Saturday 18th of June. Please cable regulation official consent immediately and keep secret. Letter follows. Love Lew.'

Jenny, of course, had to buy an outfit, and her team-mates were surprised by what seemed like an extravagant whim on her part: she had taken the morning off and returned with a new dress, blue coat, and a white pixy hat decorated with flowers. 'Hey, anyone would think you were getting married,' one of her friends jokingly remarked. Then she and Lew had to face the final moment of truth – telling Harry Hopman. At midnight on Friday 17th June – a little over ten hours before they were due at the altar – Lew asked Hopman to come to the room he was sharing with Rex Hartwig at the Kensington Hotel.

Hopman was bemused when he found Lew and Jenny together, and his jaw dropped when they announced they were to be married the following morning. He was about to explode when Lew quietly took him to one side and explained that the sudden decision was the result of 'exceptional circumstances'. His anger quickly subsided, and he turned to Jenny and said, 'Let me be the first to kiss the bride.' Having acted as a father-figure to the couple for the last few years, he also agreed to give Jenny away. Rex Hartwig, who appeared a few minutes later, was persuaded to act as Best Man; he thought the whole thing was a practical joke until he saw the look on Harry Hopman's face.

If the path of true love had not run entirely smoothly, neither did the marriage arrangements. The four of them – Lew and Jenny, Rex and Harry – set out for St Mary's Church in Wimbledon, a beautiful old, white-painted building set at Wimbledon's highest point and looking down directly onto the All England Club's famous courts. Every year, on the middle Sunday of the Championships, a service is held there for the players and officials attending Wimbledon. But the wedding party took a wrong turning and they found themselves outside the gates of the All England Club, just as Lew's friend and fellow team member, Neale Fraser, arrived for practice. He saw Hopman, Hartwig, Hoad and Jenny all dressed up in their finest, with flowers in their buttonholes – and gawped. The bags and racquets he was carrying fell to the ground. As the car reversed and sped away from the courts, up the hill to the Church, the occupants looked back to see a bewildered Fraser staring at the receding car.

Since the party had arrived at the Church late, they were late leaving – and walked smack bang into the next group waiting to be married. Lew and Jenny tried to avert their faces but there could be no mistake. Surely this blond Adonis was Lew Hoad and yes, that pretty tanned girl was another Australian tennis star! Within minutes the news of the 'secret' wedding had reached Fleet Street – in those days, home of the nation's newspapers.

Lew, oblivious to the storm that was to break around him, changed and went to Queen's Club to play that afternoon's final against Ken Rosewall, only to find the place crawling with newspapermen and photographers. Scenes reminiscent of a Pink Panther film ensued as he and Hopman were chased around bushes and hedges – sometimes even through hedges. When Lew walked on court, pressmen standing at the side of the court started shouting questions about the 'wedding'. Both he and Hopman foolishly denied the marriage rumours, but a completely baffled Rosewall retained enough composure to win the match!

With denials coming from Queen's Club, other reporters were despatched to St Mary's Church in Wimbledon, and there in the register were the names: Lewis Alan Hoad and Jennifer Jane Staley. The Australian team hotel was besieged and eventually Hopman came down to confirm the news. He said the young couple had hoped to keep the matter private and had now departed for a twenty-four hour honeymoon at a secret location in the country. Actually they were upstairs in Lew's room being 'guarded' by other members of the Australian team who had now been fully briefed. Unfortunately, because it was the weekend, Hopman had had no opportunity of letting the Australian tennis authorities know what was happening. But the news would get there soon enough. Hopman talked to Lew and Jenny – and the three of them realised the balloon was about to go up. They were right.

When Sir Norman Brookes, the President of Australian Tennis (and former Davis Cup hero), heard the news he was livid and immediately cabled an angry message demanding an explanation. He reminded Hopman that it was not simply a case of husbands and wives not being allowed to be on the same team; they were not even allowed to be in the same country as each other when playing! Hopman replied that he was well aware of the regulations but pointed out, in a nice example of linguistic hair-splitting, that the couple weren't travelling together, they had merely got married together. In any event, he said, there were 'exceptional circumstances' that justified the hasty decision. Brookes calmed down and soon a cable of congratulation was on its way from the whole of Australian tennis – with the bonus that the Australian authorities were clubbing together to buy a wedding present. This was exactly how excited team members in London had responded when they were let in on the 'secret'.

Back in Australia, Bonnie Hoad told the press: 'Lew will be happy now. I'm sure this will improve his tennis. He won't have to keep worrying and wondering where Jenny is, who she is with, or who might be cutting him out.' Later, Lew noted that Hopman's handling of the whole incident, from the time they surprised him with their news, was 'remarkably sympathetic and practical.'

After the twenty-four hour honeymoon, and on the eve of Wimbledon, it was decided Jenny should be sneaked out of the hotel and taken back to where the Australian girls were staying. With reporters still scouring London and hotels in the

Thames valley for likely honeymoon locations, the element of cloak-and-dagger intrigue persisted.

To escape the attentions of the press, Jenny would leave the hotel dressed as a man. Borrowing a long coat and a large trilby hat from Rex Hartwig to shield her face, she left escorted by Neale Fraser.

After a night's sleep, however, the young couple realised there could be no escaping the world's press on the first day of Wimbledon, and they decided to travel there together and face the music. A struggling mob of photographers greeted them on their arrival and then they had to confront a packed news conference. Lew told reporters that if the Australian LTA refused to allow wives to accompany their husbands on tour, he'd make a private tour with Jenny the following year. He recalled Sedgman had done the same thing the year before and he insisted that he was not going to leave Jenny at home.

As the tournament progressed, Jenny became increasingly apprehensive that any deterioration in Lew's play would be blamed on her, and he couldn't understand why, having responded to press questions at the news conference, they were subjected to such daily and intrusive press interest. He became more and more incensed by the continual harassment. But at least the Wimbledon crowds took the handsome young couple to their hearts. Playing in the mixed doubles, however, they had their first public tiff – though it was a light-hearted one; Jenny accused Lew of poaching her shots and he accused her of miss-hitting a shot he was trying to cover. While the press dived for their cameras, the crowd, perhaps wondering if this was a playful charade they were acting out, gave them plenty of encouragement, and their Swedish opponents smiled understandingly.

The strain of the wedding and the constant press attention got to their nerves, affecting their play but, in spite of the distractions, Jenny reached the last sixteen of the singles and Lew the last eight – and together they got through to the semi-finals of the mixed. As an Australian Davis Cup player, Lew wasn't even supposed to play in the mixed doubles, but as his mother commented back in Australia, 'Lew's pretty casual about things like that.'

Casual or not, his quarter-final loss in the singles to the American, Budge Patty, rankled. Patty, noted for his sartorial elegance and his precise volleying, was on song, winning in straight sets. His lack of speed around the court, that Lew had hoped to exploit, was compensated for, on this occasion, by his uncanny anticipation. As some consolation for this defeat, Lew and his best man, Rex Hartwig, continued their now unbeaten run as a team by winning the Wimbledon doubles title.

Love is in the air... and it brings problems!

The two Australian teams were due to travel to the United States, but it was clear that the Hoads' dream of being together throughout the year was over, and that Jenny would have to return home. Lew accepted the inevitable decision with as much good grace as he could muster. There were sad farewells: both were confronting challenges; in Jenny's case, it was a new challenge: she was flying back to Australia to start setting up a new home for them. In Lew's case, a familiar one: he was flying to America to represent Australia, and try to win back the Davis Cup.

The summer outlook had changed. From 'Set Fair' the needle on the barometer had suddenly plummeted. Instead of touring and seeing his fiancée regularly as they travelled around the world, Lew was now married – and alone. It was to be six months before he saw his wife again, by which time she had obtained a little flat overlooking Sydney harbour and was preparing to give birth to their first child. The enforced separation deeply unsettled Lew, which worried Hopman whose main concern was regaining the Davis Cup. And the way the Cup was played in those days meant that they had to win five tough Cup-ties in America and Canada against countries like Mexico, Brazil and Italy before they even got the chance to challenge the American team of Trabert and Seixas. Trabert was at the peak of his game having won the French and Wimbledon Championships, and Seixas was always an awkward opponent.

All the players agreed that Hoad at his best was unbeatable. But his mind was half a world away, worrying about Jenny's house-hunting (he shared a bedroom with one of his brothers at Wigram Road, so moving in there was out of the question) and worrying too about the baby he knew Jenny was carrying.

Hopman fretted – getting Lew ready for the trials that lay ahead was going to be tough. And Ken Rosewall also seemed to have gone off the boil. Only Hartwig appeared to be on form. Hopman realised that that summer in America was going to test his Davis Cup team to the limits. He ordered lots of road work as they prepared for their first tie against Mexico. In this tie, Lew was dropped for the first time as a singles player. Having despatched Mexico, Brazil was next. The Brazilians had a formidable ex-American player, Bob Falkenburg, in their team. Falkenburg had won Wimbledon in 1948 and was eligible because he had married a Brazilian and gone to live there. Through dint of hard work, Lew forced his way back into the singles, only for bad luck to strike again. He was hit in the groin by one of Falkenburg's heavy serves and collapsed. He recovered enough to win – and gain the Australians the tie – but he was in severe pain for several days, and ill and off-form for weeks. Nevertheless, he played his part in helping Australia beat first Canada, and then come through a tricky match against Japan.

The press reported he was 'fed up' without Jenny. The truth is the blow to the groin had done more damage than people realised and he was troubled by constant headaches. The final tie leading to the Challenge Round was against Italy. Hopman was pleased to see that for Lew a programme of running and golf, as well as practice with his team-mate, Ashley Cooper, who'd become his best friend, was beginning to pay dividends. There were signs that Lew was returning to something like his old form. An excited Australian contingent saw him play his best tennis for nearly two years to crush Fausto Gardini 6-3, 6-2, 6-0 in the tie against Italy. This inspired Rosewall to his best form, and the tie was won convincingly.

Now came the Americans. A war of nerves preceded the Challenge Cup at Forest Hills. Tony Trabert said the 'twins' had experienced success so early in their lives that the expectations people had of them were now proving to be too heavy a burden. In any event, he claimed, Hoad hadn't really achieved anything for nearly two years. Although Lew knew there was some truth in this assessment – he'd been in a slump for a long time – Trabert's remarks riled him, and he was all the more determined to make the American eat his words. Perhaps those comments also motivated Rosewall because in the opening match against Seixas he played some of the most brilliant tennis of his career. He changed his usual game plan, coming to the net at every opportunity instead of playing 'canny' from the baseline. And at the net, he was remarkably assured, picking off Seixas' attempted passing shots and directing crisp volleys to the corners of the court. Seixas seemed to get his measure in the fourth set which he snatched 6-4, but eventually Rosewall won with relative ease 6-3, 10-8, 4-6, 6-2.

What surprised Hopman about the next match was Lew's comment after Trabert won the first set 6-4. 'He's playing terrible tennis, Hop.' Hopman replied dryly, 'Maybe so, but he's just won the first set. It won't be much consolation to know he played badly, if he wins the next two. Buck your ideas up and sort him out!' Lew did, and won 4-6, 6-3, 6-3, 8-6, a fine comeback after so many months of disappointment, though he did acknowledge that Trabert might have been slightly hampered by a blistered racquet hand.

The 1955 Challenge Round doubles match is regarded as possibly the best seen in the Davis Cup. The four players, Trabert, Seixas, Hoad and Hartwig, took every opportunity to charge the net. Both teams realised that with powerful servers and volleyers on either side, the match would be won or lost by whoever dominated the net. As Lew said, 'We eyeballed it out, hammering shots straight at each other.' With the crowd on their feet, urging on the American pair, Lew went match point down on his own service, but then hit a serve so hard it sent Trabert sprawling. In an incredibly tense fifth set, the Australians finally triumphed 12-14, 6-4, 6-3, 3-6, 7-5. The stunned Americans heard the Australians in the crowd begin to sing their old anthem, 'Waltzing Matilda', a song the bushmen used to sing in Australia's early days.

Love is in the air... and it brings problems!

The Australians had regained the Davis Cup without losing a single rubber, only eight months after it had been wrested from them. A Sydney newspaper wrote, 'This is our Cup of Joy. Congratulations to Hopman and the boys, they made yesterday's sunlight all the brighter.'

Jack Kramer, the professional tennis promoter, had been watching from the sidelines, shrewdly analysing, assessing, and calculating the potential worth of these players on his professional tour, and he lost no time in persuading Trabert, Hartwig, Hoad and Rosewall to sign for him. Later, however, Lew and Kenny were to renege on the agreement, but only after frantic efforts on the part of their closest advisers to dissuade them from turning pro. At the age of twenty, Hoad and Rosewall were told anything they may have signed was not legal anyway. Kramer was upset and angry, but took the blow with the dignity he always showed as a professional. And now that Hartwig had joined Kramer, the 'twins' were able to resume their doubles partnership.

Lew was happy. He was showing some of his old, fighting form, and he knew it would not be that long before he was heading back home: to his new flat, to Jenny, and to the baby daughter who would be born at Christmas – the blonde, brown-eyed Jane. Later would come petite, grey-eyed, Sally. And later still, his son, Peter – who played tour tennis and showed considerable promise, but was never able to emulate his father's achievements. When Peter was born, Jenny said it was the first time she had seen Lew cry. The only other occasion this happened was when he stood before the joint Turkish, Australian, New Zealand and Canadian war memorial on the beaches of Gallipoli where a quarter of a million men fell in 1915 and 1916. This was the infamous campaign (movingly depicted in the film *Gallipoli*, by the Australian director, Peter Weir) in which thousands of Australians were slaughtered as they charged, bayonets fixed, to be mown down by enemy machine guns.

Two of Jenny's uncles, George and Jim Staley, had been involved in the Gallipoli campaign. Lew had met, and greatly admired, Colonel Jim Staley, who had survived Gallipoli and gone on to win the Military Cross in France. Captured by the Japanese in Malaya in World War Two, he had spent three years in the infamous Changi prisoner-of-war camp.

Chapter 9

1956: Hoad's Annus Mirabilis

Lew stood staring out over Sydney Harbour with baby Jane cradled in his arms. He thought of the moment only a few weeks ago when Jenny handed him his new-born daughter; how he'd marvelled at her beauty and vulnerability, stroked the silky down of blonde hair. In the past when friends had proudly showed him their newborn babies, he had dutifully endorsed remarks about how pretty they were, whilst privately thinking them rather scrawny, and blotchy. So he was amazed to find that he could be entirely honest with Jenny. 'Geez,' he stammered. 'She's really not bad looking.' Up to that moment, his main concern had been that she'd be born without a major handicap. And here she was, perfect – with peach-like skin, the most beautiful thing imaginable. Jenny chuckled. She recognized the tone of wonder in his voice and knew that 'really not bad looking' was the characteristic understatement of an Aussie male. Both of them realised also that with the birth of Jane, everything had changed, changed utterly; he had a beautiful daughter, and an additional burden of responsibility.

He remembered the excitement and occasional worries of those weeks preceding Jane's birth. Jenny had left Sydney to stay with her parents in Melbourne. After months of searching for accommodation, a member of the White City Club in Sydney had found this delightful unfurnished flat at Parsley Bay 'with a pleasant view overlooking Sydney Harbour and lawns for baby Jane to romp on later.' Jenny and Lew relished the task of furnishing their first home together from scratch. All that, however, would have to wait now, and with Lew contracted to play a series of exhibition matches in Japan, Jenny wanted the pampering care and support of her parents to assist her in the latter stages of pregnancy. A specialist had recommended St Vincent's, a hospital in Melbourne that he felt would cope with the inevitable media invasion, and a nun called Sister Fabian, who'd keep reporters firmly at bay when they threatened to become too intrusive.

When Lew returned from Japan, they'd talked about the future. He suddenly realised how strongly opposed she was to him turning professional. She didn't think he'd be happy and, more important, she couldn't bear the thought of them being separated again for long periods whilst he toured the world with Kramer's 'circus'.

But now – back in Sydney – tenderly rocking Jane to sleep, he wondered if he'd been right to turn down Kramer's offer. He had just turned twenty-one, had a wife, a baby, a flat – and precious little money. Sometimes his earnings from winning a tournament amounted to no more than seventy pounds. It was true that Dunlop, hearing about his negotiations with Kramer, had given him a salary increase to help with the financial problems incurred in setting up home and providing for his baby daughter. Even Lew, though, could see that the salary increase was probably due more to self-interest than philanthropic concern.

He thought again about the recent meeting with Jack Kramer. Disappointed by the way Hoad and Rosewall had backed out of the contract they'd signed, he'd flown to Sydney to try to change Lew's mind. Like most people, Lew had been impressed by Kramer, and possibly flattered by his flying all the way from California to talk to him.

It was difficult not to like and respect Jack. He was tall, suntanned, with a muscular physique, had crew cut hair and a face that was often wreathed in smiles. Yes, he had the smooth-talking charm of a successful businessman making a 'pitch', but as well as smooth-talking, you also felt he was straight-talking. You could trust him: his word was literally his bond. Furthermore, the respect he commanded from others had been well-earned. Beneath the charm and affability lay an intense desire to win. Kramer had been, and was still, a great champion. He'd won Wimbledon in 1947, and with every shot in the book at his disposal, including a powerful serve and volley, was renowned not only for his sporting ability, but also his tactical acumen. If there was an angle to be found, on the tennis court or in the business world, Jack could be relied upon to find it. He had successfully managed and expanded his troupe of professional players, recruiting new amateurs and setting up tours around the world which were now so successful they posed a real threat to the amateur game.

Some of the players occasionally complained he wasn't paying them enough, or that the signing-on fee didn't reflect their crowd-drawing potential, but they may have failed to take into account the overheads of this organisation and the day-to-day running costs, not to mention the substantial risks. However, with the notable exception of Pancho Gonzales, the players felt they were getting a good, and a fair, deal. Whilst there were still problems in finding suitable venues, and Kramer and his professional tennis troupe continued to be regarded with contempt by the amateur tennis authorities, no-one could deny they were now a major force in world tennis.

But a regular supply of new talent and new faces was still required to keep pulling in the crowds. So Kramer had been mortified when Hoad and Rosewall backed out of the deal he'd arranged.

There might still be a slim chance of changing Hoad's mind, however. Jack sensed that, subjected to conflicting advice from all sides, the young Australian was wavering. Lew had indicated that if Jack were to raise his initial guarantee to £30,000 plus an increased percentage of the profits from a proposed world tour, he might just reconsider the offer.

What Jack wasn't to know was that Lew, accompanied by his parents and Adrian Quist, had finally come to the conclusion that it was too soon to turn pro: the goal of winning Wimbledon and further major titles – possibly a Grand Slam – was too tantalising a prospect. His mind was made up. His parents had been taken aback by the size of the fee being offered their son and were amazed by his temerity not only in rejecting it, but in suggesting it should be substantially raised. It already appeared a sum beyond their wildest dreams of wealth. On the other hand, they respected Jenny's reasons for opposing the deal and leaned heavily on the advice of Quist who cautioned against the move at this time.

When Lew and his parents stepped into the lobby of the opulent hotel in which Kramer was staying, then went up in the lift to his penthouse suite, they felt intimidated by the surroundings. For a working-class family the hotel, and Jack's suite, seemed like the height of luxury.

As Kramer ushered them in, his heart sank. To have not just Adrian Quist, but also Lew's parents attending this meeting, meant all his powers of persuasion were unlikely to work. Even so, he presented his case powerfully, and Lew had begun to feel decidedly uncomfortable when Kramer pointed out that if the document he'd signed wasn't legally binding, it was certainly morally binding. Perhaps both men were going through the motions, each knowing that a counter-bid of £30,000 would be impossible for Kramer to stomach. He did, however, agree to raise the fee to £25,000 saying this was as high as he could go.

Even one last-ditch attempt by the American promoter to change Lew's mind, proved to no avail. He flew out to Melbourne accompanied by Frank Sedgman (hoping that a fellow Australian might break down Hoad's resistance), but again Lew remained obdurate.

Afterwards, Kramer attributed Hoad's rejection of his offer to the influence of Jenny. In his autobiography he suggested that she wanted Lew with her when their baby was born (which was undoubtedly true) and that the idea of a grand tour of the world with her husband as star, was just too tempting. It would involve trips to:

Paris, London, Monaco, New York, San Francisco – a couple of leisurely weeks at each stop, expenses paid, good times, and a hard match or two every week or so. That appeared a great deal nicer to Jenny than her sitting at home with a baby or maybe joining Lew for a few weeks of one-night stands – Toledo to Dayton to Columbus to Indianapolis – with Kramer or Trabert across the net every night.[1]

Kramer's speculations may not have been wide of the mark. But if he *was* right, who can blame Jenny? It was perfectly natural she should prefer, both for her sake and Lew's, the prospect of further triumphs on an amateur tour to the rigours of a professional one. Kramer also suspected that Hopman was not dealing straight from the deck. Rosewall had been employed by Slazenger; when they learned he might turn pro, they raised his 'salary, and got him another job'. At the same time Hopman informed Kramer of Rosewall's decision to remain an amateur, he intimated that Jenny Hoad might be persuaded to drop her opposition to Lew signing if Kramer 'upped the ante for her husband. It was a squeeze play Hopman had worked up'. If Kramer didn't have to spend the money on signing Rosewall, he could use the money saved to increase Lew's fee. The only flaw in this argument was what possible motive could Hopman have for negotiating a rise in the fee paid to Hoad, if he could hang on to both his Davis Cup stars by supporting Lew's change of mind?

Kramer, though, was undoubtedly right when he insisted that Hopman and Lew's advisers were 'playing with fire'. He had been double-crossed and had the signed contracts to prove it. He couldn't make them play, but he had only to wave those contracts in public and both Rosewall and Hoad would have been finished as amateurs. To be fair to Kramer, he was too honourable a man to pursue such a threat. The victims would have been naive young men rather than their advisers. Furthermore, as he admitted, it wouldn't have done him any good, apart from the satisfaction of revenge. And it would have ruined him in Australia forever, making it impossible to sign those players in the future. He'd be cutting off his nose to spite his face.

There was one other factor that clearly weighed in Lew's thinking. He was still very young; there'd be plenty of time in the future for professional tennis. He had a gut feeling that this was going to be his year. In spite of showing tremendous promise, he hadn't won a major singles title. The promise still had to be converted into results. If he could win one or two of the majors, or even win the Grand Slam, all four major tournaments in the one year – a feat only previously achieved by Don Budge – then he'd be able to negotiate vastly improved financial terms with Kramer. Not only that, perhaps more importantly for Lew, he'd have entered Tennis's Hall of Fame, and earned a place for himself in the record books.

He looked down again at the baby in his arms. He knew he had been blessed with a unique talent, and tennis, the means of expressing that talent, gave him a 'buzz', a high, a feeling of tremendous elation. There were times when, like other gifted sportsmen – Mohammed Ali or Sugar Ray Robinson in boxing; Viv Richards or Brian Lara in cricket; George Best or Pele in football – his movement and timing were so impeccable that he seemed to be performing on some kind of transcendental level. At such moments, great players have the ability to elevate their chosen sport to an art form.

But if this potential were not to be realised, if he wasted his unique talents, what would he have to fall back upon? How would he be able to support a family? He had no other marketable skills, tennis was, and had been, his whole life. He owed it to Jenny, and his daughter, to ensure that his talent was not squandered and he resolved that 1956 should be the year of his breakthrough, the year in which he stepped forward to dominate the world of amateur tennis and realise his potential.

Soon after Jane was born, Lew and Jenny moved back to Sydney to set up home in their flat at Parsley Bay. They tackled this task with all the enthusiasm and delight young couples typically bring to transforming their first home. They worked like Trojans, rubbing down, painting, putting up curtains, hanging much loved Toulouse-Lautrec prints Jenny had bought in Paris. They sorted out where new furnishings should go, where to put the knick-knacks, the various wedding presents, and the prizes they had accumulated from tournament wins. Lew found Jenny's excitement in constructing a home infectious; he almost preferred it to chilling out with a few lagers – almost, but not quite!

Perhaps these activities had the effect of taking his mind off tennis; perhaps also he needed a short break, because when he returned to tournament competition it was with renewed relish. Despite some press criticism that he was the 'problem boy' of Australian tennis, his concentration was sharp, and the strenuous fitness programme he had maintained produced some good, early season results. He won the New South Wales singles title, beating Ashley Cooper in the semi-final in three sets, and Rosewall in the final in four. He felt he was coming into his best form; he was hitting harder and with more consistency. With new responsibilities had come greater mental strength – and a steely determination to try to win the four major titles in the world: the Australian, French, Wimbledon and American Championships. A string of tournaments and exhibition matches brought him to the Australian Championships and a final against his 'twin', Rosewall, who was also on top form.

Not that there weren't mishaps for Lew along the way. In a freak car accident, he tore the nail off a finger of his racquet hand and had to cope with a good deal of pain as he fought his way through to the final of the Australian. He had a hard, five-set, battle against Mervyn Rose in the semi-final, and then a gruelling four-set final in the doubles – a total of ninety-seven games in the day before he faced Rosewall.

The papers said he would be played out, but Lew knew that his form, and his mental attitude, was stronger than it had ever been. In the final, Kenny adopted his new tactic on his service games of trying to get nearly all his first serves in, and then racing to the net. Lew countered this by moving into the court by two or three feet on the return of serve, taking the ball almost as it bounced. As he said later, 'I felt I had succeeded in harnessing my natural ability to hit hard and yet still retained control of all my shots.' In the end, big hitting overcame the wiles of Rosewall, and Lew won 6-4, 3-6, 6-4, 7-5 in what some Australian experts declared was the best tennis they had ever seen. Indeed, of all the matches they played against each other, Hoad also rated this as the best.

With the national championship under his belt, Lew was ranked the best amateur player in the world, and Rosewall No 2. Now for Europe and America – and the other three remaining titles.

It was agreed Jenny should be allowed to accompany Lew on a 'private tour' as long as he joined up with the Australian Davis Cup team later and came under the direction and organisation of the wise and kindly Pat Hughes, Director of the Dunlop Company in Europe. Lew and Jenny set off, leaving baby Jane to be looked after at home by both sets of grandparents. Jenny was subsequently criticised by some Australian newspapers for such a prolonged absence from her daughter. On their return, some seven months later, one even had a front page photograph of Jane, cradled in her grandmother's arms, looking shy and unsure at Sydney airport, whilst Jenny was in tears. The paper claimed this was because Jane had not recognised her mother – but both Lew and Jenny knew her tears were tears of joy at their reunion.

With the titles of Egypt and the Lebanon behind him, and a couple of modest cheques in his suitcase, Lew and Jenny set out for the tortures of the Italian Championships at the Foro Italico in Rome. This is one of the most amazing stadiums in the world, a vast colourful arena surrounded by huge bronze statues of naked athletes from the Roman Games of old. The Italians love to be involved as participants in the matches, shouting at every shot and becoming wildly enthusiastic in their support of favourite players. They are also the most ferociously partisan spectators: woe-betide the foreigner who comes up against an Italian player. On such occasions the stadium becomes more like a medieval bear-baiting arena. To make life even more difficult, the linesmen in Rome used to have a reputation for what can only be described as 'idiosyncratic' calls.

Lew's close friend, Larry Hodgson, recalls watching him play a match where the groundsmen started to use high-speed hoses to water the court next to where Lew was playing, so that the righthand side of his court was bathed in dizzying sunshine, and the left-hand side in a shower. Lew glared about him and slammed the ball high into the air in frustration – much to the delight of the crowd who screamed abuse.

The Italians didn't take to Lew that year, and it required a tremendous effort to maintain his concentration and temper as he plodded past a number of local heroes to reach the final against the best hard court player in the world at the time, Sven Davidson of Sweden.

Davidson was a formidable opponent, especially on clay, his favoured surface, but Lew had already beaten him in a close five-set match to take the title in Egypt, and that win boosted his confidence. He now felt he could play from the back court as effectively as at the net, and his improved stamina meant that he was a match for any player, regardless of the surface they were playing on. In fact, he beat Davidson comfortably in straight sets and headed off to the next major tournament, the French Championships in Paris at Stade Roland Garros, in exactly the right frame of mind.

Travelling separately from the team meant that Lew and Jenny had time to spare and, with her love of art, they enjoyed the typical tourist pursuits of sightseeing and shopping as Lew grew to appreciate Paris even more. Such activities also kept his nerves calm (provided Jenny didn't indulge in too many extravagant purchases!) on his path through to the final, again against Davidson. In that most romantic of cities, the young lovers were in their element. In his autobiography, *My Game*, Hoad's affection for Paris is obvious:

> *We took the train to Paris for the French Championships in high spirits. We did not stay in the hotel normally occupied during the tournament by the Australian players, but in a quiet, off the main street, hotel where few pressmen could find us. It had been booked for us by Philippe Chatrier, the former French player who is now a popular Paris sports-writer.*

> *For the first few days of the tournament we explored Paris at night, seeking out back-street restaurants and tiny bistros recommended to us by Chatrier. I worked hard during the day, but I was playing so well I could afford to relax at night. I think Jenny and I knew how lucky we were that week; you could see the glow of happiness come out from her.*

> *She fossicked about the shops in the colourful alleys and side streets of Montmartre and the Left Bank on days she did not have to go to Roland Garros to play. I would come back to our hotel at night after a match and a hard work-out, and she would say: 'Darling, you'll never guess what I've*

bought. Look, some wonderful tiles for the wrought-iron table I thought we'd have at home. You fit each tile into a design, and I've got these spares in case any break.' I thought of the air freight bills and how heavy tiles weigh, and said I liked them.[2]

Towards the end of the tournament there occurred an incident, typical of Lew, but now talked about with awe in tennis circles. Having been detained on the eve of the final by a doubles match, Lew and Jenny went for a late dinner at a quiet little bistro. After some time a waiter approached with a bottle of vodka, which he indicated was a present from two Russian 'diplomats' sitting at a nearby table. Russia was about to break into the world tennis scene and had been carefully scouting the major tournaments to get a feel for things. Lew and Jenny joined the Russians and, to cement their new friendship, decided to go back to the Russians' apartment for some more drinks.

At six o'clock the following morning, Lew and Jenny returned to their hotel and Lew slumped on the bed. As the room began to spin round, he announced with evident surprise, 'Shit, I'm drunk!' – which Jenny regarded as the understatement of the tour so far. There were only eight hours to the final; Lew got up, donned his track suit and ran several miles to the Roland Garros courts to try to clear his head, and get some much needed practice.

Luckily he came across a young Rod Laver, also looking for an early work-out, and the two set about trying to get Lew sober on an outside court. Pale-faced, and with sweat coming out of every pore, Lew then put down a hefty breakfast – which immediately returned. More work on court with Rod – then a second breakfast. With two breakfasts down and one up, Lew fell asleep on a bench in the locker room. That afternoon, in blazing heat and before a packed Paris centre court, he beat his opponent who, once again, was Sven Davidson, 6-4, 8-6, 6-1 – at one point hitting six winners in a row and taking five successive games in eleven minutes.

In the stands his overseas 'guardian' Pat Hughes was elated. But as Lew later admitted, 'If he'd known what condition I was in before I got on court, he'd have had a heart attack!' After a night-long boozing, a night that would have reduced mere mortals to a state of complete paralysis the next day, the victory – and the manner in which it was achieved – represented one of Lew's greatest tennis triumphs. Watching the match, the former great French player, Toto Brugnon (one of the legendary 'Four Musketeers') commented that not he, nor even the mighty Bill Tilden, would have taken more than a handful of games off Lew that day.

Lew now had the first two majors – the Australian and French – under his belt but he was still prone to occasional lapses. There were some who questioned the wisdom of his punishing schedule of exhibition matches and tournaments; certainly tiredness from travelling seemed partly a cause of his defeat by fellow

Australian, Bob Howe, in the final of the Spanish Championships at Barcelona. Compensation came in the visit he and Jenny made to a bullfight during their stay in Barcelona. Both found the skills of the matadors and the colourful, dramatic spectacle of the occasion, exhilarating. Lew commented: 'There is nothing quite so awesome as a 4-year-old fighting bull when it comes into the ring, or anything quite as exciting to me as a Litri or a Dominguin with the cape.'

After Barcelona it was back to England to begin his grass court preparation for Wimbledon. Pat Hughes talked to him when he stopped off in London before going on to play in the Manchester tournament. He asked Lew how he liked his racquets strung. These were the days, of course, before top tennis players toured the world with a personal retinue that included not only their own racquet stringer, but coaches, fitness trainers and practice partners.

As Dunlop's European Director, Hughes was responsible for all Hoad's equipment and sports clothing, and he was flabbergasted when Lew said he'd given away his racquets to some likeable Spaniards he'd met in Barcelona. Hughes could not believe that someone of Lew's standing in the game could be so unconcerned about turning up to play in a tournament without any racquets. And yet anyone who knew Hoad well – as Hughes undoubtedly did – should not really have been surprised by his behaviour; it was typical of the man's impulsive generosity and relaxed attitude towards life in general.

For the rest of his time in England, Lew remained under the watchful and, at times, fretful eye of Pat Hughes, as he began his run-in to the 1956 Wimbledon Championships. A run-in, it must be acknowledged, that wasn't entirely successful. He was beaten again in the Manchester final by his old tormentor, Drobny, and he realised that the 'flicking' shots he had developed on clay would not work on grass; he had to 'revert to stroking the ball again and trying to regain fluent swings on each wing.'

After Manchester, it was back down south to Bristol where, once more, weariness may have been partly responsible for his loss in the final to the engaging South African, Gordon Forbes. Forbes would be the first to acknowledge that he never quite succeeded in breaking into the very top ranks of tennis, although he was a highly respected and very talented player with a number of excellent tournament wins to his name. In later life he emerged as one of the game's most distinguished writers, with two eloquent, and often hilarious, memoirs of a life in tennis. *A Handful of Summers* and *Too Soon to Panic* have rightly become acknowledged as sporting classics, and Gordon Forbes has kindly given his permission for the authors to draw upon his memoirs more extensively at a later stage in this biography. Recalling his victory over Hoad at Bristol, Forbes writes with disarming modesty:

Defeating Hoad was extraordinary. He was a majestic player, with a superb and flawless selection of strokes, and a court presence as arresting and fearless as that of a handsome god. Blond-headed, contemptuous of caution, nervousness, or any mannerisms remotely connected with gamesmanship, meanness or tricky endeavour, I worshipped him then as only the young can worship, and remember my defeat of him as something which took place in a dream – uneasy, ecstatic, triumphant – the bringing down of an idol. He was off-form I suppose, and I exceptionally sharp, but even the defeat of an off-form Hoad was enough to lift my heart.[3]

This generous tribute to Lew perfectly sums up the feelings of almost everyone who was fortunate enough to see him play.

In spite of the tiredness that a few days well-earned rest would dispel, generally Lew felt in good shape, and approached Wimbledon with confidence. There was just a nagging doubt surrounding his back, which had become increasingly painful in the six months since he left Australia. It was arranged he should make a 'secret' visit to a Harley Street specialist, who came up with the amazing suggestion that the young man should 'take more exercise'. An odd prescription, thought Lew, for an athlete bent upon winning the world's greatest and most demanding tennis tournament in the next two weeks.

At Wimbledon, Lew was seeded No 1. For once he felt he was in charge of his game, and his mind. This would be it! The only hiccup came in the quarter-final against fellow countryman, Mal Anderson. Although he was expected to beat Anderson fairly easily, he seemed tense at the beginning of the match and lost the first set 6-4. Stung into action, he raced away with the next two sets 6-1, 6-1. Then in the eighth game of the fourth set, he got what he felt was a bad call and swatted the ball almost into the Royal Box. This petulant response upset him and his concentration faltered. Fortunately, rain put a stop to play when he was serving at 10-11 down, but it was an angry Hoad who stomped into the locker room and hurled down his racquets.

His old friend, Drobny, was waiting there to give him a quiet lecture, telling him that if he didn't calm down and regain his composure he would certainly be out of the biggest tournament of his young life. Lew, always inclined to accept the advice of an older man, especially from one he respected as much as Drobny, heeded his words and when play resumed after the rain-break, went on to win the fourth set and the match.

Only one player, he knew, could keep him from the title he so dearly wanted – the black-haired kid from Sydney, his 'twin', friend and doubles partner, Ken Rosewall. Lew had a sleepless night before the final, spending most of the time roaming around the flat he and Jenny had been lent, drinking tea. No booze before this final! This was serious preparation for Lew. He knew Rosewall had reached a peak.

Although slightly worried by his lack of sleep, he still felt confident when he walked from the locker room to the doors of the All England Clubhouse, which lead to the Centre Court. He glanced up at the famous inscription which confronts all players as they wait to go into that most dramatic arena, the quotation from Rudyard Kipling, 'If you can face triumph and disaster and treat these two impostors just the same'. Then he and Kenny walked out together.

The Centre Court was packed and the crowd, wild with excitement, looked forward expectantly to what everyone felt would be a classic final between the two best tennis players in the world. The 'twins' emerged into the sunlight, turned and bowed to the Royal Box where the Duchess of Kent, President of the All England Club, and Princess Margaret gave them encouraging smiles, and the Australian Prime Minister, Bob Menzies, who had flown in specially for the final, waved. This was a great day for Australia and he was proud of his two Sydney youngsters.

Hoad, thinking perhaps he should have gone to the toilet just one more time after all the tea he had consumed, got off to a flying start and won the first set 6-2. However, Rosewall, refusing to be intimidated by the battery of balls flying at him, settled, and fought back to take the second 6-4. With both men playing at their best, Lew just edged the third set 7-5.

Then his mind went into sleep mode and Rosewall was quick to seize his opportunity. He raced to a 4-1 lead and now appeared fully in control of a match that a little earlier had been slipping from his grasp. Lew, hands on hips, realised this was the biggest crisis of his tennis career. With one forefinger he flicked the sweat from his brow. He had to decide what to do about his serve. Hitherto, the strong, gusting wind had forced him to shorten his toss-up and slow the severity of service. Damn the wind! He prepared to serve. Tossing the ball high, he smacked down an ace. Fifteen love. With the next serve, the same high toss, the same result. That service game was easily held, and now he resolved to go for broke on Rosewall's service. He moved into the court, taking Rosewall's serves incredibly early and hitting his returns with all his might. A startled Rosewall could only stare at the ground, then up at the sky, scratch his head in that Stan Laurel-like way of his, and look on in disbelief as twenty clean winners flew past him. Lew said later: 'In fifteen minutes I played the most devastating tennis of my life.' He swept past Kenny's 4-1 lead and, taking the next five games in succession, won the set, the match and the title, 6-2, 4-6, 7-5, 6-4. He had achieved his dream. In his autobiography, Lew recalled the moment:

> Ken hit a backhand from my drive down the middle of the centre court, with the same flowing grace he had shown in almost forty matches against me since

our childhood. I thought the ball would clear the net, but it smacked the tape and hovered for a moment. Up in the grandstand, among the thousands of hushed and tense spectators, my wife Jenny watched it nervously, and the other side of the world in the Sydney my mother and father and two brothers listened anxiously by a radio set in a living room crowded with our sporting trophies.

The ball seemed to stay on top of the net for as long as history.

Then it fell on Rosewall's side of the court and in that instant I became the 1956 Wimbledon champion and the biggest gamble I've ever taken on a tennis court had succeeded against the little dark-haired youth with the nimble feet who so often stood between me and a tennis title. We had played each other in many countries for nine years and in a fairy-tale twist of fate, it was Rosewall I had to defeat to achieve the ambition which began more than a decade before, when, barefoot, I hit a tennis ball against a garage door.

The tension left me for the first time in four exciting sets of tennis as I moved up to the net to shake hands with him. I really did not feel anything for myself, I was merely very sorry for Kenny, defeated for a second time in a Wimbledon final. 'Bad luck Ken,' I said and he smiled and softly replied, 'You were too good for me today, Lew.'

The 'twins', partners and friends, went on to win the doubles.

The morning after the final, the dress designer and tennis enthusiast, Teddy Tinling, arrived early at Lew's flat armed with all the newspaper accounts of his victory. 'They are singing your praises,' said Tinling. Lew's only reply was, 'What's Peanuts doing?' – referring to his favourite cartoon.

The previous year, Hoad had agreed to wear Tinling's range of tennis clothing and the designer had been delighted to find himself scheduled to play Lew in the second round of the Manchester tournament. The only problem was he had to defeat a wily English aristocrat in the opening round to earn his place in the sun with Lew. There's a delightful account of the proceedings in *A Handful of Summers*. As Teddy acknowledged, he wasn't entirely confident about the outcome of the match, though he had the stronger forehand. 'Lords can be damned crafty. Play all day long, you see. Don't have to make dresses for a living.' Having miraculously succeeded in winning this hilarious encounter, Tinling went on to lose to Lew 6-0, 6-0. His post-match analysis, Forbes recalls, ran thus: 'I was *mentally* prepared for the match, but mental ability alone was useless. To begin with, one needs to face oneself in the right direction. I spent half the match hitting backhands with a forehand grip and forehands with my backhand grip. Lew was very polite. He'd call out to me: 'Are you ready, Teddy?' and I'd call back that I was but I wasn't. Not once in the entire match was I ready!'

Forbes comments: 'Teddy would have felt far less depressed had he realised just how many other players had gone through entire matches against Lew Hoad feeling as though they were 'not quite ready!"

At the Wimbledon Ball always held at the end of the tournament, there was a typical example of Lew's teasing Aussie humour. Tradition decreed that as men's singles champion, Lew opened the dancing with the ladies' champion, in this case Shirley Fry, and later made the Champion's speech. Naturally, there was considerable apprehension among the people attending the Ball when Lew rose to his feet. Was he about to announce he was leaving the amateur game, and signing as a professional with Kramer's 'circus'?

Lew was well aware of the rumours circulating. As he stood up, an expectant silence descended upon the assembled gathering. He cleared his throat and in that husky Australian drawl, said, 'Ladies and gentlemen – you are lucky to have me here tonight.' And there he paused for what seemed like an eternity, a pause that simply increased the tension in the room even more, especially for members of the Australian Davis Cup squad. Finally he continued, 'because by seven o'clock, my suit still hadn't come back from the cleaners.' There was a huge sigh of relief, followed by nervous laughter. What he didn't tell his listeners was that the cheap dinner suit he'd purchased had come back from the cleaners so shrunk, it would only have fitted a ventriloquist's dummy. A race around London produced another suit, which had to be altered to fit Lew's massive shoulders.

Now just the American title remained to be won and Lew's dream of being only the second man in tennis history, after the American, Donald Budge, to garner all four major titles in a single year would be fulfilled. So, on to America. But after the excitement, tension and determination of winning Wimbledon lifted, Lew realised there was something seriously wrong with his back – low down, at the base of the spine. The X-rays from the Harley Street specialist he'd seen before Wimbledon showed nothing, but the pain and stiffness sometimes made it almost impossible to get out of bed. Pat Hughes decided that rather than undergo the discomfort of a long air flight, Lew and Jenny should travel to America on the Queen Mary. He must win that all-important fourth title at Forest Hills.

With the pain and discomfort from his back increasing, Lew played mediocre tennis up to the United States Championships. He was forced to work-out more often immediately before matches to get his back warm, and he resorted to wearing a sweater during games to keep it warm. However, it was characteristic of Lew that he always dismissed suggestions that his back problems may have been a factor in his performance against Rosewall in the 1956 American final – last of the major titles that Lew needed to win the Grand Slam in one glorious year.

Although Hoad set off at a furious pace to win the first set 6-4, Rosewall's game was honed to perfection. Playing a mixture of baseline tennis and net rushing, he overcame an increasingly unhappy Hoad 4-6, 6-2, 6-3, 6-3. Lew wrote in his book:

> *I think Rosewall was almost as unhappy at the result as I was. He openly wept because he knew how much winning this last title in the hunt for the Grand Slam meant to me. He would have preferred not to be the player who thwarted me when I was so close to achieving this elusive coup and his grief for me was very solemn and genuine.*

For the rest of the American tour he shrugged off the disappointment of failing to achieve the Grand Slam, but it was a still a disconsolate Hoad who eventually headed back with Jenny to Australia, to the family, the flat, baby Jane – and the defence of the Davis Cup. To Lew's alarm, his back condition began to worsen in Australia, but with gritted teeth he played on, hoping that once he'd warmed-up, the pain and stiffness would go. On some days, though, he could barely move and for the first time he scratched from his own home state championships. This did nothing for his temper, and with the Davis Cup approaching, Hopman grew ever more apprehensive. He realised, however, that when Hoad was at ease not only with himself but, more importantly, with his back, no-one could beat him.

After several days of intense stiffness, Lew played in the Victoria State Championships in Jenny's home-town of Melbourne. He struggled through to the finals to play his 'twin' again. He didn't know that after some forty-odd matches against each other, this was the last time he was to face the 'little master' across the net as an amateur. To try to save his back from prolonged work, Lew was going for his shots, lambasting the ball, and winning as fast as he could. He was leading Rosewall by two sets to love when he considered he got a bad call. Pain made him more than usually short-tempered and he demanded that the linesman be replaced. When he was, by a woman, Lew felt disgusted with himself. Kenny looked sadly at his friend. Flowing strokes, particularly from the backhand wing, enabled Rosewall to win his last amateur title.

The Americans now publicly declared they considered Hoad the weak link in the Australian Davis Cup team, and that being a champion was proving too much for him. The Australian camp had, of course, made no reference to his back problem; this had been kept a closely guarded secret. There may also have been a touch of false bravado in the American assertions, because they knew they had a weak team.

Trabert was now a professional. Seixas, past his prime, was the new number one, Ham Richardson had refused to travel to Australia without his wife, and the rest of the team were 'green' youngsters. Nevertheless, had they known that for two days before the Challenge Round began Lew couldn't get out of bed, and was stricken with nerves when he walked on court to face the American, Herbie Flam, their morale would have been considerably boosted. But back or no back, there was nobody around in the same class as Hoad and Rosewall, and the Cup was retained 5-0, with the 'twins' playing together as a team for the last time.

Jack Kramer was in town with his touring circus and once again he approached the boys. His plan was to capitalise on the appeal of the Davis Cup and pit Australia (the 'kids', Rosewall and Hoad) against America (Trabert and Gonzales). Rosewall immediately accepted Kramer's terms and even tried to talk Hoad into it, saying the Hoad-Rosewall combination was bound to draw the crowds, but Lew declined, maintaining that he wanted at least one or two more cracks at the Grand Slam. To do this he knew he would need to cure what was wrong with his back and, following visits to several of Australia's top specialists, the news of his condition leaked out. The diagnosis of one specialist was that he had torn ligaments at the base of his spine and he was put in a plaster cast for six weeks.

In the first of the Grand Slam championships, the Australian, Lew struggled in vain. In the semi-finals against Neale Fraser, he couldn't bend, reach or jump and his dreams of another crack at the Grand Slam were shattered when Fraser won in four sets. It was then that he made the decision to become a professional. He didn't know how long he could continue playing (especially if it was to involve the unceasing nightly grind of the pro-tour), but he needed to make some big money quickly to support his growing family. He secretly signed with Jack Kramer for $100,000 minimum guarantee, and a promised $25,000 bonus if he retained his Wimbledon title and thus increased his crowd-pulling potential as the first man to win Wimbledon in consecutive years since the end of the Second World War.

With the help of one particular specialist, Dr Skougal, Lew's back began to improve. Lew had always shaved and shortened his tennis racquets – now Dunlop brought his fifteen-ounce racquets down to just over thirteen ounces to suit his wristy style. With his back on the mend, Hoad's temper and concentration improved slightly. As Wimbledon approached, he knew he had to win a second title if he was to secure that extra bonus from Kramer, plus a future for his family free from financial worries.

Chapter 10

Murder on the Centre Court

Lew set out on his 1957 world tour with a lot on his mind. He knew his agreement with Kramer must be kept secret or he would be banned from the amateur tennis circuit, and his hopes of winning a second Wimbledon (and thus Jack's bonus) would be dashed. This had happened to Tony Trabert just two years earlier when, merely by announcing that he was interested in becoming a professional, he was immediately cast out by the USLTA – even though he hadn't signed a contract or received a dime from Kramer. It was precisely this kind of blind prejudice that Kramer was fighting on the long road that eventually led to Open tennis over a decade later. Lew also knew that the prolonged lay-off caused by his back problem would make it impossible to repeat the outstanding achievements of the previous year – his best year as an amateur. He had already lost the Australian title and, as expected, on the slow red courts of Italy and France went down to lesser men. Back in Australia, the newspapers wrote him off as a 'washout', saying that he had 'physically cracked'. In America, Jack Kramer read of these defeats with growing trepidation.

However, when Lew arrived in England for the summer grass court season, there was an amazing transformation. Suddenly his back felt good, his mental agility was sharp, and he was hitting the ball with power and precision. A string of tournament wins took him to Wimbledon, where he was again seeded No 1.

Scratching about for as much money as she could find, Jenny decided to fly over to England to be with her husband as he attempted to win a second successive Wimbledon singles title. She felt it would be best for his peace of mind if they found a little flat rather than stay in an hotel. She was unaware he'd decided to turn professional. What she did know was that she would be the victim of repeated Australian criticism that she'd abandoned her baby daughter again. But she sensed winning this Wimbledon meant something very special to Lew and that cooking for him, walking and talking, and just being with him, mattered more than any criticism back home where, after all, baby Jane was in the capable and loving care of her grandparents.

So it was in a relaxed and confident mood that Lew Hoad walked on to the Centre Court at Wimbledon to open the 1957 championships – to be greeted by a standing ovation from the British crowd. The modest blond Australian, who sometimes grinned and sometimes growled, was now an idol. Lew walked to the umpire's chair and bowed his head. The boy from Wigram Road 'couldn't believe it'. He knew how much he would miss this atmosphere. So he'd do his best to please them – keeping the secret that he would never see them again within his heart until that dream of a second Wimbledon singles title was fulfilled.

On his way to the final, Lew honed his game on some of the leading players of the day. He brushed aside the Frenchman, Pierre Darmon; next in line was his mighty drinking partner and fellow countryman, Roy 'Emmo' Emerson. Then it was the turn of Mervyn Rose ('Rosie') his Davis Cup team-mate, a tricky, unpredictable adversary who was sometimes inspired and sometimes disappointing. And in the semi-final, it was again the great Sven Davidson who said after his defeat, 'Lew is a class and a half better than any other player in the world.'

At 2pm on Friday 5th July 1957 two men Hollywood would have paid a ransom for, walked out to contest the title: 'cowboy' Lew, blond hair slicked down and forearms like young oak trees, and the darkly handsome Ashley Cooper. They were of similar height and build: Cooper an inch taller than his opponent, with the same powerful physique though slimmer than Hoad. Watching the final were the Queen, the Duke of Edinburgh, the Duchess of Kent, notables from the world of movies, business, art and sport and, obviously, as this was once again an all Australian final, the beaming and waving Bob Menzies.

It was perfect weather for tennis: hot, as it had been throughout the tournament, but with the heat tempered by a gentle breeze. Hoad took control from the outset. He broke serve and began to hit winners every two or three points. Cooper knew he wasn't playing that badly. On occasions, though, his racquet just flailed the air and he was sent sprawling. Years later, Lew commented, 'This was the kind of tennis I had always dreamed I might one day be able to play.'

Throughout the match Cooper directed his serve predominantly at Lew's backhand, as if fearing the weight and penetration of his forehand return. However, Hoad alternately bamboozled him with sliced backhand returns that died at his feet, or bombarded him with crunching, topspin drives cross-court or down the lines. Hoad was playing with clinical precision, directing the ball to every corner of the court so that Cooper was often left guessing, groping for shots a fraction of a second too late. One reporter wrote that Hoad's 'own anticipation was so uncanny that you'd think he'd been fitted with radar,' and another commented, with typical journalistic hyperbole, 'Hoad hit one top-spin backhand passing shot so hard and so fast that it almost took the back of the centre court away.'

The reigning champion took the first set in exactly twenty minutes. Jenny had missed nearly all of this set because, when Lew had been having a hit with Gordon Forbes earlier in the day, he'd broken two strings in his favourite racquet. She immediately dashed of to get it repaired - what a contrast with contemporary players who come on court with half a dozen racquets and seem to have an army of racquet stringers in constant attendance. In the second set, troubled by something in his eye (a hair, a speck of dust?), Lew had to call upon a linesman for assistance. He had the same problem on two occasions later, which prompted Lance Tingay, the doyen of tennis correspondents, to observe that if Hoad could play as well as this with only one eye working, what miracles might he not perform with both!

The first game of the second set produced two points that somehow epitomised the dazzling variety and the uncanny anticipation of Hoad's game throughout the match. Cooper serving at 30-0; an excellent, deep serve to Hoad's backhand forces a scrabbled return that just clears the net, leaving Cooper, who has followed his serve in, with a range of choices. He plays a delicate drop shot and, like the rest of the Centre Court, assumes it's a winner. He's almost turned round to head back to the baseline, then catches sight of Hoad haring into the net like a whippet, and realises the point isn't over. Starting to back-pedal desperately, he watches transfixed as Lew flips a backhand cross-court, and shakes his head in disbelief.

Two points later, at 30 all, Cooper hits a second serve, this time to Hoad's forehand. Hoad's return is hard and deep, to within a few feet of the baseline and, advancing to the net, he seizes the initiative. With a slight turn of his shoulders, Cooper unleashes a classically executed off-backhand drive which Hoad does well to reach at full stretch, propelling his forehand volley once again to Cooper's backhand wing. Cooper elects to go the other way this time, and his whipped cross-court backhand looks for all the world like a winner. The champion, however, dives athletically, snakes out an arm, fades the wrist, and produces a stunning volley. Cooper, alert to the short ball, races towards the net. With both men at the net, he has a choice of passing shots, cross-court into the open court or down the line. Guessing that Hoad will move to try to cover the gap, he steers a lofted ball down the line but, as on so many other occasions, it seemed Hoad knew what he was going to do before he did it. Holding his ground, Lew put away the high backhand volley for a winner.

In the third set, at one game all, there was a fleeting possibility of a last ditch revival for the challenger. Hoad served two consecutive double faults, missed an easy volley and found himself 2-1 down; for the first time in the match, he was behind in a set. Was the inspiration that had so far fuelled his game about to fade? Could Cooper claw his way back? Unfortunately for him, the revival was snuffed out almost as soon as it had begun. That was the last game he was to win in the match.

After just fifty-six minutes, Cooper's agony was over. He had won only thirty points in Lew's 6-2, 6-1, 6-2 victory; it was the second fastest win in Wimbledon history, and one of the most one-sided finals ever. Lew played his fingers along the top of the net as a dazed Cooper slowly approached to shake hands. Then Cooper put his arms around Lew. What else could you do on a day like this? Lew pulled Ashley's head onto his shoulder and gently patted his back. Although tremendously proud of the way he had played, he felt sorry for his best friend.

The next morning, papers around the world celebrated his achievement. The *Sydney Morning Herald* said that, 'In the greatest display of severity, accuracy and aggression ever seen, the H (for Hoad) bomb burst on Wimbledon's centre court.' The London *Times* added, 'Hoad consigned his unfortunate fellow Australian, Cooper, to the realms of a mere mortal, while he himself strode Olympian Heights.' And in a more light-hearted manner, the London *Daily Mirror* commented, 'Hoad served more aces than a crooked gambler.' Cuttings kept in Lew's scrapbook at the Campo de Tenis in Spain, also contain Lance Tingay's graphic account of the match for the *Daily Telegraph*. Tingay refers to Lew's claim in a post-match interview with Peter Wilson that he had 'once or twice played rather better' (citing his defeat of Trabert in the Davis Cup challenge match in 1955). Having seen that match, Tingay observes that any difference between Hoad's form then and his expertise on this occasion, 'was purely academic'. The *Daily Express*, with the headline, 'Murder on the Centre Court', aptly summed-up: 'Hoad was out of this world, giving a non-stop exhibition of the most fluent power strokes ever seen on the world's most famous court.'

Nevertheless, watching the match on video now, one would be forced to agree with Tingay's assertion that, on the day, Cooper didn't do his own game justice. But as Tingay goes on to acknowledge: 'Cooper would have been superhuman if he had not quailed before the shots Hoad fired against him. There was rally after rally when Hoad had only to strike the ball to make a winner.' Anyone attempting to diminish Hoad's achievement would also have to take into account his opponent's seeding: he was No 2 seed, not an unseeded player or a lower order seed. He had played Hoad in three finals in Australia during the preceding year, and had won the first of these encounters. Furthermore, he returned the following Wimbledon to win the singles title.

After the crowds had drifted away at the end of the championships, Lew took Jenny to the Centre Court and, for the first time, told her he had decided to join Kramer and provide the family with the financial support he knew they would need in the future. 'Take a good look,' he said quietly, 'this is the last time we will see it.' He had won five titles on it: three doubles with Hartwig and Rosewall, and two successive singles. In a nervous speech at the Champions' Ball, he hinted he would remain an amateur and help Australia retain the Davis Cup.

Such duplicity, entirely out of character, was justified by a desire not to dampen the high spirits of everyone, especially fellow Davis Cup members, by revealing the truth. But after dancing with the American, Althea Gibson, who was the first black woman to win Wimbledon, and who would later become a film actress, he and Jenny slipped away, having informed his Davis Cup captain that he wasn't going home. He apologised for having misled so many people just a few hours earlier and explained the necessity for a secure financial base. He had won £250 for his second Wimbledon title and, back in Australia, had just £600 in the bank. Within hours he was on his way to America and Jack Kramer. He thought about Wigram Road, about Wimbledon, and about the Davis Cup; about the nine ties he had played, winning ten of his twelve singles and seven of his nine doubles for his country. When it leaked out that he had abandoned amateur tennis and turned pro, the news certainly hit Australia like an H (for Hoad) bomb!

Chapter 11

Life on the Road

By now, younger readers may well be feeling somewhat bemused by accounts of the internal divisions and internecine feuds in the world of tennis. They may be unaware of the problems faced by tennis players who decided to turn professional prior to 1968 (the start of the era of Open tennis when amateurs competed alongside professionals). To begin with, one must understand just how prevalent class privilege and snobbery was in the game – especially in Britain. In America and Australia, it was slightly easier for working-class kids to make their way to the top in tennis. But in England, tennis clubs were bastions of social exclusivity and snobbery. If you were not from the right background, you would never gain entrance to many clubs.

Someone who'd had first-hand experience of this, and who had been constantly at odds with the English LTA, was our greatest player ever - Fred Perry, three times winner of Wimbledon, and the son of a Labour member of Parliament from the north of England. In his autobiography he recounts what happened when someone suggested he compete in the schoolboys' tournament at Queen's Club. He had assumed entry was confined to boys from public schools, but then saw a newspaper article by the Queen's Club secretary denying this. So he decided to enter, and arriving at Queen's was asked for his name and school. 'Perry of Ealing [Ealing is an area of west London],' he replied. 'I beg your pardon?' queried the commissionaire, whereupon Perry explained, 'Ealing County School.' The commissionaire paused, then said, 'I'm sorry but we don't have any place assigned for you to change.'

'Never mind,' replied Perry, 'I'll change on the floor.' Later that day, seeing a dressing-room supervisor who he knew well as a member of his local club, he greeted him as 'Mr Jenkins' only to be told by a pompous official that they 'didn't address attendants like that'. Never one to kow-tow to authority, Perry informed him he'd known Mr Jenkins longer than he'd known Queen's and proposed to address him as he saw fit.

To demonstrate the social prejudice of the All England Club officials, he quotes from an *Esquire* article that appeared after he won his first Wimbledon in 1934:

> *To put things bluntly, Perry is not a popular champion at home... The members of that Holy of Holies [Wimbledon] seem to resent the fact that a poor boy without a varsity background should have yanked himself to the front – even though in the process he yanked England back into the tennis picture from which she had been absent since 1909. Extraordinary people!*

In 1936, after winning his third consecutive Wimbledon title, Perry decided that he could no longer afford not to turn pro. As Harpo Marx – the supposedly mute one of the brothers – said to him, 'You can't buy groceries with glory.' He signed up for a head-to-head series with the American, Ellsworth Vines. Considered by many commentators to be one of the greatest champions ever, Vines had turned professional in 1934, two years after winning his first and only singles title at Wimbledon.

Professional tennis had begun only ten years earlier, in 1926. Surprisingly, the star attraction had been a woman not a man; an American promoter, C.G. Pyle had lured the charismatic Frenchwoman, Suzanne Lenglen, with what was a huge amount of money in those days: $75,000.

Suzanne Lenglen had dominated women's tennis since her first appearance at Wimbledon seven years earlier. Even allowing for the limited number of women players at that time, her record is an extraordinary one: she won the Wimbledon singles title five years running from 1919 to 1923, and again in 1925 (missing out in 1924 because of ill health). In the same years she won the Wimbledon doubles titles, and the mixed in 1920, 1922 and 1925. On the clay courts of the French Championships, she notched up wins in the singles, doubles and mixed events in 1925 and 1926.

This record alone, however, would not have accounted for her extraordinary popularity. She made an electrifying impact upon crowds who flocked to marvel at her skimpy, free-flowing tennis clothes, and her balletic leaps. Whilst her opponents may not have been so distracted by her appearance or by her graceful movement, they strove in vain to find an answer to her phenomenally accurate ground strokes.

To support Suzanne, Pyle signed a further three American women and three men. Lenglen's contract required her to play exhibition matches rather than tournaments, the latter format being regarded as appropriate only for the amateur game. The first year's tour was a great success but soon the inherent lack of drama in exhibition matches, and the absence of further players with the star attraction of

Lenglen, caused gates to fall. The signing of Big Bill Tilden in 1931 temporarily reversed this decline.

However, the problem that was to dog professional tennis throughout its existence, namely a mismatch in the playing standard of the top competitors, was evident in the following years. Clearly a head-to-head series of matches was unlikely to draw such large crowds if one competitor was far better than the other. Gate receipts again started to fall until Ellsworth Vines, the United States and Wimbledon champion, made his debut in 1934 against Big Bill Tilden at Madison Square Garden. There was a sell-out crowd of 16,000 people that night and many had to be turned away. Tilden demolished Vines in little over an hour. Unfortunately Tilden was now 41-years-old, and the exhausting programme of a pro tour soon began to take its toll.

In those days there was no air travel, and railroad schedules were often too restrictive, 'so most of the travel was by night in automobiles, with a truck carrying the huge and heavy canvas court and other equipment'. In this respect, the pro game didn't basically change until its death warrant was signed with the advent of Open tennis.

In Baltzell's view, Tilden was the virtual founder of professional tennis and remained one of its leading lights right up until America's entrance to World War Two. Don Budge, first winner of a Grand Slam, who turned pro in the fall of 1938, said of Tilden, 'He just loved tennis. The last time we toured, in 1941, he was almost fifty, and I beat him something like 55-6, but let me tell you: he loved it and tried like hell every game. One time I asked him: 'Bill, what will you do when you can't play tennis anymore?' He just looked at me and said: 'Hmmph. Kill myself.' [1]

Though not above employing psychological ploys to unsettle both his opponent and court officials (he was in the habit of asking linesmen, with studied courtesy, 'Would you like me to correct your error?'), he also believed fervently in the gentlemanly ethic. He once wrote, 'For it is always to be remembered that tennis and good sportsmanship have been, are, and always will be, synonymous.'

Sadly, his liking for the companionship of young boys resulted in a seven-month prison sentence on a charge of indecency in 1947. It seems his loyalty towards the gentlemanly ethic was largely responsible for his conviction: in order to protect the dissolute 14-year-old boy he'd met at a Los Angeles Tennis Club, he decided to plead guilty (much to the consternation of his lawyer).

After his release from prison, he was shunned by most of his former friends and benefactors – only film luminaries David Selznick, Joseph Cotton and Charlie Chaplin supported him. Six years later, at the age of sixty, he was found dead, 'in a run-down apartment... just off Hollywood... he was fully dressed with bags packed, and ready to depart for Cleveland, where he was entered for the United States Professional Tennis Championships.' [2] Baltzell recounts how his memorial service held at a local mortuary the following week was attended by only a few friends, including Ellsworth Vines and Pancho Segura. There were no representatives, nor any messages and flowers, from the USLTA. An inscription on a small stone in a Philadelphia cemetery that simply says WILLIAM T. TILDEN 2ND 1893-1953, is the only monument anywhere in the world to the man regarded by many as the greatest tennis player who ever lived.

Shortly after the end of World War Two the management of pro tennis had been taken over by the gifted, often under-rated, Bobby Riggs, best remembered today for his match with Billy Jean King in 1973. This contest, played in the early years of the women's liberation movement, was labelled by some 'the libber versus the lobber'. King was 29 and Riggs, 55. An accomplished showman, Riggs made his grand entrance to the Astrodome stadium in a chariot pulled by women. He was beaten by Billy Jean in straight sets though some harboured suspicions that Riggs, never noted for his ability to resist a wager (especially if he could fix the odds) would have been shrewd enough to place a sizeable bet on his opponent. Gambling was endemic within the ranks of both amateur and professional players - Hoad and Rosewall being exceptions.

Riggs' greatest year had come in 1939 when he won 'the hat trick' (men's singles, doubles, and mixed doubles) at Wimbledon. He reputedly made a fortune by betting on himself, collecting over $100,000 - equivalent to at least a million in today's money.

After losing to the German, Baron von Cramm, 6-0, 6-1 in the final at Queen's Club in London (the tournament that's always held a week before Wimbledon begins), Riggs had got a British friend and tennis player, John Oliff, to take him to a local bookmaker. As Oliff looked on in disbelief, Bobby bargained with the bookie over the odds on his winning all three titles. He left, having bet on himself to win at odds of three to one in the singles, six to one in the doubles, and twelve to one in the mixed doubles, on a stake of one hundred pounds. There have been suggestions, probably unfair and unwarranted, that Riggs deliberately threw that match against Cramm in the final of Queen's to lengthen the odds. Be that as it may, Riggs was there, waiting at the bookmaker's the Monday after winning all three Wimbledon titles, to collect £21,600 (the equivalent of $108,000). He later recalled this as the 'biggest bet I ever won on myself in tennis, before or since.'

Afraid the bet might jeopardise his amateur standing with his association back home, he 'stashed it away in a London bank vault intending to get it out the following year. But war broke out... I sweated out the Battle of Britain from a distance and nobody rooted harder than I did for the RAF to halt the German invasion of England.' [3]

In 1952, Jack Kramer took over the organisation of pro tennis from Riggs, signing up new players and energetically promoting the pro tours. He'd turned professional four years earlier as one of the brightest stars in the amateur tennis ranks. His impressive record included the US Nationals singles titles in 1946 and 1947, four US doubles titles, and one mixed; he'd also captured the Wimbledon singles in 1947 and the doubles in 1946 and 1947.

When he joined the professional ranks, he adjusted to the higher standard of play faster than most new graduates and came out on top in a series of memorable encounters, first with Bobby Riggs, and later with Pancho Gonzales and Pancho Segura. According to Kramer, Bobby Riggs ceded control of the professional game to him largely because he'd run into contractual problems with Gonzales over his cut of the receipts, and was more interested in an easy life:

> *At this point, Bobby was divorced from Kay, his first wife, and he had just met Priscilla Whelan, who was very attractive and also very wealthy. So, Riggs figured he doesn't need the aggravation of Pancho Gonzales fouling up his happy life. Riggs wires Sedgman in Australia [Sedgman was set to turn pro and tour in a head-to-head challenge against Kramer] that the whole thing is off, and then Bobby goes off to get married and hustle golf games for the next few years.[4]*

Kramer was almost as colourful a character as the man he succeeded. There's a vivid portrait of him in *Advantage Receiver*, by Jack Pollard, who had assisted Hoad in writing his autobiography. 'Of all the colourful characters in lawn tennis,' claims Pollard, 'the most spectacular and controversial is a free-thinking Las Vegas-born gambler named Jack Kramer.' It seems that Kramer lived up to the city of his birth. He was someone for whom gambling was as instinctive as breathing and he was as likely to bet on when the next swallow would appear in the sky as the next race meeting or a speculative oil well drilling. Not that he should be regarded as a reckless or unthinking gambler – Jack always carefully calculated the odds and though he sometimes lost on the horses, most of his investments made money. 'He looks and thinks big,' commented Pollard. 'A buccaneer who has played his astonishing good luck into a fortune, a restless, imaginative egocentric... who has gambled by guaranteeing players vast sums to turn professional.'

His most important asset, though, as the man set to become the czar of pro tennis, was the respect he commanded from his fellow professionals, not only as a tough opponent on court but also as a tough, straight-talking businessman whose word was his bond. His customary method of signing deals was a handshake rather than a contract. Still able to whip most of the top professionals, he was perhaps the only player who could seriously challenge Pancho Gonzales' dominance on the pro circuit. It was not just his big serve-and-volley game that made him such a formidable adversary; his tactical acumen and his knowledge of the game was widely acknowledged, and the reason why the American LTA asked him to take charge of their Junior Davis Cup squad. Later, they even commissioned him to accompany the senior Davis Cup team to Australia and coach the players – this despite the overt hostility of the amateur establishment towards Kramer and his 'circus'.

In the late '60s and early '70s, he also emerged as the best, the most perceptive, Wimbledon commentator for BBC television, only to find himself sacked by this conservative institution for (characteristically) supporting the players' boycott of Wimbledon in 1973.

As a professional, Kramer tirelessly campaigned in support of Open tennis. Although he, and others like Gonzales, publicly attacked 'shamateurism' (the practice of under-the-counter payments in the amateur game) what really got up their noses was the fundamental dishonesty of officials within the amateur establishment. He railed against their hypocrisy in condemning professionals for earning money from tennis, even though those illicit, 'under the counter' payments offered to the top amateurs did little to prevent them succumbing to the lure of five or six figure sums offered by promoters like Kramer. As Gonzales comments in his autobiography:

> *At the frayed edge of an amateur career, when a player touches the age of thirty, it's later than he thinks. To try to carve a niche for himself [in the business world] is a mammoth undertaking. He's already lost ten productive years. He's too old to start at the bottom, too inexperienced to hold down a top position. All he's got to show for his efforts is a scrapbook, blistered feet, and tarnished trophies.*[5]

There was nothing new about top players capitalising on their talents in the professional game, or about the outrage and indignation provoked by the betrayal of their country's Davis Cup prospects. When Fred Perry turned pro after winning Wimbledon for a third time, he was widely regarded as a traitor who'd betrayed British tennis for a guaranteed $100,000 dollars for a head-to-head series with Ellsworth Vines. The All England Club's response had been to withdraw Perry's honorary membership, and request he return the tie that went with it!

With Kramer continuing to recruit top players to his pro troupe, serious concerns were expressed that the poaching of stars like Sedgman and, later, Trabert, Rosewall, Hoad and Laver, would not only destroy America and Australia's Davis Cup hopes, but also undermine the claims of major tournaments to showcase the talents of the world's best players. Certainly tennis fans everywhere recognised that the highest standard of tennis was not to be found at Forest Hills, White City, or Wimbledon but at whatever venue Kramer's professional troupe were appearing. And it was almost taken for granted that when a Wimbledon champion turned pro, he would have to endure a protracted induction as a 'rookie' before he could adjust to the higher standards and pressures of the pro game.

There were those who dismissed pro matches as 'exhibitions', rigged to produce entertaining, yet essentially phoney, contests. The experience of fans the world over [and the authors of this book] would not support this claim, and such accusations were hotly denied by players like Kramer, Gonzales and Hoad. Crucially what these allegations ignore is the pride and competitive instincts of great players. The 5,000 spectators who left the Wembley Pool at twenty-to-one in the morning, having missed the last bus or train home in order to see the end of a classic duel between Pancho Gonzales and Frank Sedgman in 1956, would certainly have laughed to scorn any suggestion of match-rigging.

In his autobiography, Hoad, clearly anxious to refute these allegations, described one of his matches with Kramer. Having joined the pro ranks, initial wins over Sedgman and Pancho Segura (the immensely talented South American) made it seem unlikely Lew would require a lengthy adjustment to pro tennis, but then he endured a spell where nothing went right for him. In Kramer he found a boss willing to persevere and encourage his new signing, perhaps not just out of self-interest, but also respect and liking. In 1957 Lew was matched against Kramer in the first round of the Wembley indoor tournament in London, an event run on amateur lines. Kramer was more concerned that his protégé should play well than with his own hopes of winning, and throughout the match he shouted advice from the other end. However, he didn't slacken the speed or accuracy of his shot-making; he was determined his opponent should earn any victory he achieved. Eventually Kramer won the match, a result that meant Hoad took no further part in the singles. 'People who hint that professional tennis is fixed,' wrote Lew, 'should have seen that match. No corrupt promoter would have allowed a player in whom he had so heavily invested to be downed so consistently as I was in my first few months as a professional.'

When Kramer made his earlier approach to Lew, there was a question mark hanging over his organisation. The pro ranks were reliant, of course, on the periodic injection of 'new blood'. But for some time it had been obvious it couldn't just be *any* 'new blood'. Kramer – and Pancho Gonzales – were searching for a player who could mount a serious challenge to the Pro Champion, especially in a head-to-head series, which was the kind of dramatic format that really gripped the public imagination. And that search was becoming increasingly desperate. Kramer himself possessed the powerful serve and volley game, and also the same determination and tactical awareness as Pancho, but though he could extend the swarthy Mexican-American, and sometimes beat him, age and aching limbs were beginning to take their toll.

In 1955 Gonzales sought him out and insisted he find an opponent who could really challenge him. Jack shook his head. 'I'd have to find a robot,' he replied. 'What about Trabert, Hoad, or Rosewall?' countered Pancho. The response was a pessimistic, 'Right now they can't beat Segura, let alone you. Maybe later...' Presumably Kramer felt he couldn't afford to wait much longer because soon after this discussion he approached the same three players and they all agreed terms, although as we have already seen, Hoad and Rosewall subsequently changed their minds.

So the following year Kramer approached Hoad and Rosewall again, and floated his idea of having a kind of professional Davis Cup with Americans, Trabert and Gonzales, competing against Australians, Hoad and Rosewall. That couldn't fail to pack them in.

Once again, however, Jack found he 'couldn't beat Jenny Hoad'. Now her baby had been born, she wanted another world tour. There's a note of bitterness in the way Kramer relates these events in his autobiography. He obviously believed Jenny knew of Lew's intention to turn pro after winning Wimbledon a second successive year. He also suspected they were aware his future career might be jeopardised by back problems.

In 1957, when Lew left the amateur game, he was paid handsomely. The terms were the best that had been offered up till that time. Also included was a performance clause (the only one Kramer had ever insisted upon) which meant Hoad's cut would go up by five per cent every time he won a match. This was Kramer's way of ensuring the young Australian did not lapse back into his old carefree habits.

When Lew turned pro, he entered a strange and unnatural world. To begin with, though he knew there was no love lost between the amateur ruling bodies and the pros, he was taken aback by the hostility of the amateur establishment, and the obstacles they put in the way of pros. The Australian authorities, for example, furious at Lew's action, declared that if Kramer brought his troupe there, he would be denied the use of any tennis facilities at all.

Kramer's men toured the world, covering vast distances; for transport, they used planes if they were lucky, but mostly a station wagon for the players, and a one-ton panel truck for the portable court they lugged around with them, which took over two hours to lay. Kramer provides a fascinating account of this court in his autobiography. It was, he writes, a canvas court, cut into two pieces about fifty-eight feet square, which made it a little short:

> *The halves were laced together at the bottom of the net. It was pulled tight on the sides by ropes that pulled through twenty-two eyes on each side. The*

driver was a regular member of the team, and then the arenas would hire about half a dozen workers (more in the big union towns) to put the court down under his supervision. The truck also carried the souvenir programs we sold and our ball supply. You would think that some tennis ball company would have been delighted to supply our balls free for the publicity, but we weren't big enough [in view of the huge signing-on fees of Kramer's top players this is a surprising admission]. We could only get the balls at cost and then try to get some of that back by selling used balls at cut-rate prices to the fans.

The canvas court would last about three years, about three hundred matches, but after that it started looking shabby. At its newest, it was faster than the Supreme Court used on tour indoors today. The canvas had French seams too, so that if you hit one, the ball would shoot a little on you. If you felt very confident, you'd shoot for the seams. If the canvas was placed over wood, the bounces tended to be lower and faster, not unlike grass.[6]

In fact, photos of the court often reveal rucking in the canvas; this made play additionally hazardous and explains why it was virtually impossible to conduct matches from the back of the court! It was imperative you got to the net at the earliest opportunity and prevent the ball bouncing.

The pros played in halls too small, halls too big, some with too many lights, others with not enough lights, in ice rinks, on cricket pitches, on courts made from freshly baked cow dung. Anywhere they found a place that could seat a crowd they played, night after night. If they were injured, or ill, or jet-lagged, it didn't matter – the 'show' had to go on. Lew told friends that they sometimes had to keep an eye on the ticket office in case the local 'promoter' skipped with the takings. It was certainly a world apart from the lovingly prepared courts of Wimbledon and the All England Club's pampering of players.

It took a special kind of individual to cope with the pressures of the professional game. There was the constant travelling, for example, when you were invariably dog-tired. Often the best time to travel would be in the dead of night after the evening's matches had finished. But then, even if you weren't driving, you would be too keyed up to sleep. The only alternative was to wait till the following morning and get up really early to arrive at the next town in time to fulfil all your publicity engagements. Jack Kramer reckoned the only American states his tours hadn't taken in were Delaware, Idaho, South Dakota and Montana. Journeys further abroad, like Australia, which Jack visited thirty-five times, meant an exhausting forty-six hour flight in those days. It was a lonely and hectic existence: you would gulp down junk food in a car driving at speeds well above the speed limit; on reaching your destination, you'd live out of a suitcase in a lonely hotel room.

Sometimes the night's takings would hardly justify those long, tiring journeys to out-of-the-way spots. One such occasion is described by Kramer in *The Game*. In 1952 he and Don Budge were touring in Europe with the two Panchos – Segura and Gonzales. They were in Falkirk in Scotland and their next one-night stand was in a seaside resort, Harrogate, on the north-east coast of England. Then they were scheduled to double back the following night to a little town, Kirkcaldy, once again near Falkirk. They were exhausted from touring so Don Budge suggested that since Kirkcaldy was close to Falkirk, they drop in on the promoter and cancel the date. The promoter was crestfallen, says Kramer, when they put this to him:

> *We were the biggest thing to hit Kirkcaldy in years. Why, he already had sixty pounds in the till. The top tickets were going for seven shillings and sixpence – about ninety cents [the Scots have a reputation for being careful with their money!]. And so, regretfully, we promised we'd be back to honour our commitment the next night. We drove all the way to Harrogate, played two singles and a doubles from around 7pm to midnight, caught some sleep at a bed-and-breakfast place, and then the next day, drove the hundred and fifty miles back over the winding roads to Kirkcaldy. And we played all evening there.*

> *When I went to settle up with the promoter, he was ecstatic. The sixty pounds advance sale had only been the start. We had drawn so well at the gate that our cut was ninety-two pounds – about $400 in those days. 'But laddie,' he said, as he gave me the money, 'you and the boys played so well, we want to give you this.' And he slipped me eight more pounds, bringing it up to an even hundred. Three figures!*

> *I went out to the car where the other three were waiting. 'How'd we do, Jack?' Budge asked.*

> *'Great,' I said. 'We got a tip.' And we all laughed ourselves silly and sat there like a bunch of two-bit hoods who had just robbed a gas station, divvying up a hundred pounds – minus the gas money and other general expenses that had to come off the top. Wouldn't you like to see Borg and Connors and Gerulitis and Vilas splitting up a few hundred bucks in the middle of nowhere, which they just drove a hundred miles to reach?* [7]

Another problem for the touring pros was loneliness and boredom. Often, the only company they had to rely on was their fellow players. Considering the claustrophobic nature of this existence, it was fortunate that relationships between players tended to be pretty good.

For those members of Kramer's troupe who were married, this was no kind of life for wives, especially if, as in Jenny's case, they had a young child to look after. So the married players would have a few beers and play cards, though Hoad and Rosewall generally avoided cards and the high-stakes gambling that accompanied them. Some found it difficult to exist without the company of women, and succumbed to female distractions (again Hoad and Rosewall were exceptions). Kramer comments:

> *Of course you would know that I'm lying if I did not say that for many of the players, there were women. There were. A lot of guys ended up divorced: Riggs, Segura, Budge, Gonzales, Trabert. (Perhaps the toughest job I ever had as a promoter was trying to convince all the wives that the photographs of Trabert and Ava Gardner together in Australia were simply 'publicity' to help the tour.) Maybe it was because they were separated so often from their wives, and maybe because of the separations there were other women. Probably it was both. Let's face it, in a business like a tennis tour, marriage is a high-risk proposition.[8]*

It was certainly frustrating for Lew, unable to be with Jenny or see Jane growing up. It would have been even harder if he'd been travelling with players who were entirely unknown to him. As it was, many of them – Sedgman, Trabert, Hartwig and Rosewall – were friends from his amateur days. Others, however, like the two Panchos, (little) Pancho Segura, and (big) Pancho Gonzales, he was really meeting for the first time.

Bandy, pigeon-toed Pancho Segura was regarded by Kramer as the model professional: he had never missed a match in ten years. Born of poor parents in Ecuador, he was one of nine children. At the age of eleven he had rickets and malaria, and children teased him with the nickname of 'parrot foot' because of his weak and spindly frame. He started to play tennis when his father became caretaker at a local club. Weakened by rickets, he developed the first two-handed forehand, which Kramer rated as the single greatest shot in the history of tennis. As Joe Stahl points out in a recent article, during his time as a pro Segura (nicknamed Segoo) had:

> *winning records over Hoad (who openly acknowledged that he learned more about tennis from Segura than from anyone else), Trabert, Sedgman, Parker and McGregor, and beat Gonzales, the greatest on many lists, for the US Professional title twice, in '51 in a 15-13 fifth-set victory, considered by Segura his greatest match, and in '52 in another five-setter.[9]*

His record was all the more amazing given his diminutive stature – he's only five feet six inches tall. He is also an ebullient entertainer, one of the most colourful, dynamic figures ever to appear on a tennis court. Still playing doubles today, at the age of 79, his boundless enthusiasm for the game leads him to 'explode with energy when his partner hits a winner, at which he yells impossibly extravagant appreciation like, 'My man! Okay, baby! That's the best shot I've ever seen!'" Stahl argues that his public drawing power was crucial in keeping pro tennis alive for decades, without which there might not have been any professional game to force the Open tennis that finally supervened in 1968, a view endorsed by Kramer:

> *The fans would come out to see the new challenger face the old champion, but they would leave talking about the bandy-legged sonuvabitch who gave them such pleasure playing the first match and the doubles.*
>
> *The next time the tour came to town the fans would come back to see* **Segoo**. [Stahl's emphasis]

Segura quickly rose to prominence, becoming quite a national hero in his native Ecuador, but he only really reached his peak in the ranks of the professionals whom he joined in 1947. Unfortunately his skills on the tennis court, admired by everyone, did not extend to driving and navigation. Stahl recounts a story told him by Jenny. She and Lew had never really been able to teach Segura how to drive. Apparently he'd almost killed a woman in a supermarket parking lot 'when he hit the accelerator instead of the brake pedal'.

One time Lew and Little Pancho were late leaving Houston because there was a post-match cocktail party all the pros had to attend. Lew then drove all the way to Tallahassee, Florida, into the next morning and told Segura to take over while he got some sleep in the back seat. Lew completed the narrative:

> *I must have slept about an hour or more when I was awakened by Segura and Virginia [Segura's first wife] having a bloody argument; Virginia was yelling at Segoo, 'If you tell me 'F... you' one more time, I'm getting out of the car.' Naturally Segura immediately told her 'F... you' again. Anyway I asked him where we were and he said, 'Damn it, I can't find my way out of Tallahassee!' That did it, I had to drive all the way to Tampa, and when we got there it was already time to practice for that night's matches, so I never got any sleep at all besides that one hour or so in the car. And you know what? I beat Gorgo that night!* [10]

Such was life on the professional circuit.

Obviously to keep interest in the pro game alive, Jack Kramer was always on the lookout for new blood. Before Lew arrived, someone suggested he might recruit the eccentric American, Art 'Tappy' Larsen, who had won the US singles in 1950. Psychologically damaged in World War Two, Larsen was advised to play tennis by his doctors, as a form of therapy. It seemed sound advice because he later acknowledged that 'I was so nervous and shellshocked that exercise in the open air, through tennis, was the only thing that cured me.' E. Digby Baltzell in *Sporting Gentlemen* describes Larsen's traumatic experiences as a front line soldier:

> *During his three years in the army, Larsen saw some of the roughest action in the European Theatre after landing on Omaha Beach on D-Day plus 30 with the 17th Cavalry Squadron of the 9th Army. Most of his buddies were killed at the landing, after which Larsen fought his way to Brest as a tommy-gunner. 'Suddenly, out of nowhere, a fleet of bombers began strafing and bombing us,' he told Jeanne Hoffman. 'Our own air force had mistaken us for Nazis.'* [11]

By the time he returned home over half the troops had been killed, but he came through it all unscathed. Larsen did not attribute such good fortune to blind chance. He had developed all kinds of superstitions and jinxes, including his compulsive habit of tapping everything to bring him luck, which earned him the nickname 'Tappy'. He would pick out a 'lucky' number every day and tap it out. On court this meant on the net, the backstop, the umpire's chair, the court, all the officials and even his opponent! When he changed ends, he carefully avoided stepping on any lines. He also talked to an imaginary bird on his shoulder.

He had one other compulsion – women. In one match, after three tight sets, a ten-minute break was called. His opponent headed for the locker room to have a cooling shower and change of clothes. Up to this point Larsen's attention had been divided between talking to his imaginary bird, and eyeing up a woman in the crowd who'd taken his fancy. During the interval she was persuaded to accompany him to the locker room. Ten minutes later, his opponent returned and waited, but there was no sign of Larsen.

As people began to look around and fidget, it dawned on outraged officials that this was no ordinary toilet break. They banged on the locker room door and, eventually, Larsen came back to the court with his clothing in a somewhat dishevelled state! For the remainder of the match he seemed curiously distracted as if his mind was on other things.

On another occasion, he went to the Lebanon with a group of players, including Lew. Arriving at Beirut airport they discovered that 'Tappy' had no passport. They fretted and fumed as the party was detained while Larsen's paperwork was sorted out. 'Tappy' thought it a great joke and went to sleep.

During the tournament he met and fell in love with a beautiful, raven-haired young woman who, it transpired, was the daughter of the country's President. On the final day of the tournament the President was the guest of honour, and the man responsible for handing out the prizes and trophies. According to Lew, Larsen accepted the cup he had just won and said, 'Thank you very much, but I'd much prefer your daughter. Would you like to swap?' The astounded President went purple with rage, and his bodyguards leapt forward and seized Larsen. The whole tennis contingent was kept under close guard and later that day taken to the airport and unceremoniously shown the Lebanese door.

These moments of light relief helped to ease the strain of an exhausting schedule, with hard fought matches sandwiched between travelling and prolonged periods of waiting. As a *New York Herald Tribune* columnist told his readers:

> *The tour life itself is hardly a laughing matter. Playing in a new town almost every night, the pros live out of suitcases, get to bed late, get up at dawn to catch a train or plane or drive long distances in cars. Sometimes they travel after the night matches, sleep until 3 or 4pm, and find it impossible at that hour to get a decent meal. Living together for months on end is something of a strain, too.*

Lew confirmed this, revealing that Trabert and Gonzales had almost come to blows more than once, and Gimeno and Buchholz had been 'getting at each other'.

Jack Kramer may well have wondered if signing a crazed man like 'Tappy' Larsen for his troupe was an entirely wise move. He already had a player whose behaviour could be frighteningly unpredictable: Richard Alonzo Gonzales – Big Pancho, 'Pancho the Tiger'.

Pancho Gonzales was born in Los Angeles in May 1928, of Mexican parents. He had started playing tennis at thirteen and seven years later won the US singles title. After repeating this achievement, he turned professional in 1949. Because he was so young when he joined Kramer, amateur players and crowds in Australia, France, Wimbledon and America rarely had the opportunity of seeing him as he matured into one of the world's best players. Certainly, until the era of Open tennis (which really came too late for Gonzales, as it did for Hoad) their only hope of watching this charismatic player in action lay in a visit from Kramer's pro tennis outfit.

A tall man, Gonzales' reach, stride, and reactions were phenomenal. He was described as a 'heavyweight boxer with the speed of a flyweight'. Like Lew, his game had everything – dynamic serve, magnificent volleys, great ground shots and an overhead almost the equal of Hoad's. What he possessed in abundance, and Lew lacked, was an intense desire to win every time he walked on court. He said of himself, 'I have never acquired a taste for losing and being second has never appealed to me.' Lew's first impression when he encountered him on court was of a man 'with vast physical toughness and unwavering mental strength who had reduced his percentage of errors lower than any man had ever done.' In Lew's opinion, 'he had the best physical equipment nature can give a tennis player –

height, reach, and a hard body, which could endure sweaty exertion for hours at a time.'

In 1954 Gonzales took the world professional title from Jack Kramer and remained world champion for seven years. His brutal approach both to the game and to his opponents made him unpopular with the other players who joined Kramer, and there were some famous on and off-court feuds with Sedgman and, particularly, Trabert. Joe McCauley reports that soon after the 1955 tour between Gonzales and Trabert began, the fact that both men:

> *virtually hated the sight of each other added spice to their contests. The ill-feeling in the air at most of their matches was tangible and the American public thrived on this sort of atmosphere. Each had considerable respect for the other's playing ability but there it ended. Neither would give an inch and, having nearly come to blows on more than one occasion, no-one surely, could doubt the genuineness of their meetings.[12]*

Gonzales' temper was legendary, and it was almost always on the boil. In what was no mean feat of strength, he once picked up a refrigerator and hurled it through his own front door, demolishing the door and part of the wall. He was married several times, and Segura said the nicest thing he'd ever heard Gonzales say to any of his wives was 'Shuddup!'

Certainly, in the latter part of his career, Gonzales' rages frequently had the effect of sharpening his concentration. Like John McEnroe, flying off the handle was a means of releasing his demons. It often distracted his opponent more than it did himself but it also attracted spectators who'd relish 'winding him up'. Bud Collins describes an occasion when Pancho was being heckled by a doctor called Edward Browne. He was playing a match against Ken Rosewall at the time, and found himself confronted by a dual irritant. Dr Browne was getting the better of their verbal exchanges, and Pancho was growing ever more annoyed by Rosewall's obdurate defence:

> *Unable to stand it any longer, Pancho stalked over to Browne and appeared ready to give the physician artificial expiration by applying hands to the windpipe. But Browne, a team doctor for the resident Celtics and Bruins, had the good fortune to be seated next to a man who stood up for him.*

> *Rising to his full and rugged six feet five inches, Jim Loscutoff, known throughout the National Basketball Association as the Celtics' 'enforcer', stepped between the enraged Gonzales and the endangered Browne. 'Now, Pancho, why don't you go back to playing tennis?' Loscutoff inquired pleasantly.*

Gonzales, a big man himself, isn't stupid. I have seen him brutalise locker rooms as a graphic commentary on defeat. But, gazing upward, as though at a lob, he saw the wisdom in Loscutoff's words, and eyes, and resumed a difficult subduing of Rosewall.[13]

On another occasion, Collins had personal experience of Pancho's stubbornness. WGBH-TV had managed to secure enough money to present local area telecasts of the US Pro tournament of 1965 at Longwood, no easy task for a public service station in Boston. Collins had been asked to get the twelve competitors to sign waivers on the understanding that since this was a non-profit venture, neither they nor their players' organisation could expect a rights fee. Eleven players were happy to sign, the one exception being Gonzales. All Collins' arguments proved futile. He tried to explain the concept of a public station, then known as educational TV: 'No commercials. No income. The station would probably lose money, but this one station in the United States believed in tennis. Didn't that mean something?'

Collins understood and sympathised with Pancho's reasons for insisting on a fee; he knew Gonzales had been around longer than anyone else, and had been conned by a variety of promoters with the promise that his appearance would be good for the game. Nevertheless, Collins told Gonzales, if he refused to join the other eleven players, there would be no show. 'Tough luck,' was the uncompromising response.

'You'd let one guy spoil it for everybody, for kids who might be watching, Richard?' pleaded Collins, using his proper name which he knew he preferred to Pancho. But Gonzales was adamant – he had to get paid. When Collins again told him that nobody was getting paid, his terse reply revealed the depth of his cynicism:

'Don't give me that crap.' For the first time he smiled, but his brown eyes were still hard. I'd been wasting his time. 'Maybe the other players are stupid, but somebody gets paid. The cameraman don't work for nothing just to advance tennis. The producer gets paid. You... you get paid.'

'Yeah.' I couldn't rebut that.

'Then why should I be a sucker?'

'Richard, you're absolutely right. I do get paid. Twenty-five bucks a show, and I'm gonna write you a check right now for the entire amount – one hundred and twenty five dollars – if you'll sign this waiver. It'll be a pleasure to do the tournament for nothing.'

Gonzales is not a small timer.

'Gimme the goddam thing to sign,' he shook his head. 'I wouldn't take your money.'

'Twenty five bucks....' He stomped out of the room.[14]

Thanks to Collins' persistence, that year was the first time the US Pro Tournament was televised.

If Gonzales went through life with a huge chip on his shoulder, it didn't get there by accident. Any assessment of his character must take into account the racist discrimination he experienced, particularly in the early years of his career. His parents were Mexican immigrants who'd settled in Los Angeles. They couldn't afford to send their son to the Los Angeles Tennis Club to learn the game, but even if they'd had the money, it wouldn't have made any difference – Richard's skin was too dark, the club had a policy of only admitting white people. As a result, he determined to teach himself, on local public courts. When he began to win tournaments and attract attention, he was subjected to various forms of racial abuse and ethnic stereotyping. He was dismissed as a typical 'lazy Mexican' and it was said the prominent scar, running from under his left sideburn and ending at his nose, had been acquired in a pool hall fight. Thousands of people, he comments in his autobiography, believed this story because 'they think a knife scar and Mexican-American youth go hand in hand.'

It's no coincidence that two of Gonzales' closest friends and staunchest supporters, Arthur Ashe and Pancho Segura, had also been victims of racial discrimination. Ashe, a Black-American, referred to Gonzales as one of the three stars who shone brighter than any others in his sky. 'Pancho Gonzales,' he wrote, 'was not only the best player in the world but also an outsider, like me, because he was a Mexican American.' [15]

As an Ecuadorian Indian, Segura knew all about racism; whilst he joked about Gonzales' explosive temper, he understood better than most the causes of it; he'd also had direct experience of racism. On one occasion he and Lew had been drinking in a nightclub after a tournament in Paris. There was a South African on the table next to them who'd clearly had too much to drink; he became increasingly belligerent, directing a stream of racist abuse towards Segura. For a time, Lew said nothing; then, unable to contain himself any longer, got up, went over to the man, grabbed his chair by the leg, and to the amazement of everyone in the room, hoisted the South African into the air. 'Why don't you shut the fuck up,' he muttered, and let go the chair.

At the time when Hoad joined the 'circus' Gonzales was in a fury – and a litigation battle – with Kramer. He went ballistic when he discovered what Lew had been paid and what his allocation of the cut would be when they played each other. Lew was to get twenty-five per cent of the take, in contrast to Gonzales' twenty. Furthermore, if Hoad won a match, he'd get thirty per cent, whereas Gonzales' cut would be twenty per cent, regardless of the result. And, as we have seen, if Lew wrested the world championship from Pancho, he'd get a bonus of $10,000. Kramer had arranged it this way to try to make Lew play hard and seriously every night, and eliminate lapses from his game.

Gonzales went to court, insisting that his contract should be changed or made illegal (he didn't succeed on either count). Some said that Kramer was bent on getting rid of Gonzales, but this seems unlikely. He probably just wanted to cut him down to size and reduce his bargaining power. As Pancho pointed out in his autobiography, *Man with a Racquet*, they may have shared a mutual dislike, but each needed the other. Kramer's organisation depended on the magnetic attraction of its moody star, especially if he could be pitted against someone who might deprive him of the crown; and Pancho relied upon Kramer's circus for his meal ticket. He was hardly in a position to set up a professional troupe of his own, though it was something he occasionally threatened.

So this was the scenario that greeted the friendly and companionable Lew as he flew into New York. Wearing a casual check jacket, his shirt unbuttoned and his tie loose, he shoved his big hand towards Gonzales, grinned, and drawled: 'Howya doin' mate?' Gonzales blinked in disbelief and his lips curled back from his teeth, 'He looked,' Lew told Larry Hodgson, 'like a tiger who'd just had his meat taken away.'

But, years later, Kramer was to write that the only player Gonzales ever tried to get along with, was Lew Hoad: 'Everyone loved Lew – even Pancho Gonzales. They should put that on Lew's tombstone as the ultimate praise for the man!'

Initially Lew arrived in New York full of confidence, proud of his achievement of having won Wimbledon a second time, and glad to be rid of the petty restrictions of the amateur game. He had money in his pocket and the promise of lucrative contracts that didn't involve hitting a single tennis ball. And yet, within a few days, 'the grinding realities of professionalism transformed me into a worried, hurt, moody figure, entirely lacking in confidence, apprehensive that my easy-going make-up might prevent me from becoming a successful professional.'

Throughout his life Lew found himself bored and frustrated by financial and business affairs. He had no desire to be as rich as Croesus; his wants were simple: to be comfortably-off and free from financial worries, play tennis, and relax with friends and a cool beer. But when he turned pro, he found himself perplexed and overwhelmed by the kind of business decisions that, these days, players employ agents like Mark McCormack to take care of. The ancillary benefits earned by top sportsman are, of course, enormous, often far exceeding the huge sums won in prize money. Sampras's earnings in racquet endorsements and related sporting products effectively double his prize money from winning Wimbledon.

Almost overnight Lew had been transformed into a commodity; a commodity where everyone 'wanted a piece of the action'. He was inundated by offers from fast-talking men asking him 'to endorse hair oils, soaps, shirts, shorts, shoes, racket gut, socks, pullovers, underwear and an incredible list of other goods.' [16] And he was plagued by sportswriters wanting him to sell them his life story, or provide articles on how to play tennis, or expose corrupt practices in the amateur game – if he knew of any! To boost attendances, he was required to appear on radio or television as often as Kramer and his staff could arrange it, and contracts he was urged to sign kept arriving in the mail. 'The telephone never stopped buzzing,' he wrote. In the past he'd have been able to turn for sympathetic guidance to Adrian Quist or Harry Hopman; here he was largely on his own. His autobiography conveys how bewildering he found the conflicting demands and pressures on him:

> I had always thought life as a top amateur was busy and disorganised – this was sheer turmoil. I took the advice of my fellow professionals as often as I could get it, but most of the time I had to make my own decisions and hope they were sensible. I had no experience to fit me for this bartering, no way of knowing whether $2,000 a year was a good or bad price for endorsing, say, a hair tonic. I just had to take a stab at it. Overnight I had become a one-man band, a combination of salesman, press relations expert, huckster, newsprint celebrity, sporting hero for pay. The bustling activity of suddenly being able to make dollars without worrying if amateur officials would catch me, unsettled my poise and my tennis. [17]

Kramer's decision to sign Lew wasn't solely determined by his being the Wimbledon champion, nor even by his winning the title in consecutive years – though that did make him an even bigger box office draw. More importantly, Kramer believed the laid-back Australian was the only man in the world capable of taking on and beating the moody, and difficult, Gonzales. And where the Mexican was prone, like Achilles, to sulking in his tent, the genial Australian was a 'pussycat'; not only would he prove co-operative and malleable, he'd be a valiant Hector, establishing himself as the new professional champion, and releasing Kramer from his dependence on Gonzales.

To begin with, the signs were propitious. Lew made his debut in Kramer's 1957 Tournament of Champions, a $10,000 round-robin affair; on paper his first opponent, Frank Sedgman, looked like a stiff challenge, but he'd just flown in from Australia and had had no time to practise. Lew won in straight sets. Next was Segura, certainly no pushover, though Lew was lucky again because Segoo was tired from three tough matches in the previous four days. Again, he won in straight sets. Commentators raved about his tennis, comparing him with the all-time greats;

privately, Lew was less confident. He'd already begun to appreciate there would be no easy opening rounds, no minnows, as there were in amateur tournaments, to get him match tight before he came up against the top competitors in the quarters or semis. Now he had to go into each match keyed-up, and anything less than his best tennis would invite ignominious defeat.

There was probably no way Lew could have sustained the heady expectations generated by these opening wins, and his fall from grace was swift. The distinguished Australian player, Dinny Pails, told reporters that Hoad looked sensational in his first two pro matches:

> *He looked just about the greatest player I had ever seen. He hit the ball with terrific power, served with tremendous pace, put away his volleys the first time and looked the fastest man you'd ever seen chase a tennis ball. At that stage I think all the players in Kramer's troupe must have thought they were in for a hiding. I know I did. And then – phhht! Lew lost it.*[18]

The man who brought Lew down to earth with a bump was his nemesis, Ken Rosewall. Any illusions he might have had about brushing aside fellow pros were shattered by the 'little wizard' who made him realise he still had to move up a couple of gears in adjusting to the far stiffer challenges of pro tennis. Of course, it was Rosewall who'd inflicted those humiliating defeats at the start of his tennis career, but in later years the balance of power had shifted, with Lew generally able to dominate his rival. When the chips were down, as in the '56 Wimbledon final, Lew's weight of shot had prevailed – though Forest Hills that same year was a notable exception. He knew he'd improved since beating Rosewall in that Wimbledon final and, in the meantime, Ken had suffered 'a morale-busting drubbing' from Gonzales. As a result, he'd figured Rosewall was the one pro he should be able to beat.

'None of this,' he recorded, 'appeared to occur to Rosewall, who showed how much he had learned as a professional.' After the big serves of Sedgman and Segura, Ken's soft serves were 'curiously difficult' to handle (how reassuring many club players will find that admission!). Though Lew left the court still convinced he was the better player, Rosewall's relentless pressure and pinpoint accuracy enabled him notch up another victory. Given Hoad's optimism going into the match, this defeat represented a huge setback.

Afterwards, analysing the match, he tried to figure out why he'd lost. Of course, he'd fluffed too many easy shots and been guilty of complacency, often coming to the net assuming he'd put the volley away, only to dump a sitter in the net, or hit too long. He'd also underestimated his opponent; though long experience had taught him to respect Rosewall's return of serve as one of the best in the game, he was unprepared for the improvement in his volleys. Time and again they were punched away, powerfully and decisively, for winners. Above all, the lesson he learnt from his friend and rival was that he had to cut down the percentage of errors in his game.

Worse was to follow; in spite of the disappointment of losing to Rosewall, he still fancied his chances of getting to the final and beating Gonzales. But first he had to overcome Tony Trabert, his adversary in so many famous Davis Cup matches. Lew was sanguine about his chances. Trabert was never the fastest man around the court, and his serve probably wasn't quite up to the standard of the top pros. Unfortunately it seemed his game also had improved since his amateur days, it had greater penetration, and he'd acquired the knack of winning those really important points. Seeing that Lew was too 'loose' he lofted several floating lobs which Lew obligingly crashed into the net. When Trabert hammered away the winning point for a five-set victory, Jenny, seated in the grandstand, was close to tears. She knew how hard Lew had been trying, and how humiliating two defeats in a row would be for someone who'd recently retained his Wimbledon title.

The pros had a point to prove: they always wanted to take a crack at the new Wimbledon champion, and cut him down to size. No respecters of reputation, they were aware that new recruits neither expected, nor desired, an easy ride. That kind of charity would have been the ultimate insult.

And one person who could definitely be relied upon to deny him charity was Pancho Gonzales. When Lew finally confronted the reigning 'King of the Pros' he knew his game would be subjected to the most searching scrutiny: Gonzales had already clinched the first prize of $2,700, beating Sedgman in five sets. Nevertheless, Lew relished playing an opponent whose style of play was similar to his own. Both men possessed powerful serves and volleys; they liked to get to the net quickly, and dominate their opponent. Gonzales had a big forehand, but he tended to slice his backhand. However, whilst some sliced shots invite the incoming volleyer to easily pick off a wafting ball at the net, Pancho's backhand slice – honed over the years – demanded both respect and caution. If he didn't have a topspin backhand drive in his armoury, as Lew did, this was more than compensated for by an intense desire to win, allied to experience and wily court-craft.

Although the American ran out the winner in four sets, Lew could salvage something from the match. To begin with, each set had turned on a single service break. Then, Pancho's serve wasn't as difficult to return as he'd anticipated, and he'd made a mental note of a weakness on the return of serve that he hoped to exploit in the future. Also, he was satisfied his strength and stamina were at least the equal of Gonzales'. Had that proved Rosewall's undoing in his hundred match series with Gonzales? Were his defeats down to the strain of playing such a physically intimidating opponent, and the constant travelling?

What Lew marvelled at in Pancho was his immense self-belief, and his astounding calmness in tight situations. 'The breaks can go against him for point after point,' he wrote, 'and his opponents come near to a crucial advantage, but big Pancho does not lose his quiet, sullen confidence. All this comes from an intense, searing belief in the pre-eminence of his own game. I would have to defeat *him*; *he* would not defeat himself.'

Despite the positive conclusions Hoad drew from his defeat by Gonzales, there was no doubt that his confidence had been badly dented. He tried to remain up-beat, but the next pro tournament, on concrete courts at Los Angeles, proved how severely loss of confidence can affect even great players. Lew was a pale shadow of the man who'd brushed aside Sedgman and Segura only a week or so before. Plagued by self-doubt, the old faults of casualness and poor concentration, as well as the new professional distractions of publicity shows, personal appearances, sponsorship deals etc, began to take their toll.

His head was in a spin, a spin far worse than that produced by too many vodkas and lagers eighteen months earlier in the French final. He stumbled to four further defeats, making a disastrous seven in a row. First, it was another humiliating straight sets defeat by Rosewall, followed by Sedgman avenging his drubbing in Forest Hills with a 7-5, 6-1 victory. Then it was veteran Dinny Pails' turn – Lew's morale slumped to an all time low after losing to the 36-year-old who, by his own admission, was no longer a threat to a good player.

The next day he hit rock bottom; Pancho Segura, fourteen years his senior, thrashed him with the loss of only three games. One reporter wrote that Hoad 'played like an amateur' and Gonzales, always nursing the grudge that as the pro champion he was underpaid and under-rewarded, growled, 'He don't look like a $125,000 investment to me.'

Hoad was to recover from these early setbacks, going on to mount a serious challenge to Gonzales' dominance of pro tennis but, in one sense, the back problems that eventually cut short that challenge were an irrelevance. Whilst he tempered his wilder excesses, trained hard, and benefitted from tutoring by Kramer, Schroeder and Segura, it's doubtful whether he could ever have sustained his concentration, and stayed motivated, over a head-to-head one hundred series match. There's no denying the fulfilment he derived from pitting his skills against a worthy adversary like Gonzales, nor his desire to be 'the best player in the world'. It's just that he lacked certain qualities essential in a true professional. Crucially, he was never able to look upon tennis as a business, he had the wrong mindset. After a recent win in the Australian Championships, Tim Henman declared, 'I'm a professional tennis player, this is my job.' Hoad could never regard the game in that light, the notion of tennis as a 'job' was foreign to him.

Also, he loved the game. Now there's nothing in the history of tennis to suggest professionalism and a love of the game are mutually exclusive. Clearly the great professionals – Tilden, Riggs, Kramer, Gonzales, Segura, Rosewall, Laver – all had a passionate love of tennis, but this didn't prevent them regarding it as a business in their pro days. That meant they were able to sustain their concentration for long periods, to cope with the grind of travelling, and get themselves 'up' for the next match. During matches, they'd assess the odds and calculate angles (like the instinctive gamblers most of them were). They knew when to coast, and when to concede a point if chasing the ball wasn't worth the energy expended; they knew not only how to pace themselves, but the kind of psychological ploys that upset opponents. And they developed strategies that enabled them to capitalise on their own strengths and exploit their opponent's weaknesses.

Lew couldn't be bothered with all this. His game expressed his attitude towards life which was, basically, a hedonistic and an easy-going one. He was a free spirit; on a tennis court, he reacted instinctively rather than plotting his every move. 'Stuff that,' would have been his response. Like a great jazz musician, he'd improvise, always striving to hit that perfect note, knowing that when the mood took him, a stream of winners would flow from his racquet. If he lost a match, there'd usually be a shrug of the shoulders, and a few beers for consolation. No lengthy post mortems, no angst-ridden sessions with the sports psychologist; therapy was a cool beer, a good work-out in the gym the following day, and the challenge of the next match.

One of the things Hoad missed most as a pro was that happy-go-lucky relaxed atmosphere of the amateur circuit, and the camaraderie between players. You'd move from tournament to tournament as part of one big, happy family. Sometimes you'd come across players you hadn't met before, but always, at the main tournaments, there'd be the top players and friends you'd made from different countries and different cultures.

On the pro tours, with a small group of people closeted together for long periods, tensions were inevitable. On amateur tours you'd have the comradeship and support of a national team squad. Though the travelling for an amateur was still irksome, at least it was comparatively relaxed and civilised – you'd sail, take a plane, or go by rail. You rarely travelled by car, and if you did it wouldn't be through the night, snatching meals at odd times. You had a niggling injury? Well, rest up for a bit, you'd be told, take a few weeks off. If you were a pro, you had to get up from your sick bed because punters had paid good money to see you perform, and the 'show must go on'.

Professionals had a tough life but they were paid handsomely, and they usually had a fair-sized nest egg in the bank. Money, however, could prove a mixed blessing, especially as far as the sport (and its future) was concerned. As players like Kramer,

Gonzales and Arthur Ashe, all testified, 'Money (big money) changes everything.' In the Open tennis era, when players have been able to command exorbitant fees for simply appearing in exhibition matches, it's often been very difficult for Davis Cup captains to persuade them to renounce lucrative engagements, and represent their country.

It's tempting, of course, to look back upon a golden age of tennis (or any other sport) that's usually set somewhere in the recent past: a pre-lapserian world untarnished by monetary considerations, when Corinthian ideals reigned supreme. Tempting, and potentially misleading. Whatever the problems caused by an enormous injection of cash and the commercialisation of tennis, few would deny that the introduction of Open tennis brought tremendous benefits.

It removed, at a stroke, the hypocrisy and deceit that had been such an unsavoury feature of the amateur game. It meant the public could now see the best players competing against each other for the major tournaments, in stadiums designed for top class tennis; and it meant those players could command the kind of huge prize money top golfers had been earning for many years. But the creation of Open tennis also meant that tennis lost its innocence, that the sporting ethic so prized by Baltzell and others was undermined.

Not that this happened to Lew – even as a professional he retained his innocence, was renowned for his sportsmanship (it's hard to think of him ever turning down a chance to represent Australia). Also, Open tennis came just too late for him. Had it occurred earlier he'd have been a millionaire several times over, and would almost certainly have escaped the financial problems that were to dog him after his retirement. In many ways, he was the last great amateur of the game.

Some might argue a better contender for this title is Rod Laver. Didn't Laver win the Grand Slam in 1962 before turning pro, and then repeat the feat in 1969, a year after Open tennis was introduced – which effectively abolished the distinction between professionals and amateurs? But we would maintain that this simply indicates Laver always had a professional *approach* to the game, whether he played in an amateur or professional set-up. Temperamentally, Lew was always an amateur, in the non-pejorative sense of the term.

The White Knight versus the Black Knight.
Lew Hoad and Pancho Gonzales pause to take refreshment

Is it rough - or smooth? On the pro tour in Florida

The ups …

... and the downs in the head-to-head pro series against Gonzales

The man who said "No" to Hollywood

Lew, Sally, Jane, and Jenny at the first ever Open Wimbledon, 1968

"Yours, partner?" Lew and son, Peter, go for the same ball at the Campo

Lew and one of the Club waiters before the "infamous" Arabian Nights evening

"Newc" (John Newcombe) and Lew - Two World Champions in tennis ... and drinking!

Jenny and Lew attending "Gangster Night" in Las Vegas

Who's that girl? Lew with Cristina Hodgson

Fred Perry, Jenny and Lew Hoad

The farm that became "Lew Hoad's Campo de Tenis"

"Lew Hoad's Campo de Tenis" - then ....

The Campo de Tenis as it is today

"Simply the most beautiful club I've ever seen." (Larry Adler)

Castellar de la Frontera. The castle retreat that became home to the Hoads

One of the pretty cobbled lanes that are a feature of Castellar

The "twins" as young men

The "twins" as veterans

"Adios amigos"
One of the last pictures of Lew, together with Maria Bueno and Salvador Gallardo

Some of the stars at the Memorial Tennis Tournament the week after Lew died.

From left to right: Manolo Santana; Ken Rosewall; Paul McNamee; Roger Taylor; Trevor Fancutt; Jenny Hoad; Charlie Fancutt; Manuel Orantes; Bob Carmichael; Buster Motram; Peter McNamara

Lewis Alan Hoad 1934-1994

Chapter 12

White Knight v Black Knight

Jack Kramer was a worried man. He'd invested an awful lot of money in Lew Hoad with one specific objective in mind: to take on and beat the professional champion, Pancho Gonzales. Crowds would come flocking to see the twice Wimbledon winner play the 'King of the Pros', gate receipts would pick up, and Kramer would start to see some return on his investment. At this stage there wasn't really anyone who could challenge Pancho's supremacy, and he'd been pestering Kramer to sign someone who could really test him.

Equally important as far as Jack was concerned, was the need to curb Gonzales' growing bargaining power. If the time ever came when Gonzales was able to call the shots in wrangles over his contract, Jack might be forced to throw in the towel and retire. Assuming his plan worked, however, Lew would crush Gonzales in a head-to-head series and get him off Jack's back once-and-for-all. No more battles in court and hefty legal bills; his morale destroyed, he'd slink away, leaving Jack to set up a series with two players who, compared to Gonzales, were both 'pussycats' to handle: Hoad and Trabert. And then, perhaps, he'd be free to set up that American-Australian professional 'Davis Cup'.

But now Jack's plans were in disarray. After a couple of encouraging wins, Lew had lost nine straight matches. Not just to the established stars in the pro firmament, but also 'make-weight' players and older members of the group looking forward to retirement. He seemed to have no defence; later Kramer was to describe him as having the 'loosest' game of any good kid he'd ever seen. 'Hoad,' he said, 'had absolutely no pattern to his game.' Jack would marvel at the shots he could even *think* of. On the other hand, he had this tendency to 'go for broke' at the most inopportune moments – there was no way you could get him to temporise on important points.

Segura tried in vain to persuade him to lob more often (but then Segura was the master of both the defensive, and the offensive, lob). Gonzales, always a perceptive commentator on the game, summed up his weaknesses:

Lew's chief fault was trying to finish a point before it was really completed. He got out of position too fast. After executing a shot, he sped for the centre of the court too rapidly. But, boy, his overheads drew raves, and if I lofted one to him, the best thing for me to do was to seek cover under the umpire's stand. Lew was an offensive player and, at that time, couldn't change the pace of his game. It was bang, bang, bang, all the way.

Assuming it's not simply the wisdom of hindsight, Hoad's autobiography reveals that he knew perfectly well where he was going wrong. His diagnosis confirmed that of Kramer and Gonzales. He castigated himself for slack volleying; his return of serve was 'miserable' – he used too much backswing and stood too far inside the baseline to cope with the booming serves of his opponents. And his second serve was getting murdered because it was so short you could run round it and hit winners off your forehand. After his first match against Gonzales, he admits he was, 'like a boxer who tries to fight every minute of fifteen rounds without resting, holding, or stalling. I sought to play every point at a fearsome, crowding pace, and every time I saw the ball loom near, I larruped it.' [1]

All this was of little help to Kramer. He knew, everyone concerned seemed to know, where Lew was going wrong. The thing was: how to put it right?

The gulf that had opened up between the amateur Wimbledon champion and the pros became apparent when the tour moved to Los Angeles. Lew proved to be the box office draw Kramer had anticipated. If anything, he exceeded expectations: fans fought to buy tickets and movie stars packed the gallery to see the blond Lew versus the swarthy Pancho. Amongst the crowd were Dick Powell, Doris Day, Ginger Rogers, Rita Hayworth, Groucho Marks and Burt Lancaster, along with many other celebrities. Unfortunately, it was Lew's play that didn't live up to expectations – though many of those expectations were unreasonably high. Every rookie needs a period of adjustment to attune to the pro game, and this was only Lew's second tournament. At the moment, though, he was clearly no match for Gonzales; the head-to-head series would have to be deferred.

Jack called on his trusty lieutenant, Ted Schroeder, who had predicted such a great future for Hoad when he saw him play as a little boy. Schroeder (the Wimbledon singles title-holder in 1949 and winner of three US national doubles titles alongside Kramer) was now Jack's manager and right hand man. Over a bottle of malt whiskey, they discussed what was to be done.

Finally, it was agreed that Lew should be withdrawn from the troupe. Segura and Schroeder would work on his game, and with Kramer and Rosewall as sparring partners, they'd embark on a tour first of Europe, and then Africa and Asia. This was to be an intensive induction course for Lew. Kramer made no attempt to hide his intentions: 'I was going to build him up, patch up the weak spots, get him so he could knock off Gonzales. Gorgo knew exactly what I was doing, and he was furious.'

In an interview for this book, Schroeder commented, 'Although he had won Wimbledon twice, Lew still couldn't play tennis when he came to us. He had no tactics or guile. He couldn't keep his cards close to his chest or read the game. He just hit the damn ball as hard as he could.'

Gonzales, on the other hand, knew that in the pro game you had to have plenty to spare. Playing night after night, and then travelling throughout the night, you had to know what you were doing when you walked on court – always play to win the next point if you get ahead or are on deuce. But if you fall behind in a game, forget it, save your energy.

Pancho believed that the amateurs he had come across, and thrashed, were hopeless because, even when they were 0-40 down they would still try and win the game, rushing round the court like headless chickens. This was not intelligent tennis. You had to know which points to win and which to lose. Kramer had been the world's greatest exponent of this strategy, aware of every trick in the book. As a rookie professional, Gonzales had been as naïve as Lew. In his first fifty matches against Kramer, he won only eight. Why was this? Well, to begin with, Gonzales had a cavalier attitude towards his diet, and never looked after himself properly. His meals consisted mainly of hamburgers and hot dogs, and he was a heavy smoker. In his autobiography, Kramer admitted taking advantage of Pancho's unprofessional approach. Describing his opponent's sleeping habits, he commented:

> He couldn't get to sleep after a match under the best of conditions – and try to sleep every night when you're losing. So he'd take an afternoon nap, grab a hamburger and come out on court dull and logy. If I won the toss I'd always let him serve first because he was half asleep, and I could break him right off the bat. Then he'd start filling up on cokes. He'd lose again, and the whole cycle would repeat itself... One of the great ironies of that tour was that he was a kid in perfect health and I beat him on stamina.[2]

So Gonzales had learned the lesson the hard way. He knew it would probably be tougher for Lew, with his happy-go-lucky temperament. And, to the astonishment of the other pros, he offered to help him with his game. Was Gonzales mellowing towards Hoad? They even had a beer or two together. Gonzales' offer was genuine, but he also knew that if Hoad got his brains kicked out night after night it would hit the turnstiles – and his own pocket.

An equally cynical interpretation advanced by one of Lew's friends, was that Gonzales' conciliatory attitude was more influenced by his obsession with winning.

Aware of Hoad's open, trusting, and friendly nature, Pancho reasoned that if Lew regarded him as a friend, he'd be less determined to beat him. A simpler explanation for Gonzales' behaviour is that, like everyone else, he was charmed by Lew's likeable personality.

As soon as Jack proposed a tour to prepare him for a head-to-head series with Gonzales, Lew's game started to pick up. One of the factors that might have helped was Jenny returning to Australia to look after their daughter. God knows he missed her, but it had become an additional strain having her witness his humiliation on court. It was agony for both of them, and they'd felt guilty about leaving Jane in the care of grandparents for a long period of time. Also, once the tour began, the distraction of publicity shows, television and radio appearances, and press interviews, was removed. Without all the American media razzmatazz, he was again able to concentrate on tennis. Gradually, under Kramer and Segura's tutelage, his game improved.

The cities they played in, 'flickered by in a dizzy kaleidoscope – La Baule, La Hague, Paris, London.' They barely had time, Lew said, for anything but eating, sleeping, travelling and playing tennis. He won some matches, lost some, and the realities of professional tennis were daily driven home to him.

What impressed Kramer about Hoad was 'how strong he was. Like a lot of strong kids, personally he was as gentle as a lamb. Once he went a whole day in Nairobi, then to Karachi, then to Lahore – more than forty-eight hours, four tennis matches.' [3] Jack realised that *motivation* was one of the keys to Lew raising his game and playing to his full potential. On that warm-up tour, he says, Rosewall beat him something like twenty-two matches to four. That was to be expected; he'd been absent from championship play for several years, and these youngsters were at the peak of their game. And yet he'd beaten Hoad, thirteen matches to twelve. Was it that he didn't regard an old champion as sufficient challenge, so he didn't pull out all the stops?

One day Jack asked him right out, why was he regularly able to beat Rosewall and yet have a losing record against him? Lew pulled a face, and his brow furrowed. 'Well, Jack,' he said, 'I guess the rivalry with Muscles goes back a long way. He thrashed me several times when we first started playing each other. Then there was that defeat at Forest Hills which cost me the Grand Slam. We're good mates but there's always an edge when he's the other side of the net.' One match Lew particularly relished was when he beat Rosewall in Dhahran. It was a 'fantastic three-and-a-half hour battle,' and they had to cope with intense heat – the temperature on court was 110°. Although he'd always disliked playing in such conditions, Lew managed to outlast Ken. 'We lost eight pounds in weight between us,' he recalled, 'and when we left the court, the beer tasted better than any I ever quaffed.'

By the end of this demanding 'toughening-up' world tour, Lew felt there'd been a vast improvement in his game – he had nearly one hundred matches under his belt and was ready to face Gonzales. He knew, of course, that Gonzales had beaten every amateur champion who had crossed the deadly line into professional tennis - Trabert by seventy-four matches to twenty-four in 1955-1956, and Rosewall by fifty to twenty-six the following year. Kramer decided to bill the head-to-head series between the Wimbledon champion and the Pro champion as 'The White Knight versus The Black Knight'. It began in Australia, in the early months of 1958.

Tickets for the thirteen matches Lew and Pancho were to play in Australia sold out at once and thousands were turned away. In all, 75,000 people saw them play. Lew was now slimmer, fitter and, under Kramer's and Schroeder's tuition, a wiser player. He'd been carefully briefed on Gonzales' game and how to play him. But Pancho had not been idle. Back in California he had brought himself to peak condition for what he knew was going to be his toughest tour.

When the series opened in Brisbane, they started off playing the best-of-five sets, and most matches went the full distance. The level of tennis played was outstanding and the crowds went wild. A Melbourne newspaper commented, 'Gonzales brings out the hate in Hoad. Lackadaisical Lew of the Centre Court is a new player, a hating Hoad, who crushes his opponents and leaves 'em crushed. What was only a game for Champion Hoad is now a grim battle between the greatest enemies ever to meet on a tennis court.'

Ted Schroeder quipped, 'Slip one of those boys a sledgehammer and they would end it quick.' At one match a spectator shouted out, 'What an act! This beats boxing.' At another, blood was seen dripping from the tightly gripped fingers of Gonzales' racquet hand. He said later, 'I had blisters on my blisters.' He'd growl, and pace around the court, and shout at the crowd.

Neither would quit, reported Kramer. Because the matches lasted so long, they were forced to abandon the doubles fixtures, and eventually Jack decided to switch to a best-of-three sets format because he grew worried he was 'going to kill them if they had to go five [sets] every day.' Of course, one of the things that made these matches such great drama was that the players' body language on court represented such a contrast in styles. The dark, swarthy Gonzales, volatile, always quick to spot a slight, or a racial slur – even where none was intended. The media loved to characterise him (perhaps justifying his anger at racial stereotyping) as the Mexican-American, from the 'wrong side of the tracks'. He prowled around the court with a feline grace, and possessed a distinctive physical tic: he was forever inserting his thumb underneath the sweat-laden collar of his shirt and jerking it free from his clammy shoulders. Then his forefinger would sweep across the forehead and he'd flick away the beads of sweat.

The blond Hoad, on the other hand, was relaxed, almost to the point where, as one friend remarked, he was comatose. His movement around the court was casual, until that moment when swiftness of foot was required, and then he covered the court with the speed of a gazelle. At times he'd appear to lose interest in a match, his mind lapsing into that tendency 'to go walkabout'. Both men had perfect, athletic physiques, but Lew's muscular build seemed more suited to feats of strength; Pancho was slimmer, built not so much for endurance as speed and grace – like a jaguar, with the same predatory instincts as he moved in for the kill.

If Lew's attitude on court was now less lackadaisical than it had been in his younger days, off court there were still moments when he'd drive Kramer to despair. One such occasion occurred in Australia. Kramer and a few others had worked out how to make a big killing on the horses. Because of the complicated in-State betting laws, the stake money would be given to Lew (as an Australian) to place the bet. He was to wait at home while the others went to the racetrack and, at an agreed time, place the bet. The horse duly won and the jubilant group returned to Lew's room. They knocked on his door. But when he opened it – yawning, and rubbing sleep from his eyes – the awful truth began to dawn on them. Schroeder laughed when he recalled Kramer's reaction. Ashen-faced, he kept repeating, 'No, Lew; no, Lew; Lew, say it isn't true; say you didn't do it. Please, Lew. Please. Say it isn't true.' But it was. Lew had fallen asleep, and failed to place the bet. As the realisation sank in that Lew wasn't joking, that he'd lost them thousands upon thousands of dollars, Jack began to cry.

It wasn't long before there was a new look of respect for Hoad in Gonzales' eyes, a respect not only for his tennis, but also for his behaviour on court, his sportsmanship, and the way he treated his notoriously irascible rival. Pancho saw in the blond Australian one of nature's gentleman, an opponent who'd have no truck with prejudice of any kind. They took to having a couple of beers together, playing a few games of snooker, and as the head-to-head tour progressed, the Wimbledon Champion and the World Pro Champion between them produced a standard of tennis unsurpassed in the history of the game – both in terms of quality and intensity.

* * *

Sadly, there is a black hole in the records of tennis history: matches involving professional players over a period of some forty years have largely been consigned to oblivion. Tennis still awaits the chronicler of those stirring contests between the best players in the world at the peak of their game. It requires someone prepared to sift through accounts of individual matches in biographies, autobiographies, and histories of the game; exhume magazine and newspaper reviews buried in the dusty vaults of archive libraries; and finally, record the recollections of people who can still vividly recall watching pro matches. However, the task of compiling such a record is a daunting one that becomes increasingly difficult as the years pass, and people's memories fade.

[Since writing this, the authors have become aware of Joe McCauley's excellent book, The *History of Professional Tennis* (2000) which fills this 'black hole'].

Unfortunately, Hoad's autobiography is of little help – it concludes in 1958 when he'd only spent a few months as a pro. Generally, we have relied on Kramer's and Gonzales' autobiographies for records of matches in this period. However, Steve Flink's *The Greatest Matches of the Twentieth Century* includes two Hoad matches, one of which is a pro match against Gonzales in the final of the World Pro Championship at Cleveland on 4th May 1958, and he's kindly given permission for the authors to quote from this account.

In the semi-finals of this tournament, Gonzales had beaten Segura 6-4, 6-3, and Hoad had accounted for Trabert 6-2, 13-11. The American and the Australian now faced each other in the final. Flink sketches in the background to this eagerly awaited clash of the Titans and reveals the enormous strain inflicted on players by a head-to-head series:

> *Throughout the spring on their tour, the American and the Australian had played an absorbing series of matches. Between March 31 and April 20, they played **twenty-one times** [our emphasis]. They moved in and out of towns like Atlanta and New Haven, Philadelphia and Montreal, Princeton and Bermuda. Gonzales held only a slim 12-9 edge in that span.*
>
> *In Cleveland, they were to play on a fast canvas court. The conditions were suited to both contestants. They were mean fast-court players. By now, they knew each other's game inside out. The edge in this final would go to the player who executed better on the big points...*
>
> *With 2,700 fans watching the American and the Australian's climactic match the first weekend in May, it became clear that service breaks were difficult but essential. Hoad got the early break for 2-0 in the opening set and held throughout to prevail, 6-3. Gonzales did not want to fall into a deeper deficit. He served steadily in the second set, but could not gain a break himself. Hoad then broke through with some blazing backhands to take a 5-4 lead. Self-assured and given the chance, Hoad held on comfortably to take the second set, 6-4, for a two-sets-to-love lead.*
>
> *The third set featured both men at their best. An obstinate Gonzales was willing to pursue any policy to keep himself in the match. He persisted with his firepower on serve backed up by decisive volleying. Hoad was anxious to finish the job in straight sets, knowing that Gonzales was a warrior who*

would not surrender. Gonzales had the advantage of serving first in the set, but Hoad was staying with the favourite through every sequence.

The pressure grew on the twenty-three year old Australian. Gonzales kept inviting him to concede the set but Hoad refused. In a battle between two premier servers in professional tennis, neither man was found wanting. Gonzales kept moving in front, only for Hoad to blast his way back to even territory.

From 4-5 down in this pivotal set, Hoad served to save it eight times. Gonzales pressed him but to no avail. Hoad answered his adversary emphatically every time. He was quick and confident in the forecourt, cutting off the volleys at short range, reading nearly every Gonzales passing shot, giving the American few second chances.

Gonzales remained on course. He held on for 13-12 and finally proceeded to set point on the Australian's serve. Hoad came in behind a penetrating approach. Gonzales responded meekly off the backhand. His passing shot was tentative. But the ball hit the tape, and somehow fell over. Set to Gonzales, 14-12.

Buoyed by this stroke of luck, Gonzales coasted through the fourth set, 6-1, behind two service breaks. He gained an early fifth set break, and there was no halting him from there. The American, five days shy of his thirtieth birthday, was much fitter and fresher in the end. Hoad was hindered by a leg injury late in the contest...

Chuck Heaton wrote in the Cleveland Plain Dealer, 'The three hour match...was the longest and perhaps most exciting in the nine years the pros have fought it out at Cleveland. The sixth straight World pro Championship for swarthy Pancho added blond Lew to a list of final victims which includes Don Budge, Frank Sedgman and little Pancho Segura.'

Tournament promoter Jack March wrote in World Tennis, 'According to Don Budge, Bobby Riggs, and Pancho Segura, it was the greatest match they had ever seen. It was also the single greatest display of shotmaking, with Aussie Lew Hoad making most of the shots but losing the match... It was the first time Gonzales was up against an opponent who surpassed him in stroke equipment, condition, anticipation, speed, and court coverage. But Gonzales won this year on brains, fight, and guts.'

March later reflected, 'For the first time, distinct weaknesses were revealed in Gonzales' game. These weaknesses were never evident before because Gonzales had never faced a stronger, faster, and better player than himself. It is a credit to a champion that he could beat a player whose stroke equipment was superior.'

Gonzales himself recognised one department of his game as instrumental in his triumph. He told Chuck Heaton, 'Lew and I both play the same kind of tennis... My serve worked as well as it ever has. In fact, it was even clicking for me in the sets I lost. Lew was just volleying too well for me in the early part of the match. Then he slowed down and wasn't getting to the net quite as fast. That always makes the other fellow look better.'

Gonzales was asked about his shrewd lobbing and semi-lobbing to work his way back into big points. He responded, 'That's a trick I learnt from 'Little Sneaky' Segura. It's a change of pace that keeps the other guy running. In a long match like this, all of those steps add up.'

Was Gonzales fortunate to overcome Hoad in their most celebrated meeting? Perhaps. The fact remains that his tenacity was crucial to his cause. He made his own breaks by competing so fiercely in the latter stages of the third set when he could easily have succumbed. He recognised one fundamental fact: Great matches are taken not only by the better player, they are won by those who want them most.[4]

The head-to-head series seesawed amazingly up until about the halfway point. First one player would get his nose in front, then the other would catch up and overtake him. Neither was able to carve out a substantial lead. Sometimes they played best-of-three sets, sometimes best-of-five, but regardless of the format many of the matches went the distance, and involved marathon sets (of course, this was long before the introduction of tie-breakers).

Gonzales recalled one such match in Australia, at Kooyong Stadium, Melbourne, where Hoad, perhaps roused by memories of his epic Davis Cup win in '53, eventually triumphed 4-6, 9-7, 11-9, 18-16. Jack was rubbing his hands with glee, this tour was beginning to exceed his wildest dreams! With interest fuelled by uncertainty surrounding the outcome, and gate receipts breaking all records, fans went crazy with excitement, and seasoned commentators rubbed their eyes in disbelief, marvelling at the sublime tennis being played.

Maybe because the tour started in Australia, on home ground, Lew made an encouraging start. Having been five matches to four down, he got on a roll, won the last four matches, and flew to the States with an 8-5 lead.

The first night in San Francisco, Kramer recalled, Hoad won 6-4, 20-18, and he sensed that the Aussie, with a few more wins under his belt, could mentally destroy

Pancho. Given the Mexican-American's famed tenacity and determination, there may have been an element of wishful thinking in Kramer's assessment.

It certainly seemed that way after the next match in Los Angeles. Hoad won the first set, 6-3, but then another marathon set, even longer than the one in Frisco, saw Gonzales eventually get his nose in front to take the set 24-22, and run away with the final set 6-1. The following day they flew to New York for a best-of-five set match and drew a crowd of 15,237, up till then the largest in US history. It was another enthralling confrontation: Hoad won the first set, 9-7, only for Gonzales to respond with tigerish ferocity, taking the next three sets in a row, love, four and four. Gonzales had now reduced Hoad's lead to only two matches.

Perhaps the person closest to the series, apart from the players, was the tour promoter. Kramer felt a crucial turning point had been reached: a turning point possibly in the history of tennis, as well as the series. At 9-7, he wrote, it looked like Gonzales was coming back:

> But no. After those back-to-back wins in L.A. and New York, Hoad took full command. He won nine of the next eleven matches. The tide had turned for him – no question. You see most of the matches remained close, three sets. And Gonzales was playing well. Some nights he was playing as well as he had ever played in his life. They raised each other's game. But that was Gorgo's problem. He was playing beautifully, and he was getting beat. Near the end of February, they flew out to the coast again for some matches, and I went out to the L.A. airport to touch base with them. When Gorgo got off the plane, I could see in his eyes he was a beaten man. I'd seen it before when I beat him on tour.
>
> As I said before, when you go one-on-one night after night, one player takes charge. Hoad could serve with Gonzales, and he was every bit as quick. But he was much stronger. He could flick deep topspin shots with his wrist that Gonzales couldn't believe a human being could hit. Hoad also had a tougher overhead, and he had better ground strokes. They both knew all this by now. The longer they played, the more certain it was that Hoad would win. I had a new champion – and he was blond and handsome and popular, and very co-operative too. If Lew Hoad could whip Pancho Gonzales, so too could he bring amateur tennis to its senses and force open tennis.[5]

Kramer's last comment is interesting. He believed if Hoad maintained his dominance over Gonzales, it would exert pressure on the amateur authorities to open up the game and end this damaging separation of amateurs from professionals.

Lew was now 18-8 up, and playing unbelievable tennis. People all over the world were flocking to see this compelling struggle for supremacy between the Australian and the American. And to top that, Kramer was starting to plan what might prove an even bigger crowd-puller: an Aussie/US 'Professional Davis Cup' competition. Soon, however, Kramer's rejoicing was to look a little premature.

The next tour match was scheduled for The Tennis Club at Palm Springs. It was the height of the tourist season, and excitement about the prospect of a new World Champion was reaching fever pitch. Demand for tickets was so great they even had to put Frank Sinatra 'way up at the back'. Many of the major Hollywood stars were there that night, including Lana Turner with Fernando Lemas, and Elizabeth Taylor arm-in-arm with husband Mike Todd. It was just three weeks before Todd was killed when his Lockheed Lodestar plane, that he'd named 'Lucky Liz', crashed in the New Mexico Zuni Mountains.

On a cold desert night, the players walked on court. They'd been competing mostly indoors and when the sun goes down, Palm Springs can get a little chilly. Lew didn't loosen up as much as he liked during the match, and Gonzales beat him. The next morning Lew woke with a stiff back. He lost in Phoenix, Albuquerque and El Paso, and clearly needed three or four days' rest to get the stiffness out of his back – but they were battling it out night after night, followed by a long haul to the next town.

With Lew's back deteriorating, Gonzales once more pulled level and then started to remorselessly grind out a sequence of wins. 'Gorgo's confidence rose,' said Kramer, 'and the assurance came back into his eyes.'

Then, one fateful night, playing in Louisville, Lew went for an arching, mighty overhead – and felt a terrific pain tear across his back like a whip. In that single, fleeting second, Lew Hoad's career was effectively over. Kramer flew in a specialist who diagnosed right sciatic neuritis. This didn't mean anything to Lew, but the words, 'Your back will never be cured,' did. 'It was the worst moment in my life,' he told friends.

It is a measure of the man that he felt he couldn't let Kramer, Gonzales, or the packed crowds, down. He played on, taking cortisone tablets to ease the pain. Sometimes he played in such agony that he couldn't stand upright. He blasted the balls he could get to, and left the rest. The pain moved to his right hip, then his right knee.

But sometimes, inexplicably and miraculously, the pain disappeared and he gave his tennis, the crowd, and Gonzales, a revealing glimpse of his true potential. At one point he won five matches in a row. At Wembley, in London, he took the first set off a blinking Gonzales, 6-0, in thirteen minutes. Larry Hodgson recalls that set as being the greatest tennis he, or anyone else there, had ever seen. Every ground stroke of Lew's seemed to hit a line, and low volleys were played with swooping elegance and beauty. But Gonzales, taking the next two sets, won the match and, having been 8-19 down, went on to win the series 51-36.

Lew was still able to look back on that tragic tour and recall amusing incidents. One of his favourite memories was of playing Gonzales in a college basketball hall, the most noticeable feature of which was a large, ticking clock at one end. Though everyone in the crowd was silent, a loud tick, tick, tick was clearly audible. Pancho began to lose the match, and his temper.

As they crossed-over, Lew sensed trouble brewing. Gonzales prepared to serve and the crowd hushed. Tick, tick, tick, went the clock. Pancho tossed the ball and hit it with all his might. Lew immediately saw it was travelling upwards, not down into the court. It kept rising as it crossed the net and flashed over Lew's head straight into the centre of the clock, which exploded like a miniature bomb, sending glass flying in every direction. With a loud whirring sound, the innards of the clock hung out from the wall for a few seconds, and then – like one of those moments of surreal violence in a 'Tom and Jerry' cartoon – crashed to the floor.

Lew stared first at the clock, and then at Gonzales who had a look of immense satisfaction on his swarthy face, though it hadn't been a difficult shot for a man of his enormous talent. Lew burst out laughing. The open-mouthed crowd cheered and cheered. Later, when Kramer and all his boys prepared to leave the hall, they found their way barred by a college chief, surrounded by his burly football team. Gonzales was solemnly given a bill for $2,500. His lips curled back. He cursed. It was left to Kramer to settle the bill.

Although Gonzales was still the World Professional Champion and would remain so for a few more years, no-one succeeded in putting him under such pressure as Lew. He said later, 'The Hoad tour was the worst strain I ever went through. I'd replay every match in my mind hours after it was over. I hope that I never meet a finer competitor. He really gave it all he had.' Pancho Gonzales, for the only time in his life, had formed a tennis friendship. As for Lew? He had a cheque for nearly $200,000 from his winnings. And a wrecked back. He headed for home, Jenny and the family.

Meanwhile, Jack shook his head, ruing the twist of fate that seemed to have deprived him of the ideal challenger for Gonzales. He wanted another head-to-head series in 1959, but when he considered the top amateurs, he knew none of them would give Big Pancho a real fight. Some would be lucky to win even a game or two. This was what made the world of amateur tennis such a sham: the smug assumption that it contained within its ranks the best players in the world. Yet he knew that the young men idolised by the tennis world, who packed in crowds at White City, the Stade Roland Garros, Wimbledon and Forest Hills, couldn't live with any of his professionals.

He dreamed of the day when tennis would be open – like golf. Then the best players would be seen to full advantage on the show courts of the world, and get paid for it, like other 'entertainers' did. He wondered how Hoad's back was shaping up – maybe there was an outside chance of a full recovery?

After that last crippling defeat by Gonzales, Lew took his back to specialist after specialist in Australia and London. No-one seemed to have the same diagnosis. Was it sciatica, arthritis, pinched nerves, calcium deposits? Nothing definite showed up on the X-rays. He tried everything from acupuncture to a new treatment where the base of his spine was bombarded with radiation. Jenny now suspects that the leukaemia that finally killed Lew may well have originated from this radiation treatment, 'which made Lew feel terrible.'

However, after a period of rest and relaxation with his family, the back was feeling much better. Thus, when the call from Kramer came, the call he'd half-expected, he felt rested, happy, and free of pain. 'Would you consider going back against Gonzales?' drawled Jack over the phone. 'Sure,' was the reply. It was a chance to get back on the tennis court and make some money – and besides, Gonzales was getting older. Perhaps he'd be easier to handle now.

Jenny accompanied him to America to make sure he was looked after, and the tour resumed. Once again Hoad and Gonzales slugged it out, night after night. There were times when, mysteriously, Lew enjoyed a remission from back pain and at one point he was leading fifteen matches to three, but he was constantly worried about the back holding up. Sometimes, if he had stiffness, he couldn't practise and would be forced to go into a match 'cold'. The nightly grind followed by the inevitable car journey, with Lew often still slightly damp from the shower, eventually took its toll, and again he began to experience agonising pain. His private nightmare of becoming a cripple, with Jenny having to spoon-feed him, loomed. The desire to continue the fight, to subject his weary body to further strain, began to ebb away. Finally, Kramer was forced to accept the inevitable and declare the series a 'no contest'. For the first time, the tour had made only modest money.

Jenny also felt it was time for Lew to stop punishing himself like this and spend more time with the family. They had made enough to get by comfortably, she said, and there were surely business opportunities where they could capitalise on the Hoad name.

Towards the end of the tour as Jenny, Lew and Pancho were speeding through the desert from Los Angeles to El Paso, a bizarre incident occurred. Suddenly all the electrics in the car failed and they found themselves in a skirt of a soft yellow light beaming down from above. To this day, the occupants of the car swear that they looked up to see a flying saucer hovering thirty feet over their heads. When the UFO swooshed away after a little while, the engine and electrics in the car came back on.

Lew 'couldn't believe it', though it made a good story to share with incredulous friends over a few beers. Jenny, being a sensible girl, took the incident calmly, but it clearly had a profound effect on Gonzales. Long ago his Mexican ancestors had believed they were in communication with gods from outer space.

Years later, Gonzales said that if there was a Universe Davis Cup, and Earth had to pick one man for all time to play one match for the planet, he would pick Lew Hoad. It may have sounded an odd way to phrase such an extravagant compliment – until one remembered the flying saucer story.

The following year Lew cut his playing schedule right down to rest his back. His electric presence and outstanding stroke-play made the crowds all the more delighted by his rare appearances. He won the London professional doubles, at Wembley, five times and was singles finalist twice – in 1961 and 1963. And, as Joe Stahl points out, few people are aware that in 1959-60, after the head-to-head one hundred match series had been abandoned, Hoad competed in a round-robin format tour with a greatly expanded roster of professionals. Unfortunately the tour was poorly attended and lost money, but Lew had the satisfaction of a winning head-to-head record over Gonzales even though the Mexican-American eventually emerged as the winner with the best overall record.

* * *

Lew would often look back fondly on his amateur days, regretting that he never achieved the Grand Slam and, like many professionals, he particularly missed competing for his country in the Davis Cup. The only thing that would have made this possible was Open tennis. There had been talk of 'open' tennis in the air for many years, but no-one seemed capable of really seizing the initiative. In 1967, however, Herman David, Chairman of the All England Club, announced that a three-day professional tournament would be staged on the famed Centre Court at the end of the Wimbledon Championships that year. Furthermore, he anticipated Wimbledon would become a fully 'open' tournament in 1968, and remain so for the foreseeable future. Lew had already promised David that, if ever this were to happen, he would come back to Wimbledon.

On the final weekend of August 1967, Rod Laver, Fred Stolle and Ken Rosewall of Australia; Dennis Ralston and Buchholz of America; and Andres Gimeno of Spain, paraded on the Centre Court. When late arrivals Hoad and Gonzales stepped out, the roars were tumultuous. As luck – or good public relations manoeuvring – would have it, the two greatest players in the world had been drawn to face each other. Fans looked forward to a mouth-watering gladiatorial contest.

And that's exactly what it proved to be! Gonzales had always wanted to show the Wimbledon crowds what they'd been missing all those years. Hoad, for his part, hadn't lost a singles match there since 1955. They were 39 and 32 years of age, and the tennis they produced that day took them back to their youth. Peter Wilson of *The Mirror* described Lew as now 'thick of waist and thigh, but still kissed with the fairy gold of genius.'

Played at a furious pace and full of drama, the match swung back and forth as they traded thunderous serves and smashes, ground shots that brought up chalk on the lines, crunching cross-court volleys, feather-like dinks, and delicate drop-shots. In a match lasting from teatime to dusk, the Centre Court provided a fitting showcase for their unique talents, demonstrating how far the game had developed.

Typically, Lew had arrived too late for any practice before the tournament, and in losing the first set 6-3 in just nineteen minutes, looked rusty and out of touch. Although he'd dropped his service only once in that first set, the power and accuracy of Gonzales' own delivery was an ominous augury. In the second set, though, Lew began to get the measure of his opponent's powerful first serve, and the tremendous kick on his second. A stunning backhand volley showed the battle was truly joined. It was nip and tuck, each holding service, until the thirteenth game when Lew was 15-40 down. Somehow the two set points were saved, service held, and six games later Hoad was presented with the first opportunity of breaking Gonzales' seemingly impregnable delivery. Two fierce backhands down the line, and a forehand passing shot on the run, brought him to 15-40. He needed two chances but then secured the set, 11-9, to square the match.

If what had gone before was tennis of an amazingly high standard, the final set, by common consent, proved one of the most memorable ever seen on the Centre Court. It gave the lie to the importance of prize money to top professionals. What was at stake here was pride, and both players seemed possessed by a passionate and steely determination to win. And both began to show signs of tiredness – but only between rallies.

Once again, games went with serve, though there were some wobbles – three times the server was 0-30 before holding serve. Then, after nearly two hours, Hoad reached triple match point on Pancho's serve in the fourteenth game.

So often in the past Gonzales had relied on his powerful serve to dig himself out of a hole, and once again it came to his aid as he pounded down an ace. On the next point he followed a good first serve into the net, and volleyed deep to the baseline. Lew met the ball almost on his toes, and instead of going for a pass, swept up a lob – an incredible shot to play. As it began to descend, Gonzales watched, initially with an almost academic interest, then with growing apprehension. 'Holy shit,' he muttered, and started to race for the baseline. Too late! The ball landed plumb on the line. Lew had won their one and only Wimbledon Centre Court match, 3-6, 11-9, 8-6. Gonzales still had one ball in his hand; he tossed it in the air and gave it the most tremendous swipe. Still travelling upwards, it shot high over the stadium roof like a rocket going into orbit, and landed in a nearby golf course.

The next day, Peter Wilson commented:

> *In the sporting sense, Hoad and Gonzales are veterans. But they put on a display of which men fifteen years their junior could have been proud. Over three sets, I don't think an amateur who played at this year's Wimbledon championships could have lived with them.*

This was 1967; by now Lew was semi-retired and had to nurse himself through those tournaments he did play, frequently fighting severe back pain as much as his opponent. Walking on court only eighteen hours after that gruelling victory over the seeded Gonzales to face Rosewall, he looked tired. There were glimpses of the old Hoad brilliance but he went down 6-2, 6-2 in forty-six minutes. John Ballantine, reporting for *The Sunday Times*, still found much to admire. Though 'Muscles' must have played 'Hoady' over a hundred times, he observed, 'their tennis was still stamped 'solid silver, made in Sydney'; Rosewall's sliced backhand set in a groove as accurately as any bacon slicer, and Hoad's Herculean ability to thrash the ball like ping pong enabling him to kill balls any other player would have had difficulty in reaching.' He concluded: 'The rallies were tremendous crescendos, Rosewall's fine string playing only rarely drowned by Hoad's percussion power. What could have proved a great symphony became a short, sweet overture.'

The following day Rosewall was beaten 6-2, 6-2, 12-10 by the new star, Rod Laver, in the first professional final played at Wimbledon. Five years earlier, in 1962, the red-haired, freckle-faced Laver had turned professional after winning his first Grand Slam. He'd gone on to play a short head-to-head series against Lew which Lew had won, prompting one British newspaper to comment on the difference between a man who was clearly one of the greatest amateurs, and a seasoned pro.

The paper declared that though Hoad was well past his physical prime because of injury, he was still, on his day, the greatest player in the world. Also noteworthy was that of all the champions who played in that first professional tournament at Wimbledon, Hoad made the biggest impact on the public, especially younger fans who'd never seen him before. The paper concluded: 'This is readily understandable for, in addition to being a splendid athlete and a wonderful stroke-player, Hoad is endearingly human in his approach to the game.'

The late Arthur Ashe believed that if Lew had stayed healthy, he would have been the tennis equivalent of golf's, Arnold Palmer, and would have hastened Open tennis by a decade. When the professional tournament concluded, Herman David sought him out, and Lew promised, yes, he'd be there next year for Wimbledon's first Open Championships – as long as his back held up.

Constantly worrying about his back and frequently hampered by it, Lew reached the quarter-finals of the Italian Open, and the last sixteen of the French, the following year, as well as winning a string of lesser titles. In Scotland, when he was competing in the Dewar Cup, all the players were asked to put in a quarter of an hour's work to get the court and hall ready. Typically, Lew stayed for two hours, re-painting the lines and adjusting the seating. Because he dared not practice for fear of wrenching his back before a game, he would sit for hours quietly reading (Lew was an avid reader) or just talk about every subject under the sun: music – which he loved (especially jazz), art, history, boxing, the origin of surnames. Without any real education, Lew had become a knowledgeable man of deep sympathy and compassion. He was also a great sleeper, blessed with that rare ability to drop off as soon as his head hit the pillow.

However, on one occasion, a final in Wales, he and Larry Hodgson stayed up all night working their way diligently through two crates of beer in the splendid home of one of the wealthy sponsors of the tournament. Without a wink of sleep, they repaired to the final. Sitting at courtside to watch the match, Larry began to yawn, and so did Lew. At one change of ends he said, 'If you don't stop yawning, I'm going to bloody well go to sleep.' Larry stopped yawning. Lew won the title.

Wimbledon champion, Arthur Ashe, revered Lew. In his autobiography, *Portrait in Motion*, he wrote that before his back injury, Lew was 'the best player ever'. He added, enviously, 'He was just so colourful and charismatic. He was the only guy in the world who would stay out drinking till five in the morning and then beat your brains out on the court by noon.'

True to the promise he'd made Herman David, Lew was determined to enter the 1968 Wimbledon Championships. However, he was seriously worried that his back injury, and lack of match play, would mean he'd cut a sorry figure. The Aussies always hung out together, and in his excellent history of Open tennis, broadcaster and writer, Richard Evans tells a story that demonstrates their devotion and loyalty towards Lew. At a party some time before the 1968 championships, the host said that 'Hoady' should give it a real go, adding. 'If your back holds up you can still beat the shit out of most of these guys on tour.' Immediately, Roy Emerson, who was at the party, offered to take six weeks off and help Lew get into shape to play his best tennis. 'You'll beat the lot of us,' he said.

It was an extraordinary offer. Emerson was a Wimbledon champion who still had hopes of another title, yet he was willing to prejudice his own chances by offering to sharpen up one of the greatest talents in the game. As expected, Lew refused the generous offer. But he did say instead, 'Emmo' could go get him another beer.

Chapter 13

Wimbledon, 1968 – A new chapter opens for Tennis

1968 was one of the most momentous years in post-Second World War history. In a decade marked by revolutionary turmoil, it stands out as the key year. The spirit of revolution was in the air, and it was infectious. It made itself felt in almost every sphere of human activity: in government, in social administration, in jurisprudence, in sexual behaviour, in fashion, in music, in culture generally. In 1968 John Lennon sang *Revolution*, and Grace Slick and the Jefferson Airplane, 'Now it's time for you and me to have a revolution'. 1968 has been described as the 'Year of the Barricades' and, in the vanguard of much of this revolutionary activity, were young people, especially students.

A wave of student protest movements broke out across Europe, Japan and the United States. In February, Paris students took over the Sorbonne, demanding control over both course content and the selection of new Faculty members. With thousands of factory workers going on strike to support them, they almost brought down the French government. The following month there were similar student demonstrations in Rome and Warsaw.

Sometimes demonstrations provoked a measured, calm response, sometimes a violent one. In America there was mounting opposition to the Vietnam War as the lists of casualties grew: young men publicly burned their draft cards, and in Washington, outside the White House, crowds chanted, 'Hey, hey, LBJ [Lyndon Baines Johnson, the then US President], how many kids did you kill today?' Violence spilled over into political life in general: America was rocked by the assassinations of Bobby Kennedy and Martin Luther King. In the same year, Mayor Daly instructed the police to use all necessary force to break up demonstrations at the Democratic National Convention in Chicago, resulting in appalling brutality.

Meanwhile, in Europe, Russian tanks rolled into the streets of Prague to suppress a popular uprising against Soviet rule.

In California, however, a rather different revolution was taking place, one that was cultural rather than political. People were 'dropping out', smoking cannabis, and wearing flowers in their hair – 'Flower Power' was taking over with the hippie slogan, 'Make Love, not War'.

In Britain there'd also been anti-Vietnam War demonstrations, and student sit-ins at universities, but as in the past, Britain remained largely insulated from the radical upheavals destabilising her Continental neighbours. Nevertheless, there was a new spirit of liberalism and permissiveness: legislation was passed legalising homosexuality for consenting adults over the age of 21; theatre censorship was abolished; and the widespread availability of the contraceptive pill was bringing about a revolution in sexual mores.

And London, a city formerly noted for its staid formality and stuffy conservatism, was now established as the trendy 'Capital of Cool'. In terms of pop culture and fashion, London led the world. If the Beatles and the Rolling Stones dominated the music scene, then Carnaby Street, the King's Road in Chelsea, Mary Quant, Vidal Sassoon, David Bailey and Twiggy, epitomised style and trendiness.

Predictably, Wimbledon remained cocooned from the violent undercurrents threatening to engulf many of the major cities of Europe and America. But it did absorb the party spirit that characterised 'Swinging London' even though it stopped short of 'letting it all hang out'. In fact, Wimbledon, that most conservative of institutions, displayed a surprising adaptability, managing to preserve its air of decorum whilst loosening its 'old school tie'. It maintained those civilised rituals that distinguished it from other major tournaments around the world: the bows and curtsies to the Royal Box, the insistence on predominantly white clothing, and the strawberry and cream teas. But there was a new brashness in the way it promoted itself.

Of course, the charm of Wimbledon has always been that it's had one foot firmly planted in the past. It's like some huge Edwardian garden party in the grounds of a great country mansion. The crowds milling around the manicured lawns, the limousines parked in the drive, the tinkle of champagne glasses, the 'pick-pock' of tennis balls, and the cries of 'Well played Gussy – good shot Cyril!' More recently there may have been an element of calculation and pretence about all this. It's what the Brits do best, what American visitors expect from 'we Limeys'. And Wimbledon has always been an essential fixture in a social calendar that included Henley and Royal Ascot. In 1968 the All England Committee may not have been about to sacrifice the distinctive nature of Wimbledon for the sake of seeming trendy, but they did employ a noticeably more relaxed approach to running a tournament still regarded by many as the greatest in the world.

What added to the party atmosphere of the first Open Wimbledon was that for many of the competitors it was exactly that – a huge party. For so many years the professionals had been pariahs, excluded from tournaments where they'd once been lionised. Now they were to be welcomed back to Wimbledon, the Holy of Holies, and not just a special event for professionals, as in the previous year. The '68 Wimbledon was like an old college reunion where famous players from the past met old friends, chatted, joked and reminisced about the good old days. Besides Lew and Jenny, there were the two Panchos, Gonzales and Segura; Australian champions and Davis Cup veterans spanning almost two decades such as Sedgman, Rosewall, Cooper, Fraser, Emerson, Stolle, Laver, and the current Wimbledon Champion, John Newcombe; the Columbian, Alex Olmedo; and the Spaniard, Andres Gimeno.

In time-honoured tradition, a number of competitors had come to England a week or two before Wimbledon began to acclimatise themselves to grass court play, and perhaps the English climate! Accustomed to playing in different countries and being exposed to different cultures, little fazed these *hommes du mond* who played as hard off court as they did on court. Two such seasoned travellers were the South Africans, Gordon Forbes and his doubles partner, Abe Segal. However, like others visiting London after a long absence, they were totally unprepared for the culture shock of this new 'Swinging London'. In his classic book about tennis, *A Handful of Summers*, Forbes records with humour, and a wonderfully precise eye for detail, the hectic, carnivalesque life of London in the summer of '68, and the author has kindly given us permission to quote extracts from his book.

Tennis tournaments have always attracted stars from the world of show business, and Wimbledon is no exception. Over the years famous celebrities have included Cliff Richard, Peter Ustinov and Charlton Heston, but many on the lower rungs of the showbiz circuit have also been attracted by the glitzy allure of the sport. In London at this time there were two entertainers, Harry Fowler and Kenny Lynch, who loved to hang out with the tennis set. Harry was a film actor who specialised in cockney parts. With a pinched, rather weasely face, he was never leading-man material but made a good living in parts as a spiv, or cockney barrow boy. Kenny was a black singer who'd done some acting – often in the *Confessions of a...* type of film.

Together, or singly, they acted as court jesters to Forbes and Segal, orchestrating a series of hilarious escapades, a manic pantomime that revolved around Wimbledon. But beneath the humour of Forbes' account, there clearly lies a real affection and respect for all those great players of the past (and especially Lew). What follows are edited extracts from the book, where diary records are interwoven with the author's memories and reflections on that historic occasion:

The ceremonial return that summer of 1968 then, as a competitor, had parcelled up in it for me about a dozen separate ecstasies, not the least of which was actually to participate. To walk onto those unbelievable grass courts on the afternoon of an English summer and play in the gentlemen's singles. Or doubles. And with Abe Segal to boot. It was too much to cope with. I was in a happy, light-hearted daze.

London bubbled. She'd changed her mood completely, Abe Segal told me when he met us at the airport. He was driving an old Rolls Royce and wearing a pair of pink velvet trousers and a kind of wide eternal grin which suggests champagne for lunch and the prospect of a thousand hearty laughs.

'Place's gone mad, Forbsey,' he said taking my suitcase. 'You'll not believe what's happening. To handle a month in London a man's got to double his insurance an' walk about with a doctor feelin' his pulse with one hand and carryin' a hypodermic in the other!'

The cases were stowed, the Rolls put into motion and all the time the snippets poured forth:

'They got these shops on the King's Road with the music and all, going like crazy and everybody's permanently high. You can blow your mind just breathin' the air!'

*   *   *

The Rolls drove sedately along the motorway while the rows of houses and corner pubs dozed in the afternoon sun.

'Everyone's here,' Abie was saying. 'Even Segura is here.' He gave a snort of laughter. 'Segoo!' he cried. 'Jesus. Movin' around on those legs of his hittin' the two-hander up the line and takin' pills.'

"Hey, Segoo,' I says to him, 'this is London, you know. The U.K. This isn't Hollywood. This is where the Queen lives."

'And he says to me, 'You theenk, beeg Abie, she's gonna want lessons from old Segoo?' he asks.'

'Sure she'll want lessons,' I say. 'How you feelin'?' an' he says: 'I steel got enough strength to get me to the Club, Abie,' an' he takes another handful of pills. Vitamin B1 to 12. They'll have to lock him up before he completely changes the habits of the English!'

I really like listening to Abie when he was happy.

*   *   *

He steered the Rolls past Barons Court Underground and into the gates of Queen's Club.

'I've got a court booked for five,' Abie said, 'to get your blood movin'!'

Queen's Club! Time rolled backwards. On the front steps, Frank Sedgman, ready for a match, rubbing some embrocation into his elbow. He shakes my hand and says:

'At twenty you don't need these lotions and at forty they don't help you!'

There is no need for a fervent greeting. Everything is back as it was – a tableau frozen into immobility for five years, then set moving again at the throw of a switch.

Lew and Jenny Hoad, Gonzales, Teddy Tinling, Drobny, Rosewall, Torben Ulrich, Luis Ayala, Gimeno, Billy Knight, Emerson, Peter Ustinov, Fred Perry, Donald Dell. Allen Fox, craftier than before. The dressing-room is still damp and smells exactly the same, and the old man with the same suspicious look hands me one of the same old towels, laundered now to a threadbare grey. Doubles against Alex Olmedo and Segura and afterwards, beer in the same little pub. The world we knew. I kept a diary for those three weeks, simply because I knew that they would soon be past and I badly wanted to remember them. Parts of it tell the story as well as any other way I can think of:

Diary Notes: London 1968

It's sunny. We're staying in a flat in Putney and if you look carefully through the bedroom window, you can see the Thames through oaks. This morning it's shopping. The King's Road, so we go via Sloane Square and join the crowds. There's madness here. A sort of happy irresponsible insanity. Definite scope for Abie's straitjackets. The British have found a stage large enough to accommodate a fair proportion of the population so they all join the cast. The result is a temporary loss of reason – a bomb attack on the mind. Gurus meditate on pavements in masses of hairy reflections. Napoleons and Nelsons, hands in jackets, scan imaginary horizons. Lord Kitchener is calling people up; a camel is tied to a parking meter. There are Zulus there and sheiks, hippies, Hindus, the directors of bowler-hatted companies, rajahs, squires, lairds, sultans, valets and jam sahibs. Monks abound, and other robed figures, and the armed forces are well represented; brigadiers, dragoons, commodores and brass. On a corner a bugler sounds a few military notes which bring a gungadin and several legionaries to attention. Skirts are up and underwear out and nipples on view through the thinnest of fabrics. The mood is sensuous, infectious and a little insanitary.

* * *

Diary Notes: Summer 1968

Queen's Club. Monday. Lewis Hoad again, on the centre court, after eleven years. I watch, transported. All the impossible majesty of his game flies through my head like a moving picture film. It doesn't matter that the shots that he now plays are off centre. Out of focus. That his service is hampered by a back injury. That he is slower. The style is the same; and with the style comes the memories. At his best, I truly swear that he was unbeatable. Unplayable. Some players do this, and others that. Lew Hoad did everything.

Select, if you like, the best tennis match ever played, and you will find quite unquestionably that Hoad played in it. And then brushed it aside with an understatement. Rod Laver is a carbon copy of the original Hoad. Only left-handed and without the full majesty. The mighty power.

Diary Notes: Tuesday

One wanders about this extraordinary Wimbledon bemused by the sensations which rise up in droves and flood the mind. First, the question of time – there is simply not enough of it. Whole blocks of conversations, friendships, tennis and laughter go to waste. Like a colour film, rife with images, crammed with humour, magnitude and pathos of this remarkable circuit; a film which can't be stopped; simply rolls past, numbing the mind.

In the player's restaurant, all at the same moment, Gonzales is saying something vital about the evolution of tennis. Peter Ustinov is imitating Nikki Pilic arguing with a linesman. Fred Perry is predicting the eventual men's singles winner. Pancho Segura is talking about a new kind of pill for the over forties, that is guaranteed to 'Get you through the night, keed!' Fowler and Moore [Ray Moore, a colourful South African player, who has a prominent role in these anecdotes] are discussing Abe Segal's weight in relation to his age, while Abie, within earshot, is trying to listen to Hoady telling him about Jenny's purchases at the 'Way In!' Diana Ross is having tea with Arthur Ashe. Teddy Tinling is on about the tigerish movements of Virginia Wade. Kathy Harter is just sitting there, all ponytail and legs – unbelievable. And two girls unknown are standing in the tea queue, wearing transparent net blouses and causing the loss of more conversational threads in the course of male conversation that could be readily totted up. And that's only inside!

[Abie, having promised to get hold of tickets for various people during Wimbledon fortnight, upsets his friends, Ray Moore and Harry Fowler, by phoning very early one morning to check if they've acquired tickets yet. They plan their revenge, which takes place several days later]

Tonight we are to try a new restaurant. London is full of these new 'in' places, very modern and upstage. Provans, the Hungry Horse, Au Père de Nico, The Spot, Angelos, Alvaros, Aretusas, Tiberios, several Dinos, Francos or Carlos. Tonight it's to be a new and remarkable place – manned, says Raymond, entirely by homosexuals. Gay Blades. 'But very funny,' says Raymond. 'Really funny. And good food, really good!' So we go; Ray [Moore] and Rose, the Segals, the Hoads and a young and earnest fellow who takes life far too seriously and who is always worrying about saving money and the price of things. We seat ourselves around our table, settle our napkins and order our wine, and Aubrey arrives.

'Raymond, darling,' he says archly, running his fingers through Ray's preposterous hair. 'Ooh dear! So wiry, and full of nice clean sweat! Such a rough, male game you play. I do love rough males, you know!'

'Aubrey, my dear,' says Raymond. 'How was your weekend?'

'Ooh, lovely weekend, darling! Went to Amsterdam! Got involved with a whole crew of Danish sailors! Very rough, Danish sailors!' A shiver of delight runs up his spine and he shifts his weight from one foot to the other.

'Sit down, Aubrey,' said Ray. 'Sit down and tell us what happened.'

'Sit down, darling!' cries Aubrey. 'Sit down? You must be joking!' and he goes off, hugging his chuckles to himself.

Laughter and mischief permeated the place. Only our serious young friend is appalled and is studying the menu with a worried frown. The wine arrives and Harry Fowler pours it, slipping, as he does so, a sleeping tablet into Abie's glass. The meal is hilarious. By the time midnight comes, Abie is nodding off and can't wait for the coffee to be served.

'Holy Hell, you guys, I'm bombed,' he says. 'I've got to leave. Let's move, Mouse, [Abie's affectionate name for his wife, dating back to their first meeting] before I fall asleep on the table.' He leaves some notes to pay the bill and they depart.

For Moore and Fowler, the night is just beginning. First, they must tease the serious one. The bill arrives. Fowler studies it, then hands it to Moore.

'Are you paying cash?' he asks in a serious voice, 'or are you going behind the curtain with Aubrey?'

'I'm short of cash tonight,' says Raymond. 'I'll go with Aubrey.'

He gets up, takes the beaming Aubrey's hand, and they disappear behind a curtain at the far end of the room. All prearranged. Sounds of ecstasy emerge.

'What's happening?' asks the serious one. 'What the hell is going on?'

'Aubrey doesn't mind how you pay him,' says Harry. 'He's very accommodating.'

'I don't like it,' mutters the serious one. 'I've never done anything like this before. This kind of thing can affect a man for life —'

'Well, pay cash then,' says Harry. 'You don't have to go.'

'Lot of money,' he replies, frowning at the bill. 'Damned expensive meal!'

Moore emerges from behind the curtain then, with a broad smile on his face, doing up his trousers.

'How was it?' says Harry.

'Two minutes for the soup,' says Ray, 'three for the main course, and two for the cheese and coffee!'

'Not bad value,' says Harry. He turns to the serious one – 'OK, your turn next.'

The expression on the serious one's face suggests the most intense mental conflict. Suddenly he gives a huge half sob.

'To hell with you guys!' he bursts out. 'I'll pay cash!' and wrenches out his wallet.

By the time we are finally ready to leave, it is just two in the morning.

'Right,' says Fowler. 'Raymond, it is time that we phoned Abie!'

We gather round the telephone at the desk, and Raymond dials the Cumberland Hotel where Abie is staying. At last the connection is made.

Abie's sleepy voice: 'What the hell is happening?'

'It's two o'clock,' Ray says urgently. 'We're all at Wimbledon and Twiggy and her friend are here. Where the hell are the tickets? You said you'd get some tickets.'

'Good God,' says Abie. 'You're joking!'

'Look at your watch, Abe! We're all waiting for you at Wimbledon. Everyone's on court!'

'Good God,' says Abie again. 'You're right. Listen, just hold it. I'll be right there. Just tell them all to hold it!'

Raymond replaces the receiver, doubled up with laughter. 'What's the odds he's jumping about, putting tennis gear into his bag?' he says.

'By the time I get to the hotel,' he says, 'I'm so tired I can't see straight, so I draw all the curtains and get into bed and sleep my brains out. Suddenly there's this phone call. It's that idiot Raymond. The curtains are so thick that I can't see too much, so I look at my watch, and sure enough it's two o'clock. I get one hell of a fright. I'm second match on court three, with Forbsey in the doubles. So I get up, shave, throw on my clothes, pack my gear, and take the lift downstairs, carryin' my bag and rackets. I come out of the lift downstairs, and there's not too many people about; but I'm in such a hurry I go up to the concierge and say:

'Listen, I need a taxi, urgently.'

"Where might you be going, sir?' says the man, looking at me kind of peculiar."

"I'm on court at Wimbledon in one hour,' I say to him.'

"I hardly think so, sir,' he says. 'It's two thirty a.m."

'A.m. or p.m.?' I shout.'

'A.m., sir,' he says.'

"It's that bloody Moore,' I say to him. 'I mean Jesus! Are you quite sure it's not p.m.?"

"Quite sure, sir,' says the concierge. 'We do try to keep in touch with these things."

'Suddenly the whole thing seems unreal. Here I am, standing in the lobby with my tennis rackets under my arm, arguing with someone about whether it's two a.m. or p.m. It's like I'm dreaming. So I go back to bed,' says Abie, 'and would you believe it, I can't get to sleep?'

Ray and Harry classed this particular incident as their ultimate in practical jokes for 1968.

It was Laver's Wimbledon. In the final he defeated, quite easily, the industrious Roche, unravelling him in much the same way as he had done Ashe. Afterwards, it was so clear and logical that he should have won. Even the tennis gods, for once, put aside their devilry and allowed justice to be served and honest history made.[1]

Few of the participants and the spectators will ever forget the very special atmosphere of that first Open Wimbledon, the sense of taking part in a unique sporting occasion, a piece of tennis history. And whilst it brought personal disappointment to Hoad – he went out in the third round to fellow countryman, Bob Hewitt – it confirmed his popularity with the crowds.

In the second round, on a damp No 2 court (the weather was living up to its unpredictable reputation with rain interrupting many matches that fortnight) he'd turned back the years again to easily despatch the Indian, Jaidip Muckerjea, in straight sets. But Hewitt, in the next round, was a sterner test, and eventually a tired Hoad lost in five sets.

As for Wimbledon, its courageous leap in the dark proved a resounding success. There had been fears that a tournament where professionals competed alongside amateurs might not draw large crowds, although the 1966 soccer World Cup (involving paid professionals competing for their country) and the 1967 Wimbledon Professional tournament, had largely dispelled such fears.

The All England Club and the British LTA were probably more concerned that by going out on a limb and unilaterally deciding to make Wimbledon 'Open', they ran the risk of expulsion from the International Lawn Tennis Federation (ILTF) and thus exclusion from the Davis Cup. Once Wimbledon had taken the lead, however, other tournaments followed meekly in their wake. Many were already finding it difficult enough to attract crowds to what were patently second-class events; relying exclusively on amateur players would simply have spelt financial disaster.

An irrevocable change in the game had obviously taken place; there could be no turning back the clock now. Open tennis had been a long time coming, but it had acquired a momentum that was to prove irresistible. There had been attempts eight years earlier to abolish the distinction between amateurs and professionals, and they had only narrowly failed. The initiative had come then from the Frenchman, Philippe Chatrier. The night before the summer meeting of the ILTF, he'd organised a dinner for Jack Kramer and Jean Borotra, the head of the French Federation. Everywhere the talk had been of Open tennis; various countries had come up with different (mostly unworkable) solutions to the rigid separation of professionals and amateurs; all agreed it was inflicting irreparable harm on the sport.

Kramer and Borotra talked long into the night about how Open tennis could work, and what Kramer's role in the new set-up might be. There was a tacit recognition on the part of both men that the ILTF vote the following day would be a formality. They'd totted up the likely votes and the Open tennis lobby seemed to possess the necessary two-thirds majority.

Chatrier, an astute visionary who was later to become President of the Tennis Federation, was delighted. He'd been acting as an honest broker, endeavouring to persuade Borotra of the need to bring Kramer back into the official tennis fold, and Kramer that the future for professionals lay in Open tennis and an integration of the two factions.

Unfortunately all these plans were nullified the following day when the proposal to switch to Open tennis failed by just five votes to secure the required majority. Kramer was shattered. He commented: 'It was an absolute fix; one man who had committed to Open tennis went to the bathroom when the vote was called. The Big Four all voted for the measure, but it was the United States that brought about its defeat. The USLTA voted one way and lobbied another.' [2]

Rightly or wrongly, Kramer attributed the proposal's failure to the animosity of some of the Federations towards him personally. For years he'd been unfairly and viciously pilloried by the media and the tennis establishment as a Dracula figure draining the lifeblood from the amateur game for selfish, mercenary ends. Wearily he decided that the future of Open tennis would best be served by his withdrawal from future negotiations, and for the next eight years he stayed true to his word. However, in 1966 he resurfaced.

During Wimbledon that year, Herman David and several other members of the Wimbledon committee dropped by the BBC tent to talk to Kramer who was commentating on the championships, and Bryan Cowgill, the BBC executive in charge of tennis. They expressed their frustration with the situation in which Wimbledon found itself. At what was arguably the world's most important tournament, audiences were being offered second-class tennis. What could be done to rectify this?

Cowgill came up with the idea of mounting an eight man trial professional tournament at Wimbledon the following year after the championships had finished. The BBC would put up the $35,000 singles prize money and Wimbledon, $10,000 doubles money. This would make it the largest prize money event ever. Jack Kramer was commissioned to recruit the eight players. Of course, he knew there'd be no problem attracting the top professionals, and the final line-up consisted of Gonzales, Laver, Rosewall, Segura, Gimeno, Buchholz, Sedgman and Hoad.

As we have seen, the crowds flocked to this trial event, and its success led to renewed pressure from England for a restructuring of the sport, a pressure that culminated in Wimbledon's decision to go it alone and stage the first Open Wimbledon the following year. The easy victory of Laver, the ex-pro, had also vindicated Kramer. With the future of Open tennis assured, the former pro tennis promoter was now free to assume an influential role in the restructuring of the game. His most significant initiative was to persuade the ILTF to adopt his idea for a Grand Prix format that would be linked worldwide, 'to a points system that would bring cohesion and understanding to the disjointed tournament circuit.'[3] Over thirty years later, the tennis circuit is still organised around Kramer's Grand Prix format.

Tragically, Lew was unable to take advantage of this new era in the history of tennis. The periods of remission from agonising back pain were now increasingly short-lived and infrequent. In 1970 he made a return visit to Wimbledon where he came up against the young Egyptian playboy, Ismail El Shafei, in the second round. Crowds queued to watch this Centre Court match between two good-looking muscle men described by one correspondent as the Robert Mitchum and Omar Sharif of tennis.

The match began inauspiciously on a wet and windy day. El Shafei, thirteen years younger than the 35-year-old Hoad, was no pushover. He'd already beaten Laver twice that year. Fleet of foot, with a vicious double-handed backhand, he took the first set 6-3, having broken Hoad's serve in the second game. Events seemed to conspire against Lew: the strong wind was affecting his ball toss and rhythm on the serve, but just when it looked as if he was getting back into the match in the second set, it started to drizzle and there was a twenty-five minute interruption. Back sufferers will tell you the worst conditions for a bad back are cold and damp; Hoad's back was no exception. When play resumed, it obviously took him some time to warm up again, and his problems were compounded by a spate of double faults, two of which occurred in the final game of the second set.

There was then a complete turnaround. Hoad broke the Egyptian's service for the first time in the opening game of the third set. 'As he did so,' wrote Lance Tingay in the *Telegraph*, 'he raised both hands high in a gesture of ironic triumph.' Eventually he took that set 6-4, recovering from 0-40 down on his own serve in the last game. Soon he was a service break up in the fourth, and the crowd, sensing an Australian revival, enthusiastically got behind Lew. However, at three all and El Shafei serving at deuce, there was a controversial incident that dominated sports headlines the following day. Hoad was aced by a serve which he was convinced had clipped the net. He questioned the net court judge who said the serve was good, and then asked El Shafei whether he'd heard a let. When the Egyptian said he hadn't, an irate Lew advanced on the net and accused him of lying. According to Lance Tingay, Lew reacted by wagging his finger at El Shafei, 'like an experienced schoolmaster, ticking off a sixth-form pupil who had let down the standards of his school.'

This was to be the only smirch on an unblemished record of good sportsmanship, but Lew's uncharacteristic action is partly explained by the fact that he believed El Shafei had turned round and was preparing to serve again, thereby tacitly acknowledging the serve was a let. Hoad was also incensed by a series of five or six net cords that he reckoned the official had already missed. He told the net court judge, 'Get your ears washed out.' Afterwards, the Tournament referee, Captain Mike Gibson, took a relaxed view of Lew's outburst, suggesting that he 'might have a quiet word with him over a drink some time.' Lew, on the other hand, whilst recognising the difficulties of officiating, made some sharp criticism of line judges. 'It's a thankless task. It's impossible to call the ball right all the time. But if a linesman realises he has made a mistake, he should have the guts to admit it – and none of them will do this.' In fairness to Hoad, it should be pointed out that he clearly believed the official was mistaken, and the crowd fully supported his protests.

Despite this setback, and some extraordinary bad luck in the last game of the fourth set when Lew was the victim of a doubtful line decision and a foot-fault call, he ran out a winner, 6-4. The match was now poised for him to achieve yet another incredible recovery from a two sets to love deficit. But it was not to be; he had nothing left in the locker to call upon. In the fifth set, El Shafei lost only one game to go through to the next round with a five-set victory.

When the authors of this book approached El Shafei recently to talk about the match, understandably perhaps, he had forgotten all about the controversy in the fourth set. All he remembered were mixed feelings of, 'joy, fear and resilience,' and the excitement of beating one of his teenage idols. 'I started the match playing very well,' he said, ' but he grew stronger each game, and I was almost cheering his great shots throughout the third and fourth sets. Fortunately for me, he ran out of steam in the fifth set and I finally won with a mix feeling of joy and sadness for a great champion trying for a comeback.'

Two years later, in 1972, Lew entered the Wimbledon singles for what was to be his swansong. He lost in the first round to a promising young German, Jurgen Fassbender, in four sets. Lithe and athletic, Fassbender was inspired by the occasional brilliance of the old champion, matching Hoad's imperious backhands with whipped forehand passes of his own. Lew had his chances: he took the first set 6-4 and was serving at 5-4 for a two sets to love lead, but two dipping returns that forced volleying errors from Lew, followed by a blistering cross-court forehand pass from Fassbender, enabled the German to level at five games all. Two games later he'd secured the set, 7-5. From then on his confidence grew, whilst Hoad's waned. Reporting for the *Times*, Geoffrey Green concluded:

Hoad's eyes burned bright but his muscles were stretched. There was no second wind and no turning the corner. The winning stroke at the third match point saw the German home with a fine running forehand pass down the line. Hoad smiled, bowed and patted his young conqueror. There was no fuss – just a longing searching look before he went, sadly.

That was enough for Lew. He never played singles again. Open tennis had just come too late for him. But he enjoyed the doubles until 1976, especially when he was playing with his friend, Abe Segal, the unpredictable and colourful giant from South Africa, who occupies such a prominent role in Gordon Forbes' memoirs. Big Abe, one of the great characters in tennis, stormed around the circuit alternately terrifying and fascinating officials and players. His feet always hurt and his extraordinary toes were a sight to behold. On his wedding night, the first thing he asked Heather, his beautiful bride, to do, was massage his feet. Life was always a chaotic whirligig for Abe. He had so many things running through his mind that he frequently forgot those small but essential matters, such as the food he'd put on to cook (with the ensuing fire in the kitchen), or the bath water he'd left running (causing the floor beneath to collapse).

At the Campo de Tenis, the tennis ranch that Lew and Jenny established in southern Spain, Abe once told a gathering of friends that he was travelling to London the next day, but had forgotten to book an hotel. Larry Hodgson's wife, Isabel, offered him the keys to their Wimbledon house. Jenny went white and rushed Isabel to the toilet, where she told her, 'Under no circumstances are you to give the keys to Abe. Your house won't be there when you get back.'

On another occasion, Lew and Abe were travelling together when their plane encountered severe air turbulence. Luggage fell from the lockers above, the drinks trolley careered down the aisle, and people began to scream as the plane bucked and skewed. Not surprisingly, Lew became very agitated. Abe, sitting next to the window, was humming quietly. Then he turned to Lew, stuck out his hefty paw and said, 'Goodbye Lew,' and calmly continued staring out of the window.

Although Big Abe was one of the most powerful hitters in the game, the ball never came off the centre of the racquet. Lew swore that if he ever did hit the ball off the sweet spot, it would travel right around the world and hit him on the back of the head!

Chapter 14

The Campo de Tenis: Tales of Old Andalucia

Throughout his years of semi-retirement, Lew's thoughts turned more and more to the idea of building a tennis club and devoting his time to coaching. He had no formal teaching himself, and his own style of play was not completely orthodox, but he could spot a fault or weakness in others immediately – and correct it. He'd done this with a number of players who joined Kramer's circus after him, and a few moments coaching from Hoad was valued like gold dust. Lew was no businessman, but he knew he was a good coach. Kramer said it was instinctive: 'He could spot what was wrong in three minutes and correct it in ten.'

A few days before he died, Lew became frustrated watching a coach working with a promising young player who just couldn't get the snap into his volleys. He struggled on court and said, 'Look, both of you, do it like this.' Within minutes, the young player was taking the balls in front of him and punching them away sharply and crisply.

Lew liked children, especially those of close friends. On them he lavished the love and attention that he felt his own children had sometimes been denied by the constant demands of his tennis career. One day he was talking to Larry Hodgson's daughter, Cristina, about her tennis progress. She told 'Uncle' Lew she was having trouble with her service. 'We'll soon sort that out, young lady,' he said, and having found a 'bat', led her onto the court. Within seconds he saw that when Cristina split her racquet hand and her ball hand for the toss-up, the movement in the ball hand projected the ball too far behind her. Sure enough, ten minutes later, the fault had been corrected.

Dressed as he was in thick check shirt, fawn trousers and brown brogues, he could easily have left it at that, but he stayed on court for nearly an hour, making sure the service was perfect and checking every other aspect of her game. Lew hadn't been on court for years, and when the news spread, everyone at the Campo crowded around the court to see the greatest tennis player of his time working with a skinny, long-legged kid. By now his shirt and trousers were sticking to him and his blond hair, wet with sweat, was falling into his eyes. His reward? Looks of admiration and an ice-cold beer.

Lew's original intention had been to open a tennis camp in Australia and put something back into tennis and the country he loved. He struggled to interest tennis officials in this project for about two years, but found them strangely indifferent. There were enough tennis facilities around, they said. Of course, he had been offered countless club and coaching jobs in America, where people like Newcombe and Laver were making a lot of money, but he wanted to be his own man and adopt his own casual lifestyle. If Australia didn't want him, he'd look elsewhere. In 1967, while Lew was playing in South Africa, Jenny took a holiday in Spain, looking at art galleries and museums. On the winding road that leads from the Costa del Sol's brash holiday resort, Fuengirola, to the quiet, whitewashed Moorish town of Mijas, she spied an old Andalucian farmhouse set in thirty acres of rolling farmland. It would make an ideal tennis camp. She phoned Lew to fly to Spain. As soon as he saw it, he agreed with Jenny; he knew if he could buy it, his dream of a tennis club could be realised.

'Mind you,' he told friends, 'it's gonna need a helluva lot of hard work.' The owner looked almost as old as the house itself; he'd existed for years by piling his onions, olives and peaches on the back of his donkey, and winding up and down the dirt road to barter for the essentials of life. He was happy to sell.

From Australia Lew brought in a long-time friend, Alan Watt, an engineer-cum-frustrated landscape gardener. Alan, Lew and Jenny then began to work on transforming the farmland into a tennis club, with Lew driving a tractor and carrying out manual tasks from dawn to dusk. It did little to improve his aching back but slowly the Campo de Tenis was taking shape. 'Lew was great when it was just a question of manual labour,' commented Jenny, 'but all fingers and thumbs where carpentry or more skilful building tasks were involved. He'd get his mates round for what would start out as a 'working party' but often end up a drinking party – or long siestas interspersed with bouts of frenetic activity.' Laughing, Jenny would say the Spanish attitude of *mañana* might have been invented for Lew. 'What the hell,' he'd respond, 'in this hot weather a bloke needs a beer or two to quench his thirst.'

Four thousand trees – many of them rare species from different parts of the world – were imported to shield the grounds from the blazing Spanish sun. Four Moorish lily-ponds were created to accommodate the Japanese koi carp that had been flown in. The exotic water lilies that graced these ponds lent an air of tranquillity, disturbed only by the croaking of frogs, whose bass chorus was one of the more unusual sounds to greet visitors. Alan Watt made the Campo a gardener's paradise with trees, flowers, orchids, jacaranda, white cacti, bougainvillaea, eucalyptus, palms and hundreds of local sweet-scented bushes and flowers. A fountain was built alongside a central swimming pool. The Andalucian farmhouse with its surrounding patio was converted into the clubhouse, bar and restaurants. In the outdoor one, which abutted the clubhouse, members could enjoy their meal shaded from the scorching sun by a bamboo veranda, partially covered by grape vines. Inside, photos of Lew in his prime, paintings (some by Jenny) and old tennis racquets adorned the walls.

Alan and Lew designed the eight courts of the complex on three levels. One, known as the stadium court, was modelled on a Roman amphitheatre that could actually seat two thousand spectators. To reduce maintenance costs, the courts were an all-weather surface, though the stadium court was deliberately laid with a slower surface than the others. This was because nearly all continental tournaments were played on red shale, so it was felt a slower court would provide better practice for European tournament players. Changing rooms, a tennis shop and boutique were added at a slightly later stage.

It only remained for local chefs and bar staff to be hired, and on 28th October 1971 the Lew Hoad Campo de Tenis was officially opened with prayers from the local Spanish priests. The opening ceremony was followed by a four-day tournament featuring Lew and Jenny, and Spanish stars Manuel Santana and Manuel Orantes.

The Campo had cost £85,000 and was, said Lew, 'A hell of a struggle. When we started there was no water, no plumbing, and no electricity.' Writing in the *Evening Standard* shortly after Lew's death, the harmonica virtuoso, Larry Adler, described the club as, 'Simply the most beautiful I've ever seen anywhere.' Few would disagree with his assessment.

It's not just the beautiful surroundings that make a visit to the Campo de Tenis such a memorable experience. Though the beauty of its setting and landscaping remain unsurpassed, there were many clubs with superior facilities, more luxurious clubhouses and accommodation. But these were clubs run on professional, commercially viable lines. Part of the Campo's charm lay in its delightful *amateurishness*. Never intended as a money-making operation, it's always been – like its creator – relaxed, laid-back, welcoming. Larry Adler described the club as 'so damned *friendly*. You are made to feel welcome, not because you're a customer but because the Hoad family likes people and they show it.'

The ethos of the club is essentially democratic: it makes no distinctions between people on the basis of wealth, class, or even tennis-playing ability. All of these qualities combine to produce a unique atmosphere that, even after Lew's death, draws visitors back to the Campo year after year. However, these were also the qualities that meant it was always going to be financially precarious.

In an interview with the authors, Hoad's long serving secretary-cum-assistant, Paloma Garcia-Verdugo, talked about Lew's overall philosophy regarding the club:

> 'Really, Lew wanted a friendly club with not too many people, who would all be his friends – from bar boys to Ambassadors and Government Ministers. He treated everyone exactly the same. And he did create a very special atmosphere. Do you know that some of the original waiters and bar staff started here as labourers when the club was being built. But they were so happy and treated like equals that they wanted to stay on in any capacity. But to have a club like that, where everyone was a friend and part of a family, requires a very great deal of money. And to turn the club into a big, crowded, money-making business didn't interest Lew at all. Sometimes the club made money. When it didn't, Lew dug into his own pocket.'

Lew admitted that if he'd hired an efficient business manager from the start, the Campo would have made a good living, but that wasn't his style. As Paloma observed, he wanted a friendly social club, where everyone could relax and enjoy themselves. Stars from the world of sport, music, film and other branches of the media, mingled with ordinary people from all over the world. The Australian and Spanish Davis Cup squads were regular visitors, using the tennis facilities by day, and relaxing (or partying!) by night. Tennis 'enfant terribles', Ilie Nastase, and Jimmy Connors dropped by, as well as Stan Smith, James Hunt (the World Motor-racing Champion) with his wife, Suzy, frequently hung out with Lew at the Campo. Film stars like Kirk Douglas, Stewart Granger and Sean Connery also stayed there, relishing its informality and the knowledge that prying cameras wouldn't disturb their privacy.

Another attractive feature of the club was the cosmopolitan make-up of its clientele. It's all too easy for clubs essentially designed for an expatriate community, to become insular and provincial. There was little danger of this at the Campo because it appealed to tennis players and fans from so many countries. Of course, English as the lingua franca fostered a lively exchange of different national viewpoints, but one could also hear a colourful *mélange* of accents, and languages, from Europe, America, Asia and Australasia. With visitors from all over the world, the Campo extended a warm welcome to people, regardless of their race, colour, or creed, and it remained an eloquent testament to the vision and personality of Lew Hoad.

One illustration of the democratic ethos Lew worked so hard to create at the Campo was the 'Mama Mia' tournament which started in the late '70s and continued until 1999. The tournament, held every September, was sponsored by Pietro, a colourful Italian. Pietro owned a string of 'Mama Mia' restaurants in towns up and down the Costa del Sol coastline, including one in nearby

Fuengirola. The 'Mama Mia' tournament was a popular week-long event that attracted a large entry of players of varying standards. It always finished with an evening meal provided by Pietro for all the competitors who were also given a 'Mama Mia' tee shirt and baseball cap. Lew and Jenny always attended the meal and tradition demanded that everyone had to wear the tee shirt and cap.

To begin with the prize money was only modest, but as the tournament grew in popularity it gradually rose to about £4,000. Inevitably, large prizes drew players of a much higher standard. At first Lew welcomed this development. Having top-class competitors attracted widespread interest and was good publicity for the Campo – and he liked watching good tennis. However, he soon began to notice a change in the atmosphere of the tournament. What he wanted to promote was a friendly, family event. But big prize money fostered cut-throat competition, and 'star' players were so fearful of injury they'd refuse to carry on if there was the slightest drop of rain. Then Lew would be called in to mediate in arguments about whether courts were fit for play.

The last straw was when the better players had to rush away to other tournaments, or were reluctant to attend the meal at the end of the week. Finally Lew told Pietro, 'Let's go back to small prizes and a tee shirt, cap, and free meal for everyone.'

When Sean Connery first settled in Estopona on the Costa del Sol coast and later bought a house in Marbella, he became a near neighbour of Lew's. He and Hoad had more in common than one might have expected. To begin with, Diane Cilento, Connery's first wife, was an Australian actress from Brisbane. Both Sean and Lew came from an impoverished background. Now, as well-known celebrities and outstanding performers in their own sphere, they enjoyed considerable wealth. They also shared a sporting interest – golf. The gruff, Scots actor had become passionately addicted to golf having learned to play for the 1964 movie, *Goldfinger*, and Lew was a natural at all ball games.

So the two men and their respective families became close friends. They would visit each other's homes, and their children, who were of similar ages, used to play together. When Lew and Jenny were visiting London for the Wimbledon Championships, they stayed at Connery's house in Putney. In 1973 Sean and Diane Cilento were divorced, and two years later he married a French-Moroccan painter, Micheline Roquebrone, who he'd met in a golf tournament in Casablanca. Over the course of the next twenty-five years, Micheline turned the house they purchased in Marbella into one of the most beautiful and stylish residences on the Costa del Sol. The friendship between the two families continued, with Jenny relishing the stimulating company of someone who shared her interest in art. Later, Lew and Jenny were to attend the wedding of Micheline's son, Stephan.

Manuel 'Manolo' Santana, the 1966 Wimbledon champion, couldn't believe his country's good fortune when Hoad decided to set up his Campo de Tenis in Spain. He immediately contacted him and asked him if he'd be prepared to coach and become non-playing captain of Spain's Davis Cup squad. He accepted the invitation, and Santana believes that the pre-eminence of Spanish tennis today is directly attributable to Lew's enthusiasm and coaching methods. Single-handed, Hoad turned Spain into a tennis-playing country, producing a series of Spanish champions in both men's and women's tennis, and encouraging such players as Carmen Perea, who was Spain's number one woman player at one time, and Anna Almansa, now the country's leading female coach. He coached Anna free of charge and his attitude was, 'I'll coach or play with anyone, from ten to seventy, so long as they are interested in tennis, and not just interested in saying they've had a hit with me.'

Santana first met Lew in Paris in 1962. He now has his own, very pretty club, the 'Manolo Santana Racquets Club' in the typical whitewashed Andalucian village of Istan, just outside Marbella, and only a few miles down the coast road from the Campo. It was there that he recalled his days with Lew.

'Of course, when we met we were world's apart. He was the glamorous idol, playing all over the world – tournaments and exhibitions – and I was just a humble Spanish player with some good results. But I was a very lucky man because my idol became my close friend.'

'In fact, he was 'my man', my coach, on and off, from 1965 to 1971.'

'I tried to emulate his game but I was not as strong. But he did wonders for my game, and for my confidence. He said, 'You can do it.' And I did.'

Santana remembers the time when Spain travelled to Australia to play against the Aussies in the Davis Cup final. 'I was so nervous playing in Australia against the world's best, and on grass. Believe me, grass is for cows, not for Spanish tennis players. I wondered if Lew would come out and hit with me for a 'leetle' bit. And you know what, he did; just like that. He worked on my game as a whole, and on my mind. Although Spain lost the tie, I played really well and, in one of the longest ever opening rubbers of a Davis Cup final, I just lost to Fred Stolle in a five-setter. Even against Emerson, the best player in the world at that time, I had another long match before going down 4-6, 6-4, 5-7, 15-17.'

It's not recorded what the Australian authorities made of their erstwhile 'Golden Boy' helping the Spanish No 1 – not, of course, that it would have mattered to Lew what they, or anyone else, thought.

Two years later, in 1967, Santana was unexpectedly beaten by George Goven, the French No 2, in the French Championships. Goven was ranked well below him, and on the slow red courts of Stade Roland Garros, so beloved of continental players and especially Spanish clay court experts, it was a sickening blow to Santana's morale. Almost immediately afterwards Spain was due to play France in the Davis Cup. Manolo phoned Lew who dropped everything and flew to join him. When Santana met Goven in the ensuing tie, he beat him so easily: 'I can't even remember the score.' Spain won the tie, 5-0.

When Lew and Jenny moved to Spain the partnership, and the friendship, was cemented. The two families frequently met up for meals and, refreshed by beers and wine, they would talk of tennis past, present and future.

Manolo recalled Lew's love of kids. 'It was well-known that if you were at a tournament and Lew wasn't to be found in the usual places, you just had to look where the kids, the juniors were playing.'

When the Campo de Tenis had established itself, Lew was appointed national and Davis Cup coach to Spain. He regularly travelled to Barcelona to train the players, and sometimes they would come to the Campo. Manuel Orantes, one of the most gifted Spanish players at that time, became a close friend of Lew's and spent two winters at the Campo under Lew's daily guidance. Orantes went on to win thirty-two career titles, the most important being the 1975 US Open. He was also a finalist on thirty-four occasions, including the French Open.

Paloma remembers helping out when the Spanish players came to train at the Campo. 'They were all so young and didn't speak a word of English. And, of course, Lew didn't speak Spanish. So I used to have to stand at the side of the court and shout Lew's instructions: 'Move your feet; bend your knees; turn your shoulder; swing like this; move your racquet this way or that way.' And so on.'

'Sometimes we'd fall about laughing. It was difficult for Lew to get across some fine point of tactics or style or some deep need to think about a certain situation. But he did it – and look at the results: Spain produced a crop of brilliant players who in turn became coaches, and now we have more players in the top 20 than any other country.'

'The young Spanish boys were lovely – and they just worshipped Lew.'

On a trip to Australia a few years after Lew's death, Santana was described as, 'The father of Spanish tennis,' by a newspaper. He was quoted as saying in reply: 'If I was the father of Spanish tennis, then Lew was the grandfather.' He was not, of course, referring to the difference in their ages.

There were other talented players at that time who benefited from Lew's help. The raw Guillermo Vilas was sent from Argentina for three months and Lew turned him into a champion who eventually notched up sixty-one singles titles, including four majors: the French and US in 1977, and the Australian in 1978 and 1979. John Lloyd, Stan Smith, Jimmy Connors, Abe Segal and Maria Bueno also worked out regularly at the Campo. All the Australians who passed through Europe during tournament time, dropped in to hit a few balls, and consume plenty of beers, with the man they idolised.

On one occasion Lew had a visit from the jazz-loving American tennis player, Vitas Gerulaitis. He was a close friend, and when Lew was in hospital in New York had visited him every day and personally looked after the Hoad family. Gerulaitis knew about suffering. He was a cocaine addict, and his addiction ruined his tennis life. Later, he became rehabilitated and went on to a successful career as a television commentator. Sadly, Gerulaitis was the tragic victim of a bizarre accident: he died from carbon monoxide poisoning from a defective heater in the house of a friend on Long Island, just a few weeks after Lew's own death.

Lew's first coaching commission had, in fact, come some time before construction work on the Campo had been completed. He received a letter from a Geoffrey Compton-Dando in England, who'd read an article in the *Evening Standard* about Lew setting up a tennis ranch in Spain. Compton-Dando's son, Ashley, was a promising Essex junior, and he wondered whether there was any chance of Lew giving his son some coaching. Ashley, he explained, had been profoundly deaf from birth, but was a proficient lip-reader. Lew replied immediately: he said he'd be happy to coach Ashley, and although the Campo was far from complete, they should come out immediately. At that time Lew and Jenny were renting a fisherman's cottage in Los Boliches, which was then a little village near Fuengirola. There were some public courts on the seafront at Los Boliches that could be used for coaching.

When the Compton-Dandos arrived, they were delighted to find that arrangements had been made for them to stay in two apartments overlooking the courts. For the next month Ashley had two coaching sessions, one in the morning and one late afternoon. Lew found the 14-year-old Ashley a receptive pupil, and eventually the teacher/pupil coaching relationship blossomed into a close and lasting friendship, with Lew acting as best man at Ashley's wedding.

Initially Lew was fascinated by Ashley's deafness: how was it possible for him to hit the ball so well when he couldn't hear? To help him get a sense of what it must be like for his pupil, Hoad put cotton wool in his ears for some of their practice sessions.

In a recent interview with the authors, Ashley Compton-Dando recalled how Lew's coaching, and the opportunities to practice at the Campo with some of the best players in the world, transformed his game:

'Lew was a wonderful man, and a wonderful coach. When coaching you, he was friendly but firm. Of course, as a player, his ground stroke production was unbelievable, and he's really responsible for me developing such a strong backhand. I used to make three or four trips a year, usually staying for about a month, and found that every time I returned from the Campo, I was winning important matches. After only a couple of visits I beat 'Buster' Mottram, 6-1, 6-4, in the quarter-finals of the Torquay Open junior tournament in 1969.'

The defeat of Mottram was a major upset. His father, Tony Mottram, was a former British No 1 and Davis Cup stalwart, and 'Buster' was regarded as one of the best young prospects around. In his heyday he achieved a world ranking of 14. The next day sports writers attributed Ashley's victory to his having 'spent Christmas at Lew Hoad's training camp in southern Spain.'

'From that moment on,' says Ashley, 'the popularity of the Campo grew, and it became a magnet for British juniors like Robin Drysdale [who later got to the quarter-finals of the Australian Open] and Stephen Warboys. They came down to Spain and formed a group, receiving instruction from Lew, and practising and training together.'

'One thing that really helped me, though, was when Lew became non-playing captain of the Spanish Davis Cup team. The team would often stay at the Campo and I was invited to practise with top-ranking players such as Manuel Orantes, Manolo Santana and Jose Higueras. And then there were other great players visiting the Campo – Stan Smith, Tom Gorman, Jimmy Connors. I remember having one fantastic doubles match when I partnered Orantes against Lew and Guillermo Vilas!'

'I developed a very close relationship with Lew that lasted right up until his death. On one occasion, when he was seriously ill in hospital with double pneumonia, only two people were allowed to visit him, and that was Jenny and me. And the day Sampras won the final at Wimbledon, I had a paging message; I was told to contact my father in Spain and when I phoned, I found that Lew had died an hour before. It was a tremendous blow.'

Ashley became a fine player: he represented Essex, winning their county championship three times, played on the satellite circuit, and eventually competed at Wimbledon. He is currently one of the leading players in veterans' leagues and tournaments in England.

Another illustration of Lew's selfless devotion to others concerns one of the coaches at the Campo, Floreal Manrique Sancho. Lew regarded him as the best children's coach he'd ever seen and even took him to Australia to show off his methods. Many of his pupils became Andalucian champions, but some years ago he suffered a stroke. After five weeks in hospital in a semi-coma, the terrible truth that he was paralysed down the right side of his body and had lost the power of speech, was broken to him – and to Lew.

For more than two years Lew looked after him, ordering, almost physically coercing him, to walk and talk. 'He forced me to rediscover life and was like a brother to me,' Floreal told friends. Until two weeks before his own death, Lew would massage Floreal's back, leg and right arm every day, stretching his dead limbs and pulling his clenched fingers, punching a racquet into them and ordering Sancho to move it. 'His hands talked to me,' he said. And slowly the body, and his vocal organs, started to respond to Hoad's treatment, so that today, although his speech is halting, he can still make himself understood.

As well as writing a book about recovering from his stroke, and another on how to teach children, Floreal is back on court and, with the aid of a ball machine, once again helping his beloved little ones from all over the area. 'It was Lew, the sheer power of him, that made me live again, while he knew he was dying.'

Close friends were not allowed to pay for anything when Lew was around. He was generous to a fault, constantly delving into his own pocket. He spent hours teaching the children of his friends how to make barbecues 'the Australian way' from the merest scratchings of wood, whilst Alan Watt refined their swimming technique. It was usually 'open house' at Lew's place and Larry Hodgson recalls many occasions when his family and Lew's would 'hang out' together. 'We'd read, talk, eat, drink and when we played tennis, he would be gentle and kind until he saw an opening he couldn't resist and then he would pound down a shot down like an express train, grinning and laughing as he did so.'

One day the Hodgson family were all invited up to the house and told there was a 'very special person' he wanted them to meet. Larry remembers how startled he was when Lew introduced him to a resplendent Prince of Wales.

'The Prince started a formal conversation, asking me about my interests and patting my wide-eyed children on the head. My Spanish wife, Isabel, almost fainted. As I tried to gather my wits, I saw Lew out of the corner of my eye, hands on hips, with tears of laughter running down his craggy face. The 'Prince', it turned out, was an actor who'd played the heir to the British Crown on American television. Having met the real Prince many times since in my job as Deputy Royal Liaison Officer for the BBC, I can assure you this man was his double, and good at it too. Lew thought it was the greatest prank ever. Those were happy, carefree, careless days. Two families just being together. The pain of financial and physical collapse were a long way off.'

An incident Larry will never forget was when Lew saved his life and that of his son, Matthew. It demonstrates Lew's ability to stay calm and relaxed in a crisis. Larry's wife had gone to North Africa and Jenny was also out of town for the day, so Lew decided to take Larry, and his two children, Matthew and Cristina, up into the mountains to a friend's house for lunch.

'As usual, we took a crate of beer with us, and as the afternoon lingered on my two children went to explore. Some time later, Cristina returned, ashen-faced, to say the dirt road they'd been walking on had given way, and Matthew had fallen into a ravine. I raced to the spot, and as I leaned forward to peer over, the edge of the road gave way again, and I found myself tumbling down to where Matthew was clinging desperately to a tree. I shouted up to Cristina to get 'Uncle' Lew, and off she scampered.'

'Soon Lew appeared with one hand clutching a huge garden hose wrapped around his waist, like a Mexican bandit. I wondered why he hadn't brought a rope, but I suppose he just grabbed the first thing that came to hand. I also thought that if the edge of the road were to give way again, and Lew came hurtling down like an oak tree with my daughter still clinging to his hand, this could turn into a major disaster. As these thoughts flashed through my mind, Lew tied the garden hose around a tree and lowered himself. Eventually Matthew and I were rescued, torn and bleeding.'

'When we got back to the house, Lew pushed us in a bath and said he needed medicinal alcohol to clean our wounds. All he could find was a bottle of cheap Spanish gin, which he poured over us. The smarting agony put me off gin for some time, and Matthew for life. He can't even look at a bottle now.'

'On her return to the friend's house, Jenny was able to see the funny side of our terrifying experience. Whilst my son and I stood in the bath, stark naked, she tried to suppress her giggles as she pulled out the splinters, spines and needles from our backsides. Her kindest comment about Lew, who stood there grinning, was that he was 'hopeless'. It was a chastened party that set off down the mountain to the Campo – and the inevitable confrontation with my wife.'

Just a couple of months before Lew died, there was the kind of bizarre incident at the Campo that he would have appreciated. David Williams, the club steward and general factotum, had a distress call from the office. Three young ladies had arrived to book into the Campo for a short May Bank Holiday break.

The booking had been made in the name of Soames, and staff thought there was something familiar about one of the women. She was an attractive blonde hiding behind a large pair of dark sunglasses. It seems the three women were complaining about the standard of their accommodation. When David Williams walked into the bar area, his jaw dropped. The 'familiar-looking' woman was none other than Princess Diana!

Apparently Diana and her bachelor girlfriends, Catherine Soames and Kate Menzies had decided on a short break somewhere in the sun. Hearing that the Campo de Tenis was a beautiful club near Fuengirola and Mijas, Catherine had made the flight and accommodation bookings under her name. So the Princess was travelling incognito; this was to be a quiet relaxing holiday free from intrusion by the paparazzi and there was no accompanying police bodyguard. Unfortunately, a crew from a satellite TV station happened to be on board the same jet as the Royal party, and they'd spotted Diana on the airport concourse, carrying tennis gear.

Williams realised immediately that the group couldn't possibly stay at the Campo. The apartments would not be the kind of five star, luxury accommodation they were used to, but more importantly, the club didn't possess the security arrangements to protect the most famous Princess in the world. There wasn't even a perimeter fence around the club – anyone could gain access.

As the *Daily Mail* gleefully reported, it was at this moment that George Guy, the charming hairdresser at the Campo, stepped forward. He suggested they transfer to a more exclusive establishment nearby which would respect their privacy and might be more appropriate:

> *With Mr Guy acting as chauffeur, the women and their luggage squeezed into his Ford Escort for the short drive to the Byblos Andaluz, a luxurious spa set amid two golf courses, five tennis courts and four pools...*

> *Yesterday, speaking with all the diplomacy of a man who has a concession at the Lew Hoad ranch, Mr Guy told how he had been leaving his salon when he literally walked into the Princess ... after driving to the Byblos, he told the Princess that nobody would believe him unless he could take 'a couple of snaps'.*

> *According to Mr Guy, Diana said he could have as many pictures as he liked, provided he came back to the hotel to take the three back to the airport on Monday.*

> *The deal was struck. 'She called me her knight in shining armour. I said I was more like a knight in a bright shining shirt.'* [1]

The Byblos, however, was unable to provide the privacy Diana craved. What she and George Guy didn't know was that an army of paparazzi was already descending on the luxury hotel. Some roamed the extensive grounds, others booked into the hotel. 'The Princess,' said the *Mail*, 'who prides herself on being able to sniff a camera from 200 yards, immediately cancelled plans to venture onto the tennis courts and retreated to the privacy of a sunlounger.'

Two Spanish cameramen managed to shoot photos of Diana from their hotel room which appeared to show her topless. The paparazzi's lair was uncovered and they were escorted off the property 'apparently without settling their bill. By Sunday, rumours of topless photos were circulating in Fleet Street.'

Newspaper reporters flocked to the Byblos, with Spain's best-known society journalist, the Marquesa de Varela, senior writer for *Hello!* also checking in. The conclusion to the holiday was reminiscent of a scene from a French farce. A posse of Spanish and British paparazzi had gathered at the hotel to trail Diana to the airport:

> *A huge convoy careered after her – once again in Mr Guy's Ford Escort. At least one driver tried to force Mr Guy to a halt during the 30-minute journey.*

> *At the airport, one cameraman leapt into a lift carrying Diana and her friends. Angry and shaken, she pushed him away and put a tennis racket in front of her face to frustrate the cameraman.*

> *For his pains, Mr Guy received a bruising kick to the shins.*

Whilst the whole affair would have amused Lew, it's also likely that he would have sympathised with the Princess remembering the way the press had constantly intruded upon his privacy when he and Jenny were in the spotlight.

Stories about Hoad and the Campo abound, and one that perfectly illustrates Lew's playful nature involves Salvador Gallardo and an infamous 'Moroccan Evening'. Salvador was trained in Switzerland as a waiter, chef, and restaurant and hotel manager. When he returned to Spain, he brought with him not only a culinary expertise and natural charm, but also the fierce 'hostier' professional code he had been taught in Switzerland. Nothing should be out of place or discredit him or his place of employment. After two years as a waiter at the Campo, Lew recognised his worth and though he was only 23, gave him the franchise for the Campo catering and bars. As Lew's club manager, he impressed everyone – friends, fellow workers, and guests – with his charm, dignity and professional integrity.

Novelty events and 'theme' nights were always being arranged by the club. Salvador prided himself on the professional way in which these events were organised and conducted. His reputation was at stake, and he was at pains to ensure that any entertainment arranged ran smoothly, and that everyone behaved with decorum and propriety. His professionalism was tested to the limit by the 'Moroccan Evening'.

For this event, a huge striped Arab tent had been erected on the Campo lawn. The waiters had their faces blackened and wore Arab dress and fezzes. Guests were asked to attend in European dinner jackets and ball-gowns. A Moroccan band was hired and, at the last moment, it was decided that a demure, Moroccan belly-dancer from a classic and reputable dancing school should be engaged to add authenticity to the proceedings. The very idea sent shivers down Salvador's spine. What embarrassing little practical joke had Lew dreamed up this time? Supposing this 'entertainment' turned into an embarrassing display of bad taste? How was he going to placate those guests, particularly the elderly ones, who would be offended by even a whiff of vulgarity? Was the evening about to degenerate into some kind of Bacchanalian orgy? One thing was certain: Lew wouldn't be losing any sleep over potential threats to his manager's *amour propre*.

Salvador's fears were well-founded. By accident (or design?) the girl who arrived was not a classically trained belly-dancer, but an Egyptian harlot. She supplemented her earnings, mostly at stag nights, by providing dancing that was outrageously suggestive, and customarily followed by service to the community in the bushes. Her red nails were almost as long as the thick black tresses hanging down her back. As the night wore on most of her skimpy costume was discarded until she danced adorned only by tassels on her well-endowed breasts, and a glistening g-string. As the drums drummed, and the horns blared, her twirling and gyrating got faster and faster. The tassels tasselled so furiously they seemed about to detach themselves from her nipples, and finally, with a triumphant flourish, the g-string was whipped away. The audience was dumbstruck. It was said that two particularly sensitive guests fled to seek sanctuary in the toilet for the rest of the evening.

Opinion was divided over whether Lew had been privy to the dancer's true vocation. Had he really known, or was it just an innocent mistake, a divertissement that went slightly wrong? Whatever the truth of the matter, an apparently incredulous Lew exclaimed, 'I can't frigging believe it.' Jenny summed-up the situation with an apt, 'Holy shit!'

Meanwhile, at the back of the tent, a distraught Salvador was rocking back and forth on his heels, crying, 'My reputation is in ruins. I am ruined on the whole Costa.' His distress produced the opposite effect on Lew who was having hysterics. Tears of laughter coursed down his craggy face, and then Jenny began giggling uncontrollably. Looking at them, the guests started to join in.

The Egyptian 'artiste', clearly accustomed to a very different reaction, regarded this merriment as an insult to her performance, and advanced menacingly upon the audience. With hair and tassels flying in every direction, and bare breasts wobbling alarmingly, she cast aside tables and chairs to launch herself at her tormentors. Her headlong charge was answered by a counter-movement from Salvador to defend his guests. Pandemonium ensued, and an international scandal seemed unavoidable. With the whole place now in turmoil, Salvador and the Egyptian girl were somehow kept apart. It was clear only skilful diplomacy could resolve the situation.

Eventually, after delicate negotiations, a large sum of pesetas changed hands, and the lady received the reward to which she felt entitled, by a handsome waiter, across a kitchen table – an arrangement that appeared to satisfy both parties. Salvador calmed down, although he looked as if he would like to murder those responsible for this outrage at the prestigious 'Campo de Tenis'. Lew and Jenny went home, shaking with mirth. For them it had been just another, typical night at the Campo. Another tale to tell from old Andalucia.

Chapter 15

Castle in the sky

Since her tour of Europe as a member of the Australian team in 1955, Jenny had taken every opportunity of buying paintings, antiques and bric-a-brac in places she and Lew visited. When, for example, they were in Paris for the French Championships, there always seemed to be some out-of-the-way little shop in Montmartre with a painting or ornament she 'just had to have'. Lew feared that each shopping trip spelt disaster for his bank balance. As an amateur he was on a tight budget, and had little money for luxuries, however much pleasure they gave Jenny.

By the time they moved to Spain in 1971, their financial situation was a good deal healthier. In spite of all the money spent on the Campo, Lew was a relatively wealthy man. He could afford to indulge Jenny's passion for antiques, paintings, carpets, china and other collectibles she purchased to adorn their large house overlooking the Campo. They loved this house but there were times when they both yearned to escape the hustle and bustle of the Campo and create a new home, a bolthole in a more isolated setting. Somewhere they could relax completely.

One Spring day Jenny came home late from a reconnaissance trip she'd made to the Gibraltar region of Andalucia in search of antiques. Though tired from a long journey, she was bubbling over with excitement and told Lew she had a surprise for him. Lew's heart sank. He still got a kick from Jenny's irrepressible enthusiasm and excitement, but talk of 'surprises' usually meant his wallet would soon be much lighter. He was told they were going on a long drive the following day so Lew should ask the Bar Manager to make up a picnic lunch.

All his efforts to extract further information about the surprise were in vain. There was nothing for it but to give in gracefully and accept defeat.

'Okay,' he drawled.

The next morning they set off early, driving along the coastal road towards the Cadiz province. Jenny still hadn't told Lew anything about the real purpose of their trip. The previous day, searching for antiques, she'd explored some of the many towns and castles dotted around the tip of southern Spain. Control of this region had shifted over centuries between Christians at one time, and Muslims at another. Many towns, like Jerez, Chiclan, Vejer, Castellar and Jimena, had the honorific title, 'de La Frontera' after their name. They were frontier garrisons, forming a defensive bulwark against either Muslims or Christians, depending on the period. Jenny had begun by looking at Jimena, and then set off on the road towards Castellar.

The old town of Castellar de La Frontera lies within the walls of a castle that historians believe was built by Muslims in the thirteenth century. It seems the castle must have been occupied prior to 1255, because that year it was captured by the Christians, only to be recaptured by the Muslims seven years later. In the course of the next one hundred and fifty years, it changed hands several times, and regularly suffered the privations of long sieges. It remained in picturesque isolation, cut off from the outside world right up until the 1960s when it was connected to telephone and electricity services, and the nearby Guadarranque reservoir was built.

It's unusual for a town to be built within the walls of a castle. In the nineteenth century, records show that there were seventy houses (about the same number as today) and a population of nearly two hundred. In 1963 its historical value was recognised when it was declared a 'National Monument of Historical and Artistic Importance'. This did little to compensate the ordinary townsfolk of the castle for the basic amenities they lacked; they wanted better schooling for their children, efficient health services, good shopping facilities, and better communications with the rest of Spain.

When the authorities offered them the chance of moving about eight kilometres to the new town of Castellar, close to the railway, few wanted to stay on top of the hill. As a result the castle was almost completely abandoned in the late '60s and early '70s.

Jenny knew nothing of this rich historical heritage as she drove into the new town. The sparkling white houses and spotlessly clean streets, which all seemed to intersect at right angles in a kind of grid-iron design, held little appeal for her. Traditionally Moorish in appearance, the buildings were attractive, but everything was so new that the town had a somewhat clinical atmosphere. She made enquiries about El Castillo and was directed along the road, past the cork factory, then up a steep, winding track to the old castle town.

After driving for about fifteen minutes along a road shaded by an avenue of trees on both sides, she suddenly emerged into dazzling sunlight, and there ahead of her, rising like a sentinel from the top of a steep hill, was El Castillo de Castellar. This was no Disney fairytale castle in the clouds; forbidding battlements and towers proclaimed its former practical and strategic importance. By this time it had been virtually abandoned, but it would not be many years before the castle housed a thriving community again, just as it had done for the previous seven centuries.

First, Jenny had to negotiate a tortuous, twisting road. There was barely room for one car, let alone two, and looking at the precipitous drop on one side, she reflected that this would not be a good road to drive on at night when you'd had too much to drink. On the side of the road leading up to the castle she passed caravans and ramshackle buildings. There were horses and donkeys tethered to some of the caravans; and people sitting outside who looked like gypsies, or hippies, smoking and drinking. They waved cheerily to Jenny.

Parking her car outside the castle walls, she walked around. Spread out before her were breathtaking views of the surrounding countryside. To the north, Jimena de La Frontera; to the east, the plains of the Guardiaro river; to the south, the Guadarranque river (and today, the azure blue water of the Guadarranque reservoir) with Algeciras in the distance; and to the west, Vejar de La Frontera.

Jenny later discovered another of Castillo de Castellar's attractions: it was situated on the edge of Los Alcornocales, one of Spain's largest natural parks. Home to the otter, mongoose, boar, roebuck and deer, Los Alcornocales' woodlands and forests are a paradise for buzzards, owls and eagles.

Already she was beginning to think this could be the perfect retreat for Lew and herself. But what she found when she walked around the castle gave her pause for thought. Almost all the houses were in a dilapidated condition: roofs had collapsed, walls needed rebuilding, and floors were thick with rotting vegetation, nurtured by the sun and rain that streamed from gaping holes above. In a few houses people were working hard to renovate and restore properties, but many had obviously been taken over by squatters. Jenny realised it would take an awful lot of work and money to make these properties habitable again, and even if you did, would there be much point if most of the town's residents were squatters? Nevertheless, exploring the maze of narrow, winding, cobbled streets that criss-crossed the small town, she could see how it might be transformed.

This was Jenny's surprise for Lew. Not a painting, nor an antique. As they reached the outskirts of Castellar, he'd begun to grow impatient. They had been driving for two hours. Surely Jenny's 'out-of-the-way' antique shop couldn't be much further?

When the castle sprang into view, the penny dropped. He guessed why she'd brought him all this way, and as he walked through the castle entrance, Lew's excitement matched Jenny's. He toured the town, stopping to peer into abandoned houses, even chatting enthusiastically with some squatters. 'Jenny, this place is amazing,' he exclaimed. 'One of these run-down properties has gotta be for sale.' The idea of a house in a Moorish fortress was irresistible.

Disappointingly though, when they contacted owners to enquire about purchasing a property, there was no response. Eighteen months later, having almost forgotten about their dream of living in El Castillo, they received a message from one of the owners. They couldn't believe their luck – the house they had singled out as the most desirable one in Castellar was for sale!

It occupied a commanding position in one of the main squares. Once the Guardia Civil Headquarters, it was now the largest residential property in the town. Its previous function probably accounts for the unusual triangular design. The house is arranged on two floors around a patio in the open space between the three sides. When the Hoads bought it, most of the roof had collapsed and the walls were in a pitiful state. An enormous amount of work was obviously going to be needed to restore the house, but if his back was okay, Lew enjoyed hard, manual labour.

Because of the steep, cobbled approach to the castle, and the narrow entrance, lorries were denied access. This meant that building materials often had to be ferried up to the house in a wheelbarrow. It took three long years, but the work was eventually completed and they moved into the house in 1980. Lew had required professional assistance for the more specialised jobs, but he'd largely carried out the task of restoration on his own.

The living room and bedroom are both on the first floor of one side of the triangle. Enormous oak beams run the length of the living room ceiling, which is decorated with beautiful paintings, sculptures and wall hangings, collected by Jenny over the years. On the ground floor is the refectory, a room dominated by a massive, antique table which seats over thirty people, and is sometimes used for banquets or wedding receptions.

On another side of the triangle are the guest bedrooms, which have now been turned into apartments for letting. The third side comprises the huge, medieval kitchen, portico, and the immense wooden and iron doors that overlook the cobbled square.

There is one particular feature of the house that Jenny delights in showing visitors. At the end of the living room, a few steps lead up to a small stone balcony. Standing out on the balcony at night, the atmosphere is magical and otherworldly. Above, there is nothing between you and thousands of stars twinkling in the canopy of the evening sky. Below, far away, one can see the lights of Gibraltar and Algeciras, and further still, pinpricks of light glimmer on the coast of Morocco.

Jenny and Lew would often escape to their Moorish fortress to be on their own, but they also loved entertaining friends and family in their new home. When it was very hot, the patio afforded some shade, and everyone would congregate there, drinking, reminiscing and setting the world to rights. In the winter they often retired to the large but welcoming kitchen, warmed by the huge, open fire at one end, on which you could spit-roast a suckling pig or a boar. And the room would resound with laughter as Lew regaled the company with his stories and wry humour. On one occasion a friend pointed to a huge pair of 's' shaped meat hooks hanging above the hearth. 'Whattcha got those for, Lew?' enquired the friend. Lew remembered Jenny picking up the hooks from an antique shop – or was it an abattoir? – on one of her shopping expeditions. 'Those hooks?' mused Lew. 'Those hooks? Waal, you see, later on, Jenny's goin' fishing to catch a couple of sharks for dinner, sport.' Having had rather too much to drink, his friend spent the next few hours looking forward to shark steaks for dinner.

Inspired perhaps by the Hoads' example, more and more people started moving into the town, and renovating properties. The tennis writer, Richard Evans, a long-standing friend of Lew and Jenny, was so impressed by their new home, and its setting, that he bought a house just a few doors away.

The town became a magnet for artists – there's now a little art gallery, a studio, and a craft shop. Touring musicians, singers, and flamenco groups often include Castellar on their itinerary. They usually perform on a floodlit stage in one of the squares, with the more intrepid members of the audience perched precariously on top of the battlements. El Castillo also has a restaurant which does a brisk trade, catering for locals and visitors. Recently, the ultimate seal of respectability was conferred on the town when the former Prime Minister of Spain, Felipe Gonzalez, acquired a weekend home there.

With houses lovingly restored, and flowers cascading from archways, bowers and hanging baskets, Castellar has transformed itself into one of the most picturesque towns in Spain, and become a popular tourist destination. Outside the castle walls an excellent exhibition centre documents changes in the town over the last two decades, and provides information on the Los Alcornocales natural park. One thing, however, remains the same; as an isolated derelict town, Castellar had attracted a migrant, hippie community. For them it provided the perfect location to – as one little guide rather quaintly put it – 'escape from the pressures of modern industrial life'. On the approach road to the castle, they congregated in makeshift buildings where a brisk trade in palliatives to those pressures took place. Beyond the pale of the castle walls, that trade continues to this day.

Chapter 16

Decline and Fall

Lew Hoad's years at the Campo were marked by financial, and later physical, decline. Even in the first few years there were disturbing signs of the financial problems that were to plague Lew, and the club. There were times, as Paloma Garcia-Verdugo pointed out, 'when the club made money; when it didn't, Lew dug into his own pocket.'

Unfortunately, the laid-back style of the Campo's owner – so instrumental in creating a friendly atmosphere – led swiftly to inefficient business practices and inadequate professional supervision. The club became a constant drain on Hoad's capital reserves. He'd earned a great deal of money with Kramer, but much of that had been sunk into purchasing the land, building the Campo, and installing the utilities.

There was nothing particularly extravagant about the Hoads' lifestyle. They didn't purchase expensive cars or luxury yachts, nor did they lavish money on huge parties. But they liked to entertain and, when it came to entertaining, Lew gave instructions that friends were either given substantial discounts or, sometimes, not charged for meals and drinks in the Campo restaurant, or at the bar. It wasn't long before this top-slicing of profits became a regular practice rather than something that only applied when the Hoads were having dinner parties or hosting larger events. There was nothing ostentatious about Lew's generosity, it was done quietly and discreetly, and continued till the day he died. Genuine friends were careful not to exploit it, but there were a few who would 'freeload' at Lew's expense, and his largesse gradually began to erode his savings.

Salvador, the brilliant, young, Swiss-trained Chef tried to explain to the puzzled owner that making a profit from the restaurant and bar was virtually impossible when so many people weren't billed for food and drink. When Peter Risdon, a friend who Lew invited over from England to sort out the club's finances in the early '80s, arrived at the Campo, the accounts he inherited from a couple to whom Lew had leased the club were in such a mess he didn't know where to begin.

Having purchased the land on which to develop the Campo, Lew thought one way of bringing in a regular income was to build apartment blocks adjacent to the tennis courts. This was an obvious step: visitors to the tennis club from abroad would like accommodation as close as possible to the club, and living 'on site' would encourage use of the bar, restaurant and other facilities. It also seemed a sound and safe investment that would provide a regular income after all the expenditure on the Campo. Of course, building the apartments required a substantial outlay initially, but Lew could relax and look forward to a healthy return on his investment.

There was a large stretch of land lying fallow on the left of the windy little road that leads from the Fuengirola/Mijas main road up past the courts to the clubhouse. The land was stepped in three or four tiers, and it seemed a perfect situation for a little whitewashed 'village' of apartments overlooking the tennis courts.

Lew originally intended managing the apartments on a time-share basis because he believed this was the best way of maximising his returns. After talking to friends, he had second thoughts. He was told he'd be responsible for the maintenance and upkeep of the arpartments. Whilst the owners of the time-share properties would pay maintenance charges, it would all need organising. 'Aw, stuff that!' was Lew's response, and he dropped the idea in favour of direct sales.

According to sources close to the Hoads, Lew was then introduced to an Englishman at the club who had experience of similar projects, and seemed to be just the right man to handle this development. He also clearly enjoyed the trappings of prosperity; he was a generous host and invited Lew to join him on his yacht at Gibraltar. Eventually it was agreed that this English entrepreneur would buy the land from Lew, build the apartments, and Lew would receive a cut on the sale of each apartment.

A lawyer friend introduced him to a local builder, and an architect was engaged to draw up plans. One, two and three bedroom apartments were to be built around a central swimming pool. However, what seemed like a sure-fire investment soon became dogged by problems. At an early stage, a well-known architect from England replaced the local one. Then there were rumoured to be problems with the mortgage that had been obtained for the construction of the apartments.

Worse was to follow. Sixty-one of the sixty-five apartments were constructed and sold when the Englishman suddenly vanished without trace – at a time when Lew had only received some of the purchase price of the land, and none of the money due to him from the sale of the apartments. The four unfinished apartments were seized by the bank in lieu of unpaid debts, and one was later sold to Jane Hoad at a discount.

If this financial venture failed to live up to expectations, the next was a disaster on a much larger scale. It all started with Jenny meeting someone she and Lew had known as a junior tennis player in Australia when they were 14-years-old. She remembered her as a precocious intellectual with a brilliant academic record. It was nice to come across someone she hadn't seen for so long and they reminisced about their experiences as junior tennis players. Over the course of the next couple of years they got to know each other better, and then one day Jenny's friend mentioned she was looking for someone who might be interested in a shopping mall project back in Australia, and Jenny asked for more details.

Eventually, the Hoads agreed to lend Jenny's friend a large sum of money. It was to be repaid with interest after two years. As usual with Lew, the deal was sealed with a handshake. Three times in the past he had loaned smaller amounts to friends to start up ventures. On each occasion the loan was agreed with a handshake. And each time the money had been repaid promptly.

Against his better judgement and the advice of friends, Lew sold fourteen flats he owned in Melbourne to fund the loan. It was a decision he soon regretted. The shopping mall venture was a disastrous failure. Legal constraints prevent the authors from going into details, but the Hoads clearly regarded the money as a personal loan, and as such Lew would be legally entitled to repayment. At no time did they consider it an investment where Lew's funds were 'at risk'. Nevertheless, he lost his money, and with it, his financial security. Worse still, given the property boom that later hit Melbourne, had Lew hung on to the flats he would have been a millionaire thrice over by the time of his death.

The Hoads retired to lick their wounds and count their losses.

Naturally, attempts were made to recover the money, with Lew and Jenny insisting they had papers which confirmed their view that it was regarded by both parties as a loan. Legal action, however, would have proved costly, and had they obtained a court judgement in their favour, they might have had difficulty enforcing it.

The experience left an indelible mark on Lew who felt he'd been exploited. 'Lew was devastated,' a distraught Jenny told friends. 'For the first time, he became quiet and disillusioned, not just because of the money he'd lost but because of the way it was done, and the way people involved had handled the situation. It showed the danger of not being business-wise. I really think it had an effect on his health.'

When the Hoads visited Australia for the medical tests that showed Lew was dying, they made repeated but unsuccessful attempts to contact (in person and by telephone) the woman to whom they had made the loan.

It's difficult to imagine that Lew could remain indifferent to financial problems of this magnitude but if he was worried about money, he rarely betrayed any sign of it in company. However, in the late '80s, friends and visitors to the Campo could hardly fail to register changes in his appearance. The 'Golden Boy' of tennis now had a paunch. The bronzed tan was replaced by a sallow complexion, the face was deeply lined and the brow furrowed. Nevertheless, his countenance was still occasionally lit up by that captivating smile, and the creased, lived-in appearance gave him a rakish attraction.

The extra inches around the waist could partly be explained by the onset of middle-age. More importantly though, he seemed to spend more time at the bar than on the tennis courts. It's true that in the '70s a more sedentary lifestyle was often forced upon him by agonising back pain, and a few beers may well have helped to deaden that pain. Had Lew's drinking become a matter for concern? Of course, he'd always had a reputation as a prodigious beer drinker, and the hot summers of the Costa del Sol did nothing to discourage this. But in the past he had been able to sweat off the beer on the tennis court or in the gym.

Jenny feels the fears of alcoholism were exaggerated. 'Lew enjoyed drinking,' she told friends, 'but he wasn't dependent on it. He could stop if he wanted to, or cut down – and he often did for periods. Also, he hardly ever drank spirits, it was always beer and it was social drinking. He liked to drink with his mates.'

By the early '90s there were major worries about Hoad's health. Since 1978 he had at least been free from back pain. Matters had come to a head in that year when Lew, bending to get into his car, felt an intense, stabbing pain at the bottom of his spine and had been unable to straighten. For the whole of that summer he was in agony and virtually unable to use his right leg, with the pain coursing down from the hip to the right knee; this was the same debilitating injury that had plagued him on the '58 tour with Gonzales. He spent a lot of time in bed or sitting on the floor with his back straight against the wall.

His eyes would light up when Larry Hodgson and his son, Matthew, used to visit him, because they could help him in and out of a hot bath. Larry recalls: 'It is no easy task, I can tell you, lowering and lifting the weight of an oak tree from a bath tub and I often wondered if my own back would stand the strain of it all.'

As the pain got worse it was clear that the one thing Lew feared most, surgery, would have to be contemplated. In September, Lew flew to the Cornell Institute at the New York City hospital to be examined by one of the world's leading neurosurgeons, the Canadian, Richard Fraser. After a fortnight of tests, Mr Fraser confirmed there was only one way out – surgery. And he spelled out that it would be an extremely dangerous operation. The bottom part of his spine was a complete mess. Throughout all the years, nobody had told Lew that he had two slipped disks with a hernia resting on one of them.

Within two hours of the operation, Lew was walking again, helped by nurses. He returned to Spain an inch shorter than when he left – but the nightmare of pain was finally over. If only he'd had this operation some twenty years earlier, before being matched in the head-to-head series with Gonzales. Back in New York, Richard Fraser asked a friend of Lew's, 'How on earth did this man walk, let alone play tennis?'

It was fifteen years later, in November 1993, that Jenny again became concerned about Lew's health. She insisted he visit Dr Nieto, the family doctor in Fuengirola, to have a check-up. In an interview with Larry Hodgson shortly after Lew died, Jenny described the outcome of this check-up.

'Dr Nieto took some tests and said Lew's liver needed treatment and recommended a course of injections, which he had. The doctor also noted that Lew's blood count was wrong, but Lew never mentioned this to me or anyone else. I knew something was wrong but couldn't put my finger on it – and I think Lew sensed it too. In January 1994, when we went to Adelaide, I told the friends we were staying with that I was worried about him, and they recommended a GP. She checked Lew thoroughly and after doing some tests, suggested he see a specialist. When he saw the specialist, he was given a bone-marrow test. I remember him lying on his side while the test was being done and looking cheerful. The specialist told him to come back in three days for the results.'

'After sitting in the waiting room with people who were obviously very ill, we were taken into a tiny room where the specialist spoke at length, explaining the kind of illness, that it wasn't good but there could be hope with bone marrow transplants etc. He never took his eyes off *my* face, and it slowly dawned on me that he was giving us dreadful news in a gradual way. He wanted me to stay calm in order to help Lew.'

'I could feel myself going numb and had to leave the room. I decided to ring a wonderful old friend of mine in Melbourne, Sister Mary Fabian – she always knew what to do in an emergency (she was with me when both Jane and Sally were born). 'Come and talk to me,' she said. When we left the clinic, I walked slightly ahead of Lew as I didn't want him to see my face. After a while I waited beside a tree until he joined me. I held him gently in my arms for a long time. Then he said, 'Let's go and have a nice, cold beer.' There was a seedy-looking pub on the corner, but this wasn't the time to be concerned with appearances or even safety – 'Great idea,' I said. We had a couple of drinks and then called in to see Lew's solicitor, a good friend, who was giving Lew some advice. 'Better hold on that,' said Lew. 'My future looks uncertain.''

'That evening I rang Manu (Dr Manuel Benavides, Sally's husband and a renowned blood specialist) and told him what the specialist had said. Manu said that when we got back to Spain he would look after Lew.'

It was with his old friend, Abe Segal, that Lew played his last tennis. In the summer of 1993, Lew decided he'd try and get in shape to play a few veterans' tournaments. He knew he was seriously ill, but thought there was an outside chance of his making some money to shore up his finances and provide for his family. He would make one last stand. Lew and Abe hit for ten minutes and then rested for ten. The routine lasted for about fifty minutes as people gathered to watch the man who had once been the best player in the world. Joe Stahl said, 'For one last time, the magic came back. It was the most beautiful tennis I have ever seen.' Several people were close to tears – everyone knew that Lew would never make it to the veterans' tournaments. After the practice with Abe, Lew knew it too. His stamina was gone.

When Lew died it was variously reported that he had had a heart attack or had been awaiting a life-saving bone marrow transplant. Neither of these explanations is correct. Dr Manuel Benavides subsequently revealed that Lew had contracted a rare form of leukaemia known as Mylelodisplastic syndrome for which there was no cure.

When Peter Hoad was asked if his father had suffered much, he replied, 'You know Dad, he never said a word.'

*　*　*

Paul McNamee idolised Lew Hoad. From next to nothing, Lew, in his view, had become the greatest tennis player ever, bewildering his opponents with the variety of his stroke-play and demolishing them with his power. His personality had dominated Australian tennis. Yet, off court, he was a humble, sincere man who had extended his limited formal education through travelling, wide reading and conversation. It was this that drew people to him and to the game of lawn tennis.

When he had seen how ill Lew was, Paul decided, with the help of the ATP, to promote a testimonial tournament at the Campo de Tenis to ease Hoad's financial problems. Lew's old friends readily agreed to participate. From Australia came Ken Rosewall, Rod Laver, Fred Stolle, Paul himself and his great doubles partner Peter McNamara, Bob Carmichael, Trevor and Charlie Fancutt. From Britain, Roger Taylor and Buster Mottram. From the USA, Butch Buchholz. And from Spain, Manolo Santana and Manuel Orantes.

When Lew died on the last day of Wimbledon, some started to head back home thinking the tournament would be cancelled, but Paul quickly recalled them. The tournament would become a tribute to Lew Hoad. Rod Laver had flown all the way to his home in California when he got a message about the rescheduled event from Daphne Fancutt. Without unpacking, he flew across America to Miami, then on to Madrid and finally to Malaga, to make sure he was on time. The Australian Ambassador also flew in from Madrid. The fabulous Los Monteros Hotel and Country Club, where Lew had once coached when he first came to Spain, gave the players and their families free room and board. Salvador brought in extra people and worked like a slave as people from all over the world crowded into the Campo to be with the Hoad family. The dining area was extended around the central swimming pool and every night, under the stars, Salvador laid on a lavish banquet for the players and guests. Although they were weighed down by grief, each member of the Hoad family tried to make sure people were happy, and felt at home. Bravest of all was Jenny. For the duration of the tournament she would have to put aside her sadness, compose herself and walk to the centre box on the decorated stadium court to join the guests in watching the evening's play.

The tournament was, inevitably, an event touched by sadness and regret, but there were plenty of light-hearted moments, as befitted a memorial to Lew. Somehow the participants felt that he would prefer to be remembered with laughter and merriment. Players pushed each other into the pool after a night's roistering. There was singing, and a flamenco show. During the day the tennis stars held clinics for children, or joined in pro-am tournaments with the local players. There was golf, and drinking bouts, and jokes. And each evening, as the night wore on, it seemed the conversation always returned to the same topic: Lew, and his exploits on and off the court.

Paul McNamee and his wife, Lesley, organised this tournament at the Campo which became such an extraordinary tribute. Paul's simple comment on his hero was: 'Lew was a credit to the human race.' The matches that week were played in an exhibition atmosphere, the players delighting the crowds with the wizardry of their shots. Sometimes, in celebration of Lew's drinking exploits, the tennis stars drank beer at the changeovers.

One day, McNamee and McNamara – the two 'Macaas', once the best doubles team in the world – teamed up against the British boys, Roger Taylor and Buster Mottram. Taylor and Mottram decided to go for broke and put these Aussie legends in their place. The play became deadly serious, and the spectators were astonished by the quality of tennis. When the 'Macaas' won, Larry Hodgson, taking over as Master of Ceremonies from Richard Evans who was on duty elsewhere, jokingly announced they had been lucky to beat the British pair. McNamee, in mock outrage, began to throttle Larry on court.

On the final day, Peter Hoad teamed up with Ken Rosewall to form for the last time, a Hoad-Rosewall partnership. This must have been a heart-rending experience for Peter, but somehow he found the courage to go through with it.

Then Jenny came on court to a standing ovation and gave every player a prize and a silver dish with the simple inscription, 'In memory of, and with love from, Lew Hoad.' For the final day of the event there were blue skies, and warm sunshine.

Larry Hodgson, who was responsible for presiding over the last day's play and the presentations on court, as well as organising the Service of Tribute to be held that night, now takes over the story.

'I was in a sweat with all these duties to carry out. The Campo was a hive of activity and emotions were rising. As hundreds packed the grounds and gardens, Salvador and his team from the bar struggled to erect a platform for the Service. Sound systems had to be installed, and speakers and musicians rehearsed and briefed. A large palm tree, which was to be planted as a memorial to Lew, had arrived and the gardeners toiled to dig a hole in the lawn for its resting place. The Hoads' chief assistant, Paloma, had to arrange thousands of flowers, and organise transport to rush a Priest from nearby Fuengirola after his last Mass of the day, to the Campo to give a final Blessing. No occasion in Spain is complete without a Priest.'

'Little Lucy Hoad, the first of Lew's eight grandchildren, had become my assistant and her big brown eyes dilated as the preparations around the Campo became ever more frenetic, with me rushing around, conscious I still hadn't written anything for my speech that night. In the midst of all this, a tall, lugubrious figure, dressed entirely in black, approached Jenny with a black plastic bag. Jenny, who'd turned very pale, came to me and said, 'I can't handle this.' The man in black was an undertaker with Lew's ashes. He bowed. 'Senor Lew's ashes,' he announced solemnly. I was aghast. Lew in a plastic bag! My distress communicated itself to the man in black and we looked at each other in mutual horror. Eventually he produced an ornate pot from the black plastic bag, and insisted that I open it and verify there were ashes inside. In a trance, I obeyed. I signed countless papers. He bowed and left. I then had to find a few minutes to compose myself and plan what I was going to say about Lew that night. There was so much to say, so much to recall, it wasn't easy.'

'I crept away to where Lew's palm tree had been placed in a deep hole, next to a mound of earth which would be used to fill it in later. The tree had been washed in milk, a traditional Spanish custom to clean and add lustre to the thick, dark leaves and fronds. I sat on the grass beside it, sweating and panicking, scribbling down words, when suddenly the tree lurched over on its side. I jumped into the hole and heaved and pushed it upright. However, moments later it keeled over a second time. Once more, I repositioned it, only for it to happen again. I was concerned the tree was going to be badly damaged. Already leaves and fronds were scattered around the hole. It obviously needed support.'

'I began to lug boulders from the Campo gardens to the hole, to hold the base of the tree in place. What with the heat and my exertions, I suddenly felt as if I was going to have a heart attack and be found dead in the hole next to Lew's tree. Well, it would be quite a convenient place to die, all things considered, two funerals for the price of one. I took a few deep breaths and carried on hauling rocks across to this damn hole. Eventually, I got the tree to stay upright.'

'Hundreds of people had gathered on the lawns for this final service. The Hoad family sat to the right of me, calm and quiet, with the grandchildren at their feet. The assembled speakers and musicians sat pensively at my back as the Campo's resident pianist, Syd Wright, played Lew's favourite music, and his wife, Dot, waited for my cues. One chair remained empty. Where was Ken Rosewall, the principal speaker? He'd been the last player on court. I left the assembly and dashed over to the locker room to see if he'd finished changing. As I entered, Ken was carefully parting his hair. He looked at me in the mirror, and seeing the look of frustration and exasperation on my face, hastily grabbed his jacket. As we walked across the lawns to the stage, I noticed Ken hadn't quite finished combing his hair, and a tuft at the back of his head was sticking up. He reminded me – as he did so many people – of a wistful Stan Laurel, and he looked so downcast my heart went out to him.'

'The time had come for me to address the assembled gathering. I spoke about Lew as I knew him, a shy and modest man, and about how I knew he remained here as long as he was always in our hearts. I left Ken to speak of the tennis player. But the task was almost impossible for him, and after a few minutes he broke down and said: 'I can't say any more.' It was left to John Barrett, who had flown in that day to represent the All England Club, to finish the tribute. Then we listened to a beautiful violin solo from Don Carney, an Australian tennis veteran who was also a talented musician, followed by some pieces for the classical guitar by Francisco Doblas, a famous Spanish guitarist and friend of the family. I saw that my wife, Salvador, Paul McNamee and Roger Taylor were in tears, as were many others. The Australian Ambassador, Warwick Pearson, concluded the tributes by reading a personal letter from Paul Keating, the Australian Prime Minister, that summed up the feelings of so many Australians, and admirers of Lew from around the world:

> *Lew Hoad remains an Australian legend. Not just because he was a great tennis player, and not just because his determination and his capacity to build on his gifts brought him from humble circumstances into the highest ranks of society.*

> *He always projected an Australian style on the most famous courts of the world – good humoured, polite, unaffected, and gracious in the most natural way. In fact, Lew did not just project that style, he largely defined it. His*

approach to the world is one which many Australians are proud to take as their model, even today.

'As darkness fell, candles were lit and there was a perfect moon and a single star in the sky. The Spanish priest spoke of 'Brother Loo' and blessed him, the tree and the crowd. Prayers from Saint Francis of Assisi, and the Lord's Prayer were said in English and Spanish. Then Jenny took my arm, and we led the family to the earth mound next to the tree and the hole. We scooped up handfuls of soil and scattered them round the tree's roots. Jenny invited everyone to do the same and a long, silent file formed. Some used silver trowels, some their hands.'

'At each side of the tree, Lew's gardeners stood, hands crossed over the handles of their long, traditional tilling spades, waiting to fill in the hole. They looked straight ahead, grim, like Knights of old Castille. When everyone had gone they were to water the tree, and the entire lawns and gardens.'

That night their services were hardly needed. That night the Lew Hoad Campo de Tenis was watered with tears.

Chapter 17

Thanks for the memory

When Hoad's death was announced, tributes poured in from around the world. Many commented on the irony that his passing should coincide with the crowning of Sampras as the Wimbledon singles champion for the second year running. In all of them, whether they were close friends, acquaintances, or fans who'd never spoken to Lew, sadness was mixed with admiration and affection. And in the press, leading sportswriters paid tribute to his warmth and generosity, and his contribution to the game.

In his *Guardian* obituary, Frank Keating, like so many others, celebrated his sportsmanship and his tennis prowess, as well as his legendary reputation as a beer drinker:

> *Hoad in his prime was contemptuous of caution, nervousness, or any mannerisms remotely connected with gamesmanship, meanness, or tricky endeavour. He had the wolfish grin of a Miller, or a Botham and although when in the mood, and in trim, he also had the wolfish competitiveness, losing seldom hurt if it happened dead on opening time. As the always colourfully apt Rex Bellamy of the Times, who was closest to the players of his time, remarked one day, 'When it came to hitting the grog, Lew was also a world champion, even by Australian champion's standards. He drunk enough beer to irrigate the Nullabar Plain.'*

Keating went on to recall an exchange between Lew and Ian Chappell, the former Australian cricket captain, that nicely captures Hoad's impish sense of humour. Chappell, who was working on television at the time, asked if he could interview him, not about tennis but about the Pamplona bull run, which he felt Hoad, as an exile in Spain, might know something about:

> *Hoad looked at Chappell, and his eyebrows popped up quizzically. 'Are you looking to run with the bulls next week, boy?' Chappell said, 'Yes, and they are going to film me, any advice?' Lew looked his squat and cocksure little cricketing compatriot up and down again – and then laconically advised,*

'Well, boy, if you're running the bulls for the first time, make sure you have a bloody good crap beforehand.' He loved Spain.

He said he had no regrets. 'We had fun. These millionaires now don't know the meaning of the word 'fun', do they? When I played Davis Cup for the first time – and we won in front of 25,000 people – I was given £5 for the week's expenses. But I had a fantastic life. I was only sorry in a way that I had to turn pro – but you can't eat silver cups, can you?' And he laughed, and the fair hair bobbed around just like it used to three decades before when the wrist-whip and top-spin not only hit tennis balls, but hurt them. The only things, mark you, that Lew Hoad ever hurt in his life. His generosity was genial, and so was his immense talent. And his sportsmanship.

Richard Evans, in the *Sunday Times*, wrote of Hoad's hatred of adulation, how he'd prefer to 'hit on an outside court away from the gaze of spectators on the [Campo's] terrace.' Evans points out that in their quest for greater privacy and seclusion, Lew and Jenny retreated even further into the hills of Andalusia, to their house at Castellar:

Jenny brought furniture over from Morocco and turned it into a home of extraordinary originality. I sensed Hoad was happiest here, unbothered and un-noticed, far from the madding crowd, a taciturn Aussie wedded to the splendour of Spain.

At night, the silence around Castellar was broken only by the sound of goat bells and faint echoes of a million tennis balls, hit with such awesome power all those years before.

In *Tennis Week,* Bud Collins celebrated the comradeship of Hoad's generation of Aussie players, rounding off his eulogy on a lyrical note:

Hoady lived as he pleased, a carefree natural of no pretentions. His was the rollicking outlook of the down-to-earth Aussies in their galactic days. They'd drink beer with anybody and beat the world the next day. Their intake of brew and titles was prodigious.

They were the Carthaginians of tennis, vanished conquerors, and their beloved Hannibal is dead.

Jenny was touched by the messages of sympathy, condolence, and appreciation that flooded in from all parts of the world. Many were from well-known tennis players, others from members of the tennis club at the Campo, or people who'd stayed there, yet others from fans, well-wishers, or people who'd had first hand experience of Lew's kindness and generosity. They helped, in some measure, to ease the pain of bereavement for Jenny.

A top American player, Bob Lutz, who – like so many others – had been drawn to tennis by Lew, wrote about the time Hoad was in America, playing a Californian, Ed Atkinson, a man with a tremendous service. During the warm-up, Atkinson thought he'd try to intimidate his opponent by showing him how hard he could hit his serve. He crashed down a serve with all the might and power he could muster. Lew caught it off the bounce with his left hand and said, 'Ready to play mate?'

Bob Lutz commented, 'Well that was it for Atkinson. He was so totally deflated he didn't even remember the match, except that it went very quickly.' Lutz, whose physique was similar to Lew's and was something of a power player himself, was competing in the US Open one year when Lew paid a visit. Hoad hadn't played in ages, but Lutz was looking for a hit and Hoad said he would give him one. Lutz went on, 'I was just amazed at how cleanly he hit the ball and with so little effort. It really seemed that I was doing all the work.' Lew always said tennis was a walking game. When incredulous listeners queried this, he'd explain, 'Well, the secret is to make your opponent run for the ball, while you walk.' Exactly how you put this advice into practice is another matter – but the thinking behind it is sound.

Fred Perry took the time to pen a short note to Jenny: 'Lew was a great player and a credit to the game. To me he was a special and valued friend. The many happy times we spent together will always be remembered.' In Australia's *Sunday Sun*, Perry declared, 'The game has lost someone and something that really mattered.'

From the world of cricket, Richie Benaud said, 'sadness and shock must be the two things associated with someone's passing, but very high on the list with Lew must also be the pleasure of having known him. There have been a lot of good sportsmen in Australia, some very good ones, and a handful of greats. Lew was one of the greats, not solely because of his deeds, which were legendary but because, while he was with us, no-one had a bad word to say about him. That is the ultimate test.'

When friends reminisce about Lew, the conversation returns again and again to his kindness, generosity, and mischievous humour. Philip Barnatt, a frequent visitor to the Campo, recalled these qualities which, he said, 'became more and more apparent the more you got to know him.'

'I remember even in April, [1994] when he must have already been suffering greatly, he was still helping out others who were sick or had fallen on hard times. For a tennis player like myself, he was also the best possible role model, with lovely wit and humour. This seemed to come to the fore on a rainy day at the Campo. Lew would stand at the bar with that quizzical look on his face and a twinkle in his eye, ready for discussion. I kept a diary of my days at the Campo with many anecdotes. One involved an intense discussion between a few of us over the likely winner of the Wimbledon singles in 1994, the year Lew died. One of the club regulars,

'Chinese' Hans, opted for Thomas Muster. Lew gave him a kind but pitying look. 'But he can only play on clay.'

'Yes Lew, but you say you should be able to play anywhere.'

'Exactly, Hans, and he can't. Thomas Muster has as much chance of winning Wimbledon as my daughter's dog.'

'I'll bet you Lew, what odds?'

Quick as a flash came the reply, 'Any f***ing odds.'

A figure was agreed, followed by a long pause. Then came that familiar drawl. 'D'you wanna give me the money now?'

[Muster subsequently withdrew from the 1994 and 1995 men's singles]

Hoad was always giving away clothes as mementos to his friends. One grateful recipient was Joe Stahl, the lawyer from New Orleans: 'I was staying at the Campo and noticed Lew wearing the kind of impossibly smart beige windbreaker that made me crazy to have one like it. It was a trim, snappy-looking thing, rakishly bristling with little zip pockets here and flap pockets there. One pocket, at chest level, even had a little window above it for the insertion of a name tag. I interrogated Lew. 'Whose design is that? Where'd you get it?'

'We've sold them in the boutique here at the club.'

'I've got to have one!'

'They're out of them right now.'

'To make a long story short, Lew swore that he was tired of his, took it off and gave it to me. I was thrilled but I felt like a criminal, taking the clothes off his back, although he made it clear that he didn't want it anyway. I put it on, delighted. Suddenly Lew's eyes opened wide and he exclaimed, 'Wait a minute! I forgot something!' and he took out a pen and began writing on a little piece of paper. When he finished, he inserted the paper into the jacket's breast pocket window. I didn't bother to look at it just then, figuring it was just a little 'to Joe from Lew' sort of note, an impression reinforced by the smiles of appreciation that spread over the faces of everyone who scanned it. That night, in my flat, I took off the jacket and read Lew's inscription. It said, 'My name is Joe Stahl. I'm lost.' I have it still.'

One of the most eloquent tributes to Hoad came, predictably, from Gordon Forbes. In *Too Soon to Panic*, a companion work to his earlier book, *A Handful of Summers*, he writes about one of Lew's favourite haunts when he visited Wimbledon – the Last Eight Club. Members of this exclusive club (to be eligible you must have reached the quarter-final stage of a Wimbledon event) meet in a marquee close to Court 17. The atmosphere is convivial; the surroundings are comfortable, there's a bar, and food is served. It is a place where players and their friends can relax and unwind, reminisce about the 'old days', and discuss the merits – or drawbacks – of the contemporary game. For Forbes, it is 'impossible to think of the Last Eight Club without thinking of Lewis Hoad':

> *Lew died in July 1994 and with him died a part of all those who played tennis in his time. He loved the Last Eight Club. Even though he had won Wimbledon twice... and was welcomed in the inner sanctuaries of the All England Club as an honoured member, he always chose to base himself near the little bar. I can see him now, beer-mug in hand, with one eye on the tennis and the other half-closed against the smoke of a cigarette – on his face the quizzical, half-surprised frown he used to wear nearly all the time. He liked to have a friend beside him, but there did not have to be a conversation. In his later years he had a beat-up look, as though he had been ravaged by a life which had somehow seemed to puzzle him – a life in which the most lovely rose-garden always beckoned – but one to which he never really found the door. ('Shut up, Forbsey!' I can hear him growl.)*

> *But a few more words must be said. Lew played as an amateur for only a few years, but while he played he was invincible – a quiet man who never spoke a word about himself, who never complained, who scorned cheating, who respected the game he loved and the people who tried their best to play it; who was able to play, without fuss or effort, the most harmonious, majestic and creative tennis of all time.[1]*

Forbes' assessment of Hoad inevitably raises the question of his ranking in comparison with other great players. It's the kind of question that's applied to all sports and is guaranteed to provoke heated debates in bars all over the world. Who's the greatest ever athlete/footballer/baseball player/cricketer etc? Ultimately, of course, there can be no definitive answer; so many variables have to be taken into account. In tennis, some of the factors one has to consider are:

- the quality of the opposition faced;
- the respective ages of the contenders for the 'greatest ever' title and their contemporary rivals;
- changes to the rules and improvements in equipment (racquet technology, for example) that make such comparisons difficult if not impossible;
- the different surfaces on which the game is played, with only one Grand Slam tournament (Wimbledon) now being played on grass.

An additional problem with tennis is the separation of amateurs and professionals up to 1968. Where should one place legendary figures like Gonzales and Segura who turned pro before they could win many major titles in the amateur game? Acknowledging all these difficulties, the veteran broadcaster, Max Robertson, boldly offered his own league table of the greatest post-war tennis players in his book, *Wimbledon 1877-1977*. One needs to point out that the publication date of the first edition of the book (1977) precluded a consideration of the later achievements of Bjorn Borg, John McEnroe and the career records (to date) of Agassi and Sampras. Robertson's ranking is as follows: 1. Hoad; 2. Gonzales; 3. Laver; 4. Borg; 5. Kramer; 6. Sedgman; 7. Rosewall; 8. Trabert; 9. Newcombe; 10. McEnroe; 11. Connors; 12. Emerson.

Whilst the authors of this biography are naturally sympathetic to a rank order that places Hoad first, there are clearly problems with this and other selections (Trabert above McEnroe?). Nevertheless, for a period, albeit a brief one, it was undoubtedly the case that Hoad bestrode the tennis world like a colossus. Most expert observers of the game would agree that Hoad – on his day – would have beaten any other player in the world, past or present.

Perhaps the best solution to this contentious (and ultimately irresolvable!) ranking problem is that offered by Frew McMillan, who certainly qualifies as one of the best doubles players of all time, and is now a highly respected tennis commentator. In 1996, he was commentating with Christine Jaynes for BBC Radio Wimbledon on a Sampras match. At a changeover of ends, Jaynes asked him whether Pete Sampras wasn't the most complete player he'd ever seen. There was a pause; then Frew replied, 'Well, he's certainly up there with the greats, but no – I'd have to say the most complete player I've ever seen was Lew Hoad.'

In assessing Hoad, this is a viewpoint we'd like to develop. If you wanted to claim that a particular player was the 'greatest ever', you'd need to establish the criteria used to arrive at that judgement. Presumably, this would include some reference to the duration of that 'greatness', the number of major titles won, and the quality of the contemporary opposition. But as we have already seen, such criteria are open to serious question. Judged by the number of major titles won, Emerson and Sampras would be way out in front and Gonzales nowhere. If the length of time you were at the top was a primary consideration, Hoad wouldn't get a look-in – because of when he turned pro, and (in terms of the pro game) because his career was so tragically and cruelly cut short by back injury. If, however, you consider claims for Hoad as the most 'complete' player ever, then it's possible to mount a very strong case.

Hoad was one of those players responsible for the dominance of the serve-volley game on fast surfaces (especially grass) in modern tennis. He had a very powerful serve, which he could hit flat or with spin. His speed about the court was phenomenal – he could get into the net swiftly and his volley on both sides was punched away crisply and decisively. He was also adept in seizing the initiative from the incoming serve by racing to the net behind his return. What made Lew such a charismatic player to watch was that power was combined with balletic grace: when a mighty serve was delivered, or a penetrating volley executed, he maintained a perfect balance.

Great players all agree that Hoad had every shot in the book. Seasoned observer, Jack Kramer, confessed to being amazed by some of the shots Hoad could even think of playing, so dazzling was the variety of his stroke-play. And contrary to popular belief, he could, and did play delicate drop volleys and teasing lobs. He was also one of the first players to employ a rolled topspin backhand off the return of a fast serve. Even Don Budge, whose backhand is regarded by many experts (including Kramer) as the best ever, tended to block the ball back when returning a cannonball or kicking serve on the backhand wing.

Rod Laver was certainly one player to be influenced by Hoad's topspin backhand. Laver realised that to pass the incoming volleyer, you had to able to hit the backhand with topspin. In watching Lew, he noted the brute power of his shot and 'this wonderful roll with the whole arm' that, along with a wrist-flick, produced the overspin. Hoad, he acknowledged was his 'idol, I emulated almost everything he did both on and off-court.'

Perhaps the last word on Lew's place in the pantheon of tennis heroes should be left to his indomitable rival, Pancho Gonzales. 'If I had to play a huge match,' said Pancho, 'a major final or a Davis Cup match, the one man I would fear is Lew Hoad. Not only was he great – a lot like Pete Sampras, a can-do-everything great – but no-one was ever so geared, physically and mentally, for such a match.'

* * *

The demands of the modern game are frequently said to be greater than they have ever been: the season's longer, standards of play at all levels have improved, the game is faster, and matches go on longer. However, it could be argued that the demands on a player's strength and stamina (especially in pro tennis) were far greater in Hoad's day. The amateur season may have been shorter but there were foreign tours, and in many tournaments it was assumed you'd compete not just in the singles but in the men's, and even the mixed, doubles. As we have already noted, the top singles players at Wimbledon today invariably shun other events.

Whilst it's undeniably the case that standards of play in the modern game have improved, comparisons are more difficult when one thinks of the professional game where the top players in the world were competing against each other night after night. The game is manifestly faster than it used to be, but racquet technology and changes in the pressure of balls may partly account for that. Another factor determining the speed of serves which has changed is the foot fault rule which now allows the server to have both feet off the ground as he hits the ball.

However, in terms of the demands on a player's strength and stamina, there would appear to be no case to argue. If one thinks of racquet technology, wielding a fifteen-ounce wooden racquet is far more tiring than the light metal racquets used today. Matches may often last longer now but how much of that is due to ninety-second rest periods in a chair at change of ends – and thirty seconds spent bouncing the ball before serving! The introduction of the tie-break in the '70s marked another significant reduction in the time the ball was actually in play in a match – as opposed to the time the match lasted. Prior to the tie-break system it was not uncommon to have sets of thirty games or more, which was the equivalent of an additional two or three sets of average length.

It was to meet these demands on a player's strength and stamina that Harry Hopman put his squad through such rigorous and punishing fitness programmes. He told his players that if they were physically fit and mentally fit, well-trained and well-prepared, they gave themselves a chance of winning matches just because of their condition – especially if the match went to a fifth set. This is why Hoad's contemporaries tend to deride the claims that tougher demands are made on players today.

When it came to physical strength and fitness, there were few players to compare with Hoad. Kramer testified to this, and so did Gonzales, who said of him:

> *God, he was such a strong son of a bitch! He had such strong wrists that he could hold the racquet high up the handle. In those days, Australian racquets were shorter than ours anyway, but even then he'd chop another half-inch off the end so he could wield it like a ping-pong bat.*

> *On his day, when he tried, you just couldn't beat him. He hit the ball harder than anyone I ever played. He would take the ball low inside the court and whip it at your head, and you knew the damn thing would drop six inches inside the baseline if you let it go. But it was coming so fast, egg-shaped with top-spin that sometimes you couldn't even get a racquet on it. He was the only guy, if I was playing my best tennis, could still beat me. The series we played was ball-busting, every day fraught with drama. I think his game was the best game ever. Better than mine. He was capable of making more shots than anybody. His two volleys were great. His overhead was enormous. He had the most natural tennis mind with the most natural tennis physique.*

The tennis history books will record Hoad's great feats: his Davis Cup triumphs, his major titles, successive Wimbledon victories, epic battles with Gonzales. What they may not get round to recording is perhaps his most significant achievement: Lew is justly celebrated as a uniquely gifted tennis player but, as Jack Kramer commented, 'he will also be remembered for being just about the nicest guy that ever walked the court.' And that is Richie Benaud's 'ultimate test'.

Chapter 18

Epilogue

After Lew died, Jenny took over some of his coaching commitments and flew around the Mediterranean giving tennis clinics for a German company, 'Ever-Court', whose director, Reinhold Comprix, has been immensely supportive to her. She had to try and raise money to keep the Campo operating because virtually all the money the Hoads had invested in the Australian shopping mall had disappeared. Peter Hoad, who had the same deep Australian drawl and casual manner as his father, continued to shoulder for a time the burden of the coaching in Spain. He was assisted by Daniel Lascano, a very good coach and player from Argentina, and Derek Harvey, an Englishman known as 'the Silver Fox', because of his long mane of silver hair. Eventually Peter decided to move to Australia, where he is now settled with a growing family. Until recently, Sally worked part-time at the Campo, and both she and Jane continue to visit the club.

For a few years Jenny struggled to ensure that the club stayed in the hands of the Hoad family, but it soon became obvious she was fighting an uphill battle. The club was saddled with mounting debts, unpaid bills were accumulating, and a programme of renovation was urgently needed. The swimming pool required repairs to meet safety regulations, and the tennis courts were getting to a point where the club would lose regular bookings from tennis groups if they weren't resurfaced or relaid.

All Jenny's valiant efforts to raise money through coaching couldn't stem the rising tide of debts and financial liabilities. Apart from the house in Castellar, to which she was becoming ever more attached, her only realisable asset was the Campo de Tenis. Ownership of the club was divided between members of the Hoad family, and Jenny was urged by her children to consider the painful option of selling the Campo – there would be no shortage of people interested in purchasing it.

In fact, Jenny and the other owners of the Campo had already had one approach. When the scale of the club's financial problems became apparent, Salvador Gallardo, the restaurant manager, formed a consortium that put together an attractive proposal. The consortium would purchase the club and pay off its debts;

Jenny, would be employed as consultant, continue her coaching role at the club, and retain ownership of the *caseta*, the little cottage within the grounds.

In a recent interview with the authors, it was clear that Salvador was profoundly affected by Lew's death. He obviously regarded him as a father-figure, someone prepared to take a risk by appointing a young man with very little experience to manage the restaurant at the Campo.

The day before Lew died, Salvador had been having a drink with him at the *caseta*. They'd been chatting about the Wimbledon finals, and Lew advised him, 'Have a bet on Conchita Martinez – I reckon it's her year.' (Martinez duly won)

A few years earlier Salvador had been offered two or three jobs at other establishments. One, in particular, presented a marvellous opportunity. The managing director of the Byblos Hotel (where Princess Diana was later to stay) visited the Campo and was so impressed by Salvador that he invited him to become the Manager of his exclusive hotel. Salvador talked it over with Lew. What should he do?

'You've got to take it, my son,' replied Lew 'I didn't want to turn pro but I realised if I didn't I'd be missing the opportunity of a lifetime.' He paused, and sighed. 'But there were real drawbacks. D'you know I didn't see Sally till she was nine months old?'

Nevertheless, the feelings of loyalty and devotion to Lew were too strong – Salvador couldn't bear the thought of leaving him in the lurch without a manager. To give Lew time to find a replacement, he asked the Byblos if they'd keep the offer open for six months. That was too long for them to wait, however, and the opportunity was lost.

Thus, when Salvador put the consortium's proposal to the Hoad family, he didn't view it simply as a business proposition: it would be a dream come true, the 'son' coming to the aid of the Campo. The Hoads conferred; then Jenny thanked him and said that though the offer was an attractive one, giving up ownership of the Campo would be too great a wrench. They had decided to keep it in the family.

At this point in the interview, Salvador said: 'I always thought I *was* part of the family.'

There's a happy postscript to this story for Salvador. In the first year of the twenty-first century, he opened his own luxury hotel a few miles from the Campo, the Hotel Tamisa Golf. By contrast, in the same year, Jenny was forced to bow to the inevitable and sell the Campo to an English businessman.

It was a decision she took with obvious and understandable reluctance. For over thirty years it had been the home she shared with Lew. The creation of the Campo was a joint vision which reflected the personalities of a triumvirate: Lew, Jenny and Alan Watt. Jenny had spotted the farmland on which the Campo took shape. If, as *Tennis Week* claimed, 'It was the most beautiful club in the world,' then that was due, in no small measure, to her guiding hand. It had also been the home where their children grew up; where they'd enjoyed good times (and a few bad ones); where they'd entertained sporting and media celebrities, and where they'd formed a network of close friends.

Understandably, the transfer of ownership was accompanied by tensions: 'take-overs' are rarely easy at the best of times, and this was no exception. Different owners inevitably have different ideas about how they want things run. But once the decision to sell the Campo had been made, Jenny was relieved - happy even. Freed from the financial and administrative responsibilities that had been bearing down on her, she could enjoy the club and look forward to a far more relaxed and enjoyable future.

New ownership has provided the necessary injection of cash to renovate the club. The courts have been completely relaid, the clubhouse refurbished, and the restaurant extended. A gym and beauty salon have also been added. Though Lew might feel ambivalent about the perimeter fence that now provides security, he would be gratified to see the Campo preserved as a beautiful tennis club - with courts and facilities befitting a centre of excellence.

Endnotes

Chapter 3

1   Richard Evans, *The Davis Cup* (1998) p.130.

Chapter 4

1   E. Digby Baltzell, *Sporting Gentlemen* (1995) pp.66-67

2   Baltzell pp.67-68

3   In Evans p.19

4   In Evans p.32

5   In Baltzell pp.78-79

6   Baltzell pp.77-78

Chapter 5

1   Arthur Ashe, *Portrait in Motion* (1973) p.189

2   Ashe p.189.

3   Harry Hopman, *Aces and Places* (1957) p.123

Chapter 6

1   Evans p.139

2   Steve Flink, *The Greatest Tennis Matches of the Twentieth Century* (1999) p.62

Chapter 8

1   Ashe p.196

2   Ashe p.195

3   Bud Collins, *My Life with the Pros* ( ) p.230

4   Collins p.231

5   Collins pp.233-234

Chapter 9

1   Jack Kramer (with Frank Deford), *My Game* (1979) p.229

2   Lew Hoad (with Jack Pollard), *My Game* (1958) p.171-172

3   Gordon Forbes, *A Handful of Summers* (1997 paperbk. edition, 1st pub. 1978) p.155-156

Chapter 11

1 Baltzell p.202

2 Baltzell p.216

3 Baltzell p.308

4 Kramer p.218

5 Pancho Gonzales (with Cy Rice) *Man with a Racket* (1959) p.172

6 Kramer pp.193-194

7 Kramer p.56

8 Kramer p.196

9 Joseph Stahl 'The Mirthful Mr Segoo' in *Tennis Week* Oct. 12, 2000 p.9

10 Stahl, 'Grand Master' Lew Hoad' in *Tennis Week* Dec. 17, 1998, p.36

11 Baltzell p.326

12 Joe McCauley, *The History of Professional Tennis* (2000) p.16

13 Collins p.128

14 Collins p.130-131

15 Arthur Ashe (with Arnold Rampersad), *Days of Grace* (1993) p.66

16 In Caryl Phillips, *The Right Set* (1999) p.98. This is from the later edition of Hoad's *My Game* pub. In the USA in 1959

17 ibid.

18 Phillips p.99

Chapter 12

1 Phillips p.100

2 Kramer p.200

3 Kramer p.231

4 Flink pp.66-69

5 Kramer p.234

Chapter 13

1 These edited extracts are taken from pp. 285-320 of Gordon Forbes, *A Handful of Summers*

2 Kramer p.235

3 Richard Evans, *Open Tennis* (1988) p.35

Chapter 14

1 *Daily Mail* May 4, 1994

Chapter 17

1 Gordon Forbes, *Too Soon to Panic* (1997) p.217